ADVANCE PRAISE FOR

Movements for Change

"Rauf Arif's *Movements for Change* is a rare account of how the worlds of traditional media, politics, and policy-making revolutionize under the disruptions of interactive media venues, technologies and savvy user/producers. The book will be of interest to activists, journalists and political leaders alike because it delves behind the binary headlines of Pollyanna 'social media liberates the developing world' versus 'old authoritarians reassert control in the streets.' There is, indeed, much more to understand and appreciate about how large media organizations as well as ordinary concerned citizens are creating, distributing and using media content with political intent. *Movements for Change* is an insightful look behind the curtain and prophecy for the future."

—David D. Perlmutter, Professor & Dean,
College of Media & Communication, Texas Tech University

"Rauf Arif argues that popular uprisings against authoritarian rulers in the Middle East and North Africa during the 'Arab Spring' were in fact part of a global phenomenon that cut across wide swathes of the Muslim world. He persuasively demonstrates that there were continuities of discontent between the popular revolts in Pakistan, Egypt and Tunisia. His case studies demonstrate that despite governmental use of the traditional media as components of their architectures of repression, Al-Jazeera and social media platforms provided cascades of information, and alternative avenues for creative expression of discontent that were instrumental in the overthrow of the authoritarian rulers of the three countries."

—Lyombe Eko, Professor of Journalism & Creative Media Industries,
College of Media & Communication, Texas Tech University

Movements for Change

This book is part of the Peter Lang Media and Communication list.
Every volume is peer reviewed and meets the highest quality
standards for content and production.

PETER LANG
New York • Bern • Berlin
Brussels • Vienna • Oxford • Warsaw

Rauf Arif

Movements for Change

How Individuals, Social Media and Al Jazeera Are Changing Pakistan, Egypt and Tunisia

PETER LANG
New York • Bern • Berlin
Brussels • Vienna • Oxford • Warsaw

Library of Congress Cataloging-in-Publication Data

Names: Arif, Rauf, author.
Title: Movements for change: how individuals, social media and Al Jazeera are changing Pakistan, Egypt and Tunisia / Rauf Arif.
Description: New York: Peter Lang, 2020.
Includes bibliographical references and index.
Identifiers: LCCN 2019031220 | ISBN 978-1-4331-6669-3 (hardback: alk. paper)
ISBN 978-1-4331-6670-9 (ebook pdf)
ISBN 978-1-4331-6671-6 (epub) | ISBN 978-1-4331-6672-3 (mobi)
Subjects: LCSH: Al Jazeera (Television network) | Social movements—Pakistan—History—21st century. | Protest movements—Pakistan—History—21st century. | Social media—Pakistan. | Social movements—Egypt—History—21st century. | Protest movements—Egypt—History—21st century. | Social media—Egypt. | Social movements—Tunisia—History—21st century. | Protest movements—Tunisia—History—21st century. | Social media—Tunisia. | Pakistan—Politics and government—21st century. | Egypt—Politics and Government—21st century. | Tunisia—Politics and government—21st century.
Classification: LCC HN690.5.A8 A75 2020 | DDC 303.48/4095491—dc23
LC record available at https://lccn.loc.gov/2019031220
DOI 10.3726/b15293

Bibliographic information published by **Die Deutsche Nationalbibliothe**.
Die Deutsche Nationalbibliothek lists this publication in the "Deutsche Nationalbibliografie"; detailed bibliographic data are available on the Internet at http://dnb.d-nb.de/.

29 Broadway, 18th floor, New York, NY 10006
www.peterlang.com

To My Parents: Mr. & Mrs. Malik Rashid Ahmed;
Mr. & Mrs. S. M. Zia

Contents

PART V What Happens Now?

Figure

Acknowledgements

Many people contributed to the creating of this book. I am forever indebted to my mentors, family, and friends for their guidance, support, and love that led me to this path of success. I find writing acknowledgements to be the most difficult task because sometimes words are not enough to express my gratitude to all the amazing people who contributed to make my life more meaningful in one way or another. My expression of this brief gratitude is just a formal way to thank you all even though it means a lot more than the words printed on this piece of paper.

To my family: First and foremost, I am in dearth of words to thank my parents who were, indeed, helpful with their ideas and assistance throughout my life. They are the ones who put me on the path of learning and respecting all humans equally. I will never forget those countless moments when they preferred to pay for my school and college fees over their own food. Dear mom and dad, for everything you both have done for me, I am eternally indebted. Thank you! Most importantly, I want to thank my wife, Lamia, who has been a great support and motivation in all the stressful moments involved in the creation of this book. It is because of her true friendship, love and understanding that I was able to finish this task successfully. I owe all my successes to you, my dear soul mate!

To my mentors: My true gratitude and thanks goes to my mentors for their limitless support, guidance and advice throughout the process of writing this manuscript. This project, which in fact started as a doctoral research initiative in 2012, was only possible because of the genuine guidance and intellectual support of my professors. First of all, I would like to thank Dr. Leo Eko for all of his contributions in setting the stage for the creation of this book. Both as a chair (during my doctoral program) and an expert on the Middle East, he was always there for me to help and lead me whenever I lost hope or direction. In 2018, when I shared my plans to build upon my doctoral research work to write this book, Dr. Eko immediately endorsed my plans with such a positive energy and started helping me with the structure and publishing guidelines right away. Dear Professor, Eko, I cannot thank you enough for all of your help at each and every stage of this book writing process! Finally, if I must pick one person who has literally changed the tracks of my professional life from being a journalist to becoming an academic, I have no other name, but of Dr. David D. Perlmutter, Dean of College of Media & Communication at Texas Tech University. My sincere gratitude and thanks go to Dr. Perlmutter, who has been my mentor and a real source of inspiration for me since 2007 when I first entered the United States as a grad student to start my Master's degree program at the University of Kansas. Without his support and guidance, I would not be here. Therefore, my gratitude for Dr. Perlmutter is not only to thank him for this book project, but to acknowledge his contributions as my professor during my doctoral years, and then as my mentor, guide and inspiration when I joined academia as an assistant professor in the field. In my culture, it is a famous saying that your parents bring you to the planet earth, but it's your teacher who makes you shine like a star on the skies. And Dr. Perlmutter is the true representation of that teacher! I am indebted to Dr. Bob Boynton for all his help and hard work in making sure that I understand the concepts correctly, during my days at the University of Iowa. My weekly meetings with Dr. Boynton were the best part of my learning process. I remember having long conversations with him on the Arab Spring, Social Movements, and the miracles happening around us in the age of social media.

To my friends: I would like to also thank my friend, Jesse Starkey, who read and edited several drafts of this manuscript. Her invaluable suggestions helped me to improve and clarify my writing. As a Ph.D. student when Jesse herself had a crazy busy schedule, she never refrained from taking on new challenges in the successful completion of this book. I will never forget that Jesse kept on helping me on this project even when her official RA assignment was over by the end of Spring 2019. I will forever remain indebted to Jesse for all the hard work and dedication that she put in this project, not to mention the strict deadlines that Jesse had created and enforced for me to stay on track. I am so fortunate to say that it was because of this book project, Lamia and I found two amazing friends, Jesse and her husband, Ian Lertora. I wish Jesse all the success in her Ph.D. program and beyond! My sincere gratitude also goes to Ali Gul Pir and Adil Omar for letting me use the lyrics of their song, *Kholo BC* in one of my chapters. I owe special thanks to my friends, Sana Ali, Michael Kugelman, Kevin Dilley, and Christie Perlmutter for their endless support and genuine friendship that goes beyond this book project. I am so fortunate to have you all in my life.

PART I

Introduction

The 2011 uprisings in the Middle East, commonly referred to as the Arab Spring, were widely seen and celebrated as a turning point in the history of the Muslim world (Bayat, 2017; Falk, 2016; Ghannam, 2011; Harb, 2011; Khosrokhavar, 2016; Mendel, 2011; Mir, 2011; Ryan, 2011; Salamey, 2015; Volpi, 2017). These political uprisings, which shook up several countries in the Muslim world, started in Tunisia in 2010, when a Tunisian street vendor, Mohamed Bouazizi, doused himself with gasoline and self-immolated in an attempted suicide to protest poor economic conditions and police brutality in his country (Harb, 2011; Mir, 2011; Zayani, 2015). This incident paved the way for online and real-world political protests in 18 Arab countries in North Africa and the Middle East (Ghannam, 2011), and points toward a new era of social movements and protests in the digital age (Gerbaudo, 2018; Hänska Ahy, 2016; Volpi & Clark, 2018).

The Problem

This book argues that the term Arab Spring is unnecessarily limiting in scope because of its tendency to interpret the political insurrections that have taken place in many Muslim-majority countries only in the context of the Arabic-speaking

Middle East. In fact, the ongoing political struggles in Muslim-majority countries are part of a much bigger phenomenon than the Arab Spring.

For purposes of simplicity, this book will use the term Muslim world instead of Arab world. By Muslim world, the author means all the countries that are members of the Organization of Islamic Cooperation (OIC). Currently, there are 57 OIC member states, including the 22 states and territories of the Arab League (OIC, 2018). The total population of Muslims around the world in 2017 was approximately 1.7 billion, with the highest percentages (47%) in the Asia-Pacific region (World Atlas, 2017). According to Pew Research Center statistics and the World Atlas, more Muslims live in India and Pakistan (350 million combined) than in the entire Middle East-North Africa region (317 million) (DeSilver & Masci, 2017; World Atlas, 2017).

Numerous academic and non-academic writers praise social media as the sole driver of the Arab awakening (Lewontin, 2016; Dencik & Leistert, 2015; Mitchell, Brown & Guskin, 2012; Robertson, 2015; Shirky, 2009; Shirky, 2011). In other words, the Arab Spring is considered to be the direct outcome of the popularity of the Internet and digital media in the region. However, little scholarly research is available that helps us understand what factors and types of content on these alternative media platforms led to the political uprisings of the region. Therefore, understanding the circumstances and the nature of content in the case of political uprisings in non-Western settings will help us recognize the fundamental question of how social media are contributing to the new era of global social movements.

Moreover, it is important to revisit how social media in developing countries such as Pakistan, Egypt and Tunisia became an agent of change when conventional news sources failed to play their role in society because of strict governmental control. Different pressure groups such as extremist religious groups and others with vested interests have a history of creating hurdles against the smooth and free-functioning news media in Pakistan, Egypt and Tunisia. These factors may contribute to the popularity of social media as an alternative to traditional media (Peer & Ksiazek, 2011). Well before the political uprisings in Pakistan, Egypt and Tunisia, an increasing percentage of the public in these three countries had started to rely on the Internet for information about current events and to give feedback on critical issues (Farooq, 2018; Freedom House, 2018; Ghannam, 2011; Mendel, 2011). This continues to be a common practice. For example, by December 2017, Pakistan witnessed a 22.2% penetration rate of the Internet with 44,608,065 Internet users in the country (IWS, 2018b). For Egypt, the Internet penetration rate for the same period was much higher (49.5% of the population, or 49,231,493 users) (IWS, 2018a). Among the three countries, however, Tunisia wins the race in terms of its Internet penetration rate, as 67.7% of the population (7,898,534 users) had already joined the online world by late 2017 (IWS, 2018a).

Since this book is about political protests in authoritarian regimes—where speaking up against dictators and monarchs involves risk—anonymity and long-distance participation are important tools to examine, because they allowed online protesters to engage in political dialogue without fearing for their lives (Rohlinger & Brown, 2009). Bennett and Segerberg (2011) argue that the anonymity factor makes online activism more popular in authoritarian regimes than in open societies:

> It is easy to grasp why personalized networking is so appealing in authoritarian regimes such as Tunisia, or Egypt, where conventional political organization—particularly of the democratic reform variety—is often policed and punished. Joining online protest networks offers at least a measure of anonymity and safety in the numbers of people with mobile phones, access to Internet cafes, or friends with tech skills, often resulting in dense recombinant networks. (p. 41)

Furthermore, it is difficult to find literature that acknowledges the fact that political uprisings similar to the Arab Spring had actually taken place or were ongoing well before the Tunisian revolution. Pakistan, the second-largest Muslim country in terms of population (over 200 million), is an example of a country where such political activism took place as early as 2007 (Arif, 2018; DeSilver & Masci, 2017; Hashim, 2012; Ricchiardi, 2012). In his book, *The Dispensable Nation*, Middle East scholar and a former foreign policy advisor to the White House, Vali Nasr, states that those who believe that the ongoing political and economic crisis in Pakistan could produce a Pakistan Spring are actually mistaken. In fact, argues Nasr, "Pakistan had its spring in 2008 when its lawyers, media, students, and civil society joined hands to send General Musharraf packing" (Nasr, 2013, p. 92). Likewise, Egypt witnessed its social movement, "We are All Khalid Said," in June 2010, which was also before the Tunisian Jasmine Revolution started. Yet the academic world continues to look at Tunisia as the starting point of mass political uprisings in the Muslim world. This order of understanding needs to be changed to truly comprehend the chronology of events that unfolded to become mass political uprisings in these Muslim-majority countries, commonly referred to as the Arab Spring. This book argues that Pakistan, not Tunisia, was the epicenter of social movements in the Muslim world, which then witnessed similar activism in Egypt and finally in Tunisia in the form of the Jasmine Revolution. The Tunisian revolution of 2010, however, should be seen as a catalyst for all of the political uprisings that followed. Therefore, in order to get a clearer picture of political activism in the Muslim world outside of the Middle East, we will investigate the scope of political activism in Muslim-majority countries prior to the Arab Spring of 2011.

Also, it is important to determine whether social media platforms were the sole factors that served as alternative channels of communication during the political uprisings in the Muslim world or whether there might be other factors that need to be explored and acknowledged to make sense of the social movements of the digital age. For example, the Qatar-based, pan-Arab television network Al Jazeera was seen as a channel of revolutions during the political uprisings in countries with Muslim majorities (Galander, 2013; Harb, 2011). A number of media scholars believe that social media, especially YouTube, not only served as a platform for the protesters but also benefited Al Jazeera, since the Arab TV network could upload and disseminate videos of political uprisings online (Eko, 2012; Ghannam, 2011; Harb, 2011). This was particularly beneficial when the channel was banned from airing its transmissions in Tunisia and Egypt during the political unrests.

Moreover, this book argues that because English dominates as a language of communication on social media platforms, this may be a contributing factor to consider when looking at social media and social movements in the global context. Also, this book highlights an important aspect of the rising youth population in Muslim-majority countries—as most of them not only are educated and technologically savvy but also share a common backdrop of poor economic conditions and dismal employment outlooks. Hence, they are a group participating in levels before unseen of collective action, hoping for a better tomorrow.

This examination into the content and place of social media as an alternative form of communication during political protests will contribute to our understanding of social uprisings in Muslim-majority countries, commonly known as the Muslim world. This book explores how this political activism is related to the broader concept of social movements. The term "social movements" refers to group actions in which individuals or organizations join a collective action to achieve a common goal (Hirschman, 1970; Jenkins, 1983; Olson, 1965; Skocpol, 1979; Tarrow, 1998; Tilly, 1992). For this investigation, however, the term social movements should also be interpreted as contentious (Tarrow, 1998) political uprisings and mass protests in the three countries. Furthermore, the term networked social media refers to Internet-based human communication that involves audiences as the active producers, consumers and disseminators of content online (Burgess & Green 2018; Green & Jenkins, 2011). Two scholars, Kaplan and

Haenlein (2010), define social media as "a group of Internet-based applications that build on the ideological and technological foundations of Web 2.0, and that allow the creation and exchange of user-generated content" (p. 61). Scholars like Bennett and Segerberg (2011) believe that these "emergent social media networks often achieve impressive results, from toppling corrupt regimes to putting pressure on governments to consider popular feelings" (p. 5). This book makes no such claims. However, this study may contribute to our understanding of social media platforms as part of the "cascade of information" against authoritarian regimes, as well as an alternative source of information and communication during these crises (Eko, 2012; Lohmann, 1994; Mitchell, Brown & Guskin, 2012).

Why Pakistan, Egypt and Tunisia?

This book is a comparative analysis of social media in political uprisings in three countries (Pakistan, Egypt and Tunisia). The three countries are comparable as related to several variables ranging from culture, religion and politics to their geographic and economic similarities (Eko, 2012). For example, the three countries under discussion are members of the Organization of Islamic Cooperation (OIC) and are Muslim-majority countries. In Tunisia, the population is 99% Muslim, while 97% of the population of Pakistan is Muslim, and 90% of Egyptians are Muslim (CIA, 2018 a, b, c).

The three countries also have a history of dictatorial regimes. Egypt and Tunisia were "led by long-serving authoritarian military leaders turned civilian presidents (Gen. Ben Ali of Tunisia was president for twenty-four years, Air Chief Marshal Hosni Mubarak was president [of Egypt] for almost thirty years" (Eko, 2012, p. 133), and Pakistan witnessed more than thirty-two years of interrupted dictatorial regimes starting from General Ayub Khan (1958–1971), followed by General Zia-ul-Haq (1977–1988) and President Musharraf, from 1999 to 2008 (Lieven, 2011; Hashim, 2012).

Furthermore, Pakistan, Egypt and Tunisia all have a history of government-controlled mass media. As it is common knowledge that the biggest casualty of war is truth, likewise the biggest casualty of authoritarian regimes and dictatorships is the free functioning of mass media. Historically, the mass media in these three countries were subject to strict governmental control, particularly whenever they tried to report on the plight of common people. We have seen in the cases of the political crises in the three countries under examination that at the time of the uprisings the traditional media were being blocked by the government and citizens were being punished for expressing views against the regimes. For example, in Egypt bloggers were punished, beaten and jailed for criticizing the military and the Mubarak regime (Mendel, 2011; Stack & Bronner, 2011). During the Jasmine Revolution in Tunisia, President Ben Ali banned Al Jazeera and other independent news sources in the country to curb the political uprisings against his regime (Mir, 2011). Similarly, Pakistan has a long history of banning media that does not support the leadership, with YouTube and other social media sites being banned for varying periods of time in 2006, 2008, 2010, and 2012 (Nabi, 2013), before a local version of YouTube was launched in 2016, which the government can censor at its will (CPJ, 2018; Ricchiardi, 2012; Wilkes, 2016). Additionally, scores of journalists have been killed in each of the countries over the past decade, many murdered for reporting against the regimes (CPJ, 2018).

In addition to these similarities in terms of dictatorial rule and questionable media and individual freedoms of speech and expression, Pakistan, Egypt and Tunisia have identical economic conditions, with burgeoning populations and rising unemployment among educated youth. Also, unlike many other oil-rich Arab states such as Saudi Arabia and the United Arab Emirates, these three countries lack such natural resources to appease their frustrated and unemployed educated youth.

Thinking in terms of Perlmutter's (1998) conceptualization of icons of outrage, which suggests that some images in photojournalism have the iconic power to get public and elite attention simultaneously and thus can create upheavals if turned into action, this book argues that during the political uprisings in Pakistan, Egypt and Tunisia, certain images of political protests became icons of outrage among citizens. These helped the formation and sustainability of social movements in the three countries. One example of such images can be those of the self-immolation of Mohamed Bouazizi. The image travelled with the speed of light to the rest of the world, resulting in online and offline (real-world) political activism inside and outside of Tunisia.

This book reminds its readers that political protests have not been uncommon in the three countries. In fact, all three countries have a long history of resistance, which goes all the way back to their struggles against their respective colonizers. Likewise, even after these three countries won their freedoms from foreign invaders/rulers, political activists continued struggling for their rights and kept marching toward the federal capitals of Pakistan, Tunisia and Egypt in ongoing attempts to achieve equality for all citizens. One possible reason for choosing capital cities—and particularly sites in front of presidential palaces—is that protesters wanted to get noticed. Also, in all three countries, the traditional media cluster in their federal capitals because they are supposed to serve and report on the activities of rulers, not the plight of people (Arif, 2010; Ciftci, 2018; Ghannam, 2011; Harb, 2011; Lieven, 2011; Mendel, 2011; Stack & Bronner, 2011; Zayani, 2015). Thus, if people manage to protest in front of a parliament building or a presidential palace, they are sure to get media attention. This means their dissenting voices have a better chance of being heard on a bigger scale. In the three countries under discussion, the dictatorial regimes were well aware of this fact. Thus, when these dictators could not control the political protests, they blocked the traditional media coverage of the protests to suppress the voices of the protesters.

However, in 2007 and 2010–11 circumstances were different. For the very first time in the history of the world, people had an alternative to traditional media in the form of social media including YouTube, Facebook, Twitter and blogs. Protesters used their cellphones to record the ongoing protests against their dictators and uploaded them on social media platforms. From audiences perspective, such a phenomenon of witnessing political protests as live, resembled with the traditional practices of reality television or live broadcasts. Thus, the informational cascade regarding people's unhappiness and disapproval of the regime kept flowing on social media platforms, even though the mass media had vanished from the scene.

This book is divided into five parts. *Part I* begins with an exploration of social movements in the context of communication, then takes readers through an overview of creative political protests in each of the three countries under investigation. The first part concludes with a detailed discussion about the pivotal role of Al Jazeera and how this "channel of revolutions" used social media content from protesters to make the uprisings a global conversation.

Parts II, *III* and *IV* of this book are dedicated to Pakistan, Egypt and Tunisia, respectively. For each country, an in-depth examination of a specific revolutionary icon is presented, followed by an overview of social movements and the politico-cultural context at the national level in each country. In its closing, *Part V: What Happens Now*, this book offers an understanding of how the theoretical paradigm of "collective memory" is being transformed into "connective" and "globital" memory themes. Such global "connective memory" themes, which are omnipresent on social media platforms, are no longer static but are porous and flexible in nature, morphing with each new digital protest movement. Digital protest movements are transforming the future of political uprisings, particularly because protesters can deploy more and more global memory themes, rather than just local ones, to sustain their movements.

Furthermore, after summarizing common themes that emerged during the comparative analysis of political uprisings in the three countries, the concluding chapter of this book puts forward the idea of "flash social movements" to understand the dynamics of the new era of digital activism and how these flash movements are different in their nature and scope as compared to the real-world (offline) movements of the past. Moreover, the chapter proposes a new model of collective action in the digital age. In this model, the role of communication is treated as central, not the peripheral, reason for a political collective action. The final chapter also invites future researchers and scholars studying social media and social movements to test this new paradigm in their investigations to further enhance our knowledge and understanding of online social activism.

The second part of this concluding chapter highlights the most recent political uprisings in Algeria, Sudan and Morocco and examines how these uprisings are a part of the same phenomenon that was witnessed during the political upheavals of 2007 (Pakistan) and 2010–11 (Tunisia and Egypt). It further hypothesizes what can be expected as an outcome from these newly emerging political uprisings in Muslim majority countries. Finally, the chapter concludes by predicting that these social movements in Muslim-majority countries are the beginning of, not an end to, a new era of protest politics. This means that the countries that have already had their versions of "Springs" may witness more episodes of social movements and political uprisings with far stronger and wider collective actions, through both online and offline (real-world) platforms. Likewise, we may see newer and smarter tactics being deployed by the authoritarian regimes and monarchs to counter such future social movements (Hintz, Dencik & Wahl-Jorgensen, 2017). In other words, not only the citizens and common people but also the powerful elites might tap into the resource of social media to benefit, strengthen and prolong their exploitative regimes in the days to come.

References

Arif, R. (2010). *How terrorism killed the news: Pakistani journalism after 9/11*. Saarbrucken, Germany: Lambert Academic Publishing.

Arif, R. (2018). Social networks, social movements and politico-cultural situation of Pakistani media. In Julie Dee (Ed.), *From Tahrir Square to Gezi Park: Social networks as facilitators of social movements*. New York, NY: Peter Lang Publishing.

Bayat, A. (2017). Revolution without revolutionaries: making sense of the Arab Spring. Redwood City, CA.: Stanford University Press.

Bennett, L. & Segerberg, A. (2011, August). *The logic of connective action: Digital media and the personalization of contentious politics.* Paper presented at the meeting of 6th General Conference of the European Consortium for Political Research, Reykjavik Iceland.

Burgess, J. & Green, J. (2018). *YouTube: Online video and participatory culture* (2nd ed.) Medford, MA: Polity Press.

Central Intelligence Agency (CIA). (2018a). Egypt. In *The World Factbook.* Retrieved February 18, 2019, from https://www.cia.gov/library/publications/the-world-factbook/geos/eg.html

Central Intelligence Agency (CIA). (2018b). Pakistan. In *The World Factbook.* Retrieved February 18, 2019, from https://www.cia.gov/library/publications/the-world-factbook/geos/pk.html

Central Intelligence Agency (CIA). (2018c). Tunisia. In *The World Factbook.* Retrieved February 18, 2019, from https://www.cia.gov/library/publications/the-world-factbook/geos/ts.html

Ciftci, S. (2018). Self-expression values, loyalty generation, and support for authoritarianism: evidence from the Arab world. *Democratization, 25*(7), 1132–1152. doi: 10.1080/13510347.2018.1450388

Committee to Protect Journalists (CPJ). (2018). *Journalists killed since 1992/Motive confirmed.* Retrieved January 20, 2019, from Committee to Protect Journalists website https://cpj.org/data/killed/?status=Killed&motiveConfirmed%5B%5D=Confirmed&type%5B%5D=Journalist&start_year=1992&end_year=2019&group_by=year

Dencik, L., & Leistert, O. (2015). *Critical perspectives on social media and protest: Between control and emancipation.* New York: Rowman & Littlefield International.

DeSilver, D. & Masci, D. (2017). Update: World's Muslim population more widespread than you might think. *Pew Research Center.* Retrieved October 9, 2018, from http://www.pewresearch.org/fact-tank/2017/01/31/worlds-muslim-population-more-widespread-than-you-might-think/

Eko, L. (2012). *New media, old regimes: Case studies in comparative communication law and policy.* Lanham, MD: Lexington Books.

Falk, R. (2016). Rethinking the Arab Spring: Uprisings, counterrevolution, chaos and global reverberations. *Third World Quarterly, 37*(12), 2322–2334. doi: 10.1080/01436597.2016.1218757

Farooq, M. (2018, April). Pakistan's mobile Internet users stand at 21 percent of the population: Report. *Pakistan Today.* Retrieved March 02, 2019, from https://profit.pakistantoday.com.pk/2018/04/21/pakistans-mobile-internet-stand-at-21-percent-of-the-population-report/

Freedom House. (2018). *Pakistan Freedom Report.* Retrieved March 09, 2019, from https://freedomhouse.org/report/freedom-world/2018/pakistan

Galander, M. M. (2013). Al-Jazeera, advocacy and media value determinism re-conceptualizing the network's coverage of the Arab Spring of revolutions. *Global Media Journal, 12*(22), 1–17.

Gerbaudo, P. (2018). *Tweets and the streets: Social media and contemporary activism.* London: Pluto Press.

Ghannam, J. (2011). Social media in the Arab world: Leading up to the uprisings of 2011. *Center for International Media Assistance, 3*(1), 1–44. Retrieved March 07, 2018, from http://www.cima.ned.org/wp-content/uploads/2011/02/Ghannam-Jeffrey-Arab_Social_Media-Report-10-25-11.pdf

Green, J., & Jenkins, H. (2011). How audiences create value and meaning in a networked economy. In V. Nightingale (Ed.) *The handbook of media audiences* (109–127). West Sussex, UK: Wiley-Blackwell

Hänska Ahy, M. (2016). Networked communication and the Arab Spring: Linking broadcast and social media. *New Media & Society, 18*(1), 99–116. doi: https://doi.org/10.1177/1461444814538634

Harb, Z. (2011). Arab revolutions and the social media effect. *M/C Journal, 14*(2), 1–5. Retrieved March 10, 2019, from http://journal.media-culture.org.au/index.php/mcjournal/article/view/364Two

Hashim, A. (2012, April 30). Pakistan: A political timeline. Al Jazeera. Retrieved April 06, 2019, from https://www.aljazeera.com/indepth/interactive/2012/01/20121181235768904.html

Hintz, A., Dencik, L., & Wahl-Jorgensen, K. (2017). Digital citizenship and surveillance. *International Journal Of Communication, 11*, 9. Retrieved May 09, 2019, from https://ijoc.org/index.php/ijoc/article/view/5521

Hirschman, A. O. (1970). *Exit, voice, and loyalty: Responses to decline in firms, organizations, and states*. Cambridge, MA: Harvard University Press.

Internet World Stats (IWS). (2018a). *Africa internet users*. Retrieved February 12, 2019, from https://www.internetworldstats.com/stats1.htm

Internet World Stats (IWS) (2018b). *Usage and population statistics*. Retrieved February 12, 2019, from https://www.internetworldstats.com/asia/pk.htm

Jenkins, J. C. (1983). Resource mobilization theory and the study of social movements. *Annual Review of Sociology, 9*(1), 527–553.

Kaplan, A. & Haenlein, M. (2010). Users of the world, unite! The challenges and opportunities of social media. *Business Horizons 53*(1), 59–68.

Khosrokhavar, F. (2016). New Arab Revolutions That Shook the World. London, UK: Routledge.

Lewontin, M. (2016). Five times Internet activism made a difference. *The Christian Science Monitor*. Retrieved October 24, 2019, from https://www.csmonitor.com/Technology/2016/0105/Five-times-Internet-activism-made-a-difference/Arab-Spring

Lieven, A. (2011). *Pakistan: A hard country*. London, England: Allen Lane.

Lohmann, S. (1994). The dynamics of informational cascades: The Monday demonstrations in Leipzig, East Germany, 1989–91. *World Politics, 47*(1), 42–101.

Mendel, T. (2011). Political and media transitions in Egypt. A snapshot of media policy and regulatory environment. *Internews*. Retrieved February 17, 2019, from http://hrlibrary.umn.edu/research/Egypt/Internews_Egypt_MediaLawReview_Aug11.pdf

Mir, J. (2011). Political and media transitions in Tunisia: A snapshot of media policy and regulatory environment. *Internews*. Retrieved February 18, 2019, from https://internews.org/sites/default/files/resources/Internews_Tunisia_MediaLawReview_Aug11.pdf

Mitchell, A., Brown, H., & Guskin, E. (2012). The role of social media in the Arab uprisings. *Pew Research Center: Journalism & Media*. Retrieved April 20, 2018, from http://www.journalism.org/2012/11/28/role-social-media-arab-uprisings/

Nabi, Z. (2013, August). *The anatomy of web censorship in Pakistan*. Paper presented at the 3rd USENIX Workshop on Free and Open Communications on the Internet, Washington, D.C.

Nasr, V. (2013). *The dispensable nation: American foreign policy in retreat*. New York, NY: Doubleday.

Olson, M. (1965). *Logic of collective action*. Cambridge, MA: Harvard University Press.
Organization of Islamic Cooperation (OIC). (2018). Member States. Retrieved October 9, 2018, from https://www.oic-oci.org/states/?lan=en
Peer, L., & Ksiazek, T. B. (2011). YouTube and the challenge to journalism: New standards for news videos online. *Journalism Studies*, *12*(1), 45–63. doi: 10.1080/1461670X.2010.511951
Perlmutter, D. D. (1998). *Photojournalism and foreign policy: Icons of outrage in international crises*. Westport, Conn.: Praeger.
Ricchiardi, S. (2012). *Challenges for independent news media in Pakistan: A report to the Center for International Media Assistance*. Washington, DC, National Endowment for Democracy. Retrieved June 03, 2018, from http://www.centerforinternationalmediaassistance.org/wp-content/uploads/2015/01/Challenges-for-Independent-News-Media-in-Pakistan_Ricchiardi-updated.pdf
Robertson, A. (2015). What's going on? Making sense of the role of the media in the Arab uprisings. *Sociology Compass*, *9*(7), 531–541.
Rohlinger, D. & Brown, J. (2009). Democracy, action, and the Internet after 9/11. *American Behavioral Scientist*, *53*(1), 133–150. doi: 10.1177/0002764209338791
Ryan, Y. (2011, January 26). How Tunisia's revolution began. Al Jazeera. Retrieved May 06, 2019, from https://www.aljazeera.com/indepth/features/2011/01/ 2011126121815985483.html
Salamey, I. (2015). Post-Arab Spring: Changes and challenges. *Third World Quarterly*, *36*(1), 111–129. doi: 10.1080/01436597.2015.976025
Shirky, C. (2009). *How social media can make history* [Video file]. Retrieved April 10, 2019, from https://www.ted.com/talks/clay_shirky_how_cellphones_twitter_facebook_can_make_history
Shirky, C. (2011). The political power of social media. Foreign Affairs. Retrieved April 10, 2019, from http://www.foreignaffairs.com/articles/67038/clay-shirky/the-political-power-of-social-media
Skocpol, T. (1979). *States and social revolutions: A comparative analysis of France, Russia, and China*. Cambridge, England: Cambridge University Press.
Stack, L. & Bronner, E. (2011, April 12). Egypt sentences blogger to 3 years. *The New York Times*. Retrieved July 17, 2019, from https://www.nytimes.com/2011/04/12/world/middleeast/12egypt.html?ref=todayspaper
Tarrow, S. G. (1998). *Power in movement: Social movements and contentious politics*. Cambridge, MA: Cambridge University Press.
Tilly, C. (1992). *Coercion, capital, and European states, AD 990–1992*. Hoboken, NJ: Blackwell.
Volpi, F. (2017). Revolution and authoritarianism in North Africa. Oxford Scholarship Online. DOI: 10.1093/oso/9780190642921.001.0001
Volpi, F. & Clark, J. A. (2018). Activism in the Middle East and North Africa in times of up-heaval: Social networks' actions and interactions. *Social Movement Studies*, *18*(1), 1–16.
Wilkes, T. (2016, January 18). Pakistan lifts ban on YouTube after launch of local version. *Reuters*. Retrieved March 24, 2019, from https://www.reuters.com/article/us-pakistan-youtube/pakistan-lifts-ban-on-youtube-after-launch-of-local-version-idUSKCN0UW1ER
World Atlas (2017). How many Muslims are there in the world? Retrieved October 9, 2018, from https://www.worldatlas.com/articles/how-many-muslims-in-the-world.html
Zayani, M. (2015). *Networked publics and digital connection: The politics of everyday life in Tunisia*. Oxford, England: Oxford University Press.

1 Understanding Social Movements in the Context of Communication

Overview

In the 21st century, the Internet continues to redefine, challenge and change the overall scope of human communication, and social media has become an integral part of political communication (Edgerly, Vraga, Dalrymple, Macafee & Fung, 2013; Milan, 2015; Treré, 2016). This book analyzes the use of social media—including YouTube videos involving political protests by social movements in Pakistan, Egypt and Tunisia—and compares Pakistan's political crisis of 2007 with the political uprisings in Tunisia and Egypt. These latter uprisings are part of what is commonly known as the Arab Spring of 2011. By situating the North African uprisings in the broader concept of the Muslim world, this book explores how online political activism is related to the broader concept of social movements (Dewey, 1954; Gerbaudo, 2016; Ghannam, 2011; Habermas, 1989; Harb, 2011; Milan, 2015; Skocpol, 1979; Tilly, 1992; Volpi, 2017) and what role communication plays in the formation and sustainability of these political uprisings.

To begin, this chapter will discuss (1) what social movements and revolutions are; (2) the historical development of the concepts of social movements and revolutions; (3) Hirschman (1970), Tarrow (1998) and Lohmann's (1994) perspectives on the ideological paradigms of social movements and revolutions;

(4) the importance and contribution of iconic images for social movements; and (5) an explanation of the significance of digital communication in the creation and sustainability of social movements during the political uprisings in Pakistan, Egypt and Tunisia.

What Are Social Movements?

Introduced by German scholar Lorenz von Stein in 1848, the term "social movement" refers to group actions in which individuals or organizations generate and join a collective action to achieve a common goal (Hirschman, 1970; Jenkins, 1983; Olson, 1965; Skocpol, 1979; Tarrow, 1998; Tilly, 1992; von Stein, 1848). Social movements can be peaceful (e.g., Gandhi's nonviolent movement for Indian independence of the 1940s or the American Civil Rights movement of the 1950s and '60s), violent (e.g., terrorist organizations, such as the Taliban's movement in Afghanistan and Pakistan), organized (e.g., gay rights and feminist movements), and/or unorganized (e.g., the Occupy Wall Street Movement of 2011).

Most of the literature on group actions treats social movements as an umbrella term (Dahl, 1971; Huntington, 1965; Ross, 2001; Tarrow, 2012), and so it is difficult to provide a single agreed-upon definition of social movements. Thus, this chapter will spotlight some of the key historical developments in the study of social movements and revolutions before discussing the role of communications in protest politics.

A majority of scholarship during the 1960s and '70s was concerned with *how* and *why* individuals participated in social movements (Jenkins, 1983). The resource mobilization approach to group actions and social movements provides an explanation of the rational decision of individuals in a collective action (Hirschman, 1970; Jenkins, 1983; Olson, 1965). Put this way, historically the scholarship on group actions and social movements oscillates between traditional and rational views of collective behavior and group actions. According to the traditional view, group actions and social movements are deviant, irrational, random occurrences of individuals based on their emotional reaction to circumstances out of their control (Blumer, 1939; Boudreau & Meyer, 2009; Imig & Tarrow, 2001; Ostrom, 1998; Shibutani, 1988; Tilly & Tilly, 1981). The rational view, on the other hand, treats individuals as rational actors who strategically analyze the cost and benefits of joining a group action (Kolb, 2007; Kousis & Tilly, 2005; Olson, 1965; Tilly & Wood, 2012).

Olson (1965) argues that rationality, self-interest and the size of a group determine participation and collective action in groups. His argument challenges the traditionalists' view of participation and collective action, which suggests that a common interest is sufficient for people to take a group action. Olson (1965) adds that traditionalists do not entertain the economic logic of self-interest and rationality in their model. The most important factor for the traditionalists is a common interest among individuals that forces them to organize and participate in a group action without evaluating the associated cost/benefit. Rationalist scholars in the comparative literature, however, argue that individuals participate and pursue their collective interests only when they find it cost effective and rational to do so (Olson, 1965; Verba, Nie & Kim, 1987). For example, if the size of a group is smaller in a collective action, the reward of that group action will be distributed to a majority of participants. However, in medium-sized and larger-sized group actions, only a small number of participants (mostly elites) will benefit from the outcome of a group action (Olson, 1965). That's why, according to rational choice model, it is difficult to persuade people to join a larger group action, which might result in a free riders' problem (Olson, 1965). More discussion on the free riders' problem is provided later in this chapter.

In his work *Exit, Voice and Loyalty*, Hirschman (1970) applies similar economic logic to political participation and collective action. Hirschman argues that the choice to leave or protest the problems of an institution depends largely on the subject's level of freedom and choice. According to the author, there are two possible responses to the decline of organizations, firms or states: (1) exit, which means to leave the organization, and (2) voice, which means to resist and protest to reverse the decline. Individuals' decisions to leave or resist are determined by their rational evaluation of the costs and benefits involved. Hirschman's main contribution to the debate is to introduce the factor of loyalty, which was missing in both the traditional and rational models of participation. The loyalty factor can influence an individual's choice whether or not to participate in a group action. For example, if a country or state is declining because of poor administrative policies, some of the people may decide to raise their voices to reverse the decline by protesting against the policies of the government, even though they had a choice to leave that country and migrate to a better and more stable country/state. According to Hirschman's logic, people's decision to raise their voices against the regime, and not to exit, must have been influenced by the loyalty that they have for their country/state.

According to Jenkins (1983), since group actions don't form because of one or two specific reasons, a multi-factor approach is necessary to study movement formation. He provides a threshold model of movement formation. The threshold model suggests that all specific reasons, including grievances, organization and opportunities, should be present at a threshold level for a movement to form. Also, tangible and intangible assets are needed for the mobilization of groups, where tangible assets include money, facilities and the means of communication. Intangible assets refer to human beings as assets. Jenkins describes two models for the organization of a social movement:

1. The centralized bureaucratic model: social movements that are a result of modernization. Such social movements are aimed at institutional change.
2. The decentralized, informal model: These kinds of social movements are known as leaderless group actions, which are aimed at system change.

Jenkins argues that professional Social Movement Organizations (SMOs) fall mostly between the bureaucratic and decentralized models to reap the benefits of both models as needed for their goals.

So far, the literature that this chapter has discussed has focused on social movements in the context of Western or democratic societies. This is because resource mobilization theorists are focused largely on liberal democratic settings and do not provide any justification for the formation of social movements in non-democratic settings. Therefore, there is a need to apply the existing approaches to social movements and group actions in authoritarian and one-party systems to see whether they will produce similar results (Jenkins, 1983). Furthermore, Jenkins believes in the role of mass media in making or breaking social movements.

A lot has been debated on the problem of "free riders" in a group action. The free rider problem refers to a situation in which individuals benefit from the efforts of others without paying the cost for that benefit (Olson, 1965). Think about a situation when some people manage to ride public transportation for free, while others pay the price for tickets so that the public service continues to function. Similarly, some individuals may decide not to join a group action or social movement thinking that they will eventually benefit from others' sacrifices and hard work. Even though Olson's explanation of the free riders' dilemma was primarily attributed to the parasitic intentions of some people, free riding might be caused by more than just immoral intentions. Jenkins (1983) observes that sometimes free riders fail to join a movement simply because of ignorance of the movement's existence, or because they were not communicated to by the movement's organizations. That's where the role of effective communication via mass media or alternate media (social media in this case) becomes more important. In other words, free riders' ignorance can be resolved by proper and effective communication with them. Also, the better informed the public is about a group action, the more inclined they would be toward participating in that particular group action.

Using the analogy of Isaac Newton's micro level versus Albert Einstein's macro level physics, Boudreau and Meyer (2009) emphasize the need for a larger, contextual understanding of how social movements relate to other political phenomena. Their logic enables the development of broader comparisons across political contexts. Boudreau and Meyer divide the literature on social movements in three stages. During the first stage, most scholarly literature of the 1960s studied social movements using the rational choice approach—i.e., that individuals strategically analyze costs and benefits before joining a group action—and focused on the group size and collective action factors (e.g., Olson, 1965).

During the 1970s, scholars challenged the rational choice model by arguing that it does not explain social movements like gay rights, environmental, peace and feminist movements. These scholars argued that social movements were both alternative and additional modes of decentralization in advanced and post-industrialized societies. Put this way, the rational choice model—which is based on wanting more rather than less of a good—does not provide solid justification for social movements that emerged in industrialized societies (Boudreau & Meyer, 2009; Jenkins, 1983; Tilly, 1992). For example, the gay rights movements, feminist movements and environment-related social movements do not fit into the economic logic of rational choice model, as the participants in these movements seem to be motivated on ideological grounds rather than rational or economic reasons.

The third stage began at almost the same time in the 1970s, when another group of scholars studied political rebellions and revolutions. These scholars argued that revolutionary campaigns emerged when the economy's capacity to deliver benefits was outstripped by growing expectations. Tilly (1992) and Tarrow (1998) advanced the idea of "contentious politics," which helped distinguish reform-oriented social movements and revolution-oriented social movements in terms of the outcomes of these movements. While reform-oriented social movements are aimed at getting accepted in the system, revolution-oriented social movements have an entirely different goal. They want regime change.

Boudreau and Mayer (2009) suggest that the study of social movements should be divided into two categories: social movements in the global North (Western, developed societies) and social movements in the global South (developing societies). These scholars observed that most of the social movement-related work is conducted in the United States within a Western perspective.

These movements differ in nature from the social movements in the developing world. In order to understand the nature of social movements in the global South, we need to focus on the interaction of challengers and authorities through actions of resistance and repression.

Protest movements in wealthier settings may result in greater openness in the policymaking process and the willingness of authorities to resolve grievances, as these movements advocate broader policy reforms. However, protest movements in weaker states or poorer settings may have very different outcomes because policy reform is less likely in such settings. Since such movements may result in unresolved grievances on the part of challengers; these movements advocate broader displacement goals, which could result in regime change and even revolutions. Boudreau and Mayer (2009) suggest that the comparison between the global North and the global South may provide the basis for some of the broader comparisons in the field. Thinking in terms of Boudreau and Mayer's logic of social movements, we can make a case that the political uprisings in the three countries (Pakistan, Egypt and Tunisia) were aimed at system change, not system reform.

The Role of Communication in Social Movements

After this quick overview of social movements literature, let's explore how and why communication becomes relevant to this complex phenomenon of group actions. Scholars of political science and communications disciplines agree on the inevitable role of communications and media in forming and sustaining social movements that emerge for all kinds of political and/or social purposes. Nor is this role associated exclusively with modern online social media; in fact, social movements and media share a long history. Studying the media coverage of Students for a Democratic Society (SDS), the United States' anti-war movement of the 1960s, Gitlin (2003) observed that the mass media have the power to shape a social movement's narrative. In fact, he believed that journalists and the mass media hold the exclusive power to validate a social movement and determine whether a movement's goals and objectives matter to the society. Since Gitlin's work covers the anti-war social movement of the 1960s, when the Internet and online social media did not exist, his book, *The World is Watching*, attributes absolute power to the mass media in shaping the narrative of social movements. It is interesting to note that Gitlin's (2003) work provides a good example of a top-down model of journalism, wherein journalists and their newsrooms reinforce the hegemonic norms and roles of a society (Berkowitz, 1997; Gitlin, 2003; Robinson, 2011). However, as a result of technological developments and networked social media, which make it possible for audiences to shape their own narratives in an online world, the top-down model of journalism is no longer applicable (Robinson, 2011; Singer et al., 2011).

In order to understand the role of communication in protest politics, the works by Hirschman (1970), Lohmann (1994) and Tarrow (1998) on social movements are of critical importance. This review of these seminal theoretical works will help explain how these theorists are helpful in the study of the role of digital communication during the political upheavals in Pakistan, Egypt and Tunisia. Also, this discussion will help us understand the inevitable connection of Perlmutter's theory of icons of outrage (1998) to the political uprisings of the three countries under discussion.

Hirschman's Perspective of *Voice*

In his seminal work, *Exit, Voice and, Loyalty*, Hirschman (1970) used economic logic to explain people's choices and responses to the decline of organizations, states or firms. According to Hirschman, individuals' choices to leave or complain depend upon the level of choice and freedom they have. Using the analogy of a firm's decline, he adds that people may choose two possible options in response to the decline of an organization: "exit," which means to leave the organization, and "voice," which means to resist or complain to reverse the decline. However, the interplay of the "loyalty factor" can affect these two situations. The following paragraphs will explain the interplay of loyalty factor in a relatively more elaborative way.

Hirschman's (1970) argument can be understood using the following example: Let us think about a situation in which consumers of a product decide to stop buying the product because of its declining quality. Consumers will most probably shift to another product if alternate choices are available in the market. In order to switch to another product, they need to have competitive options available in the market; if there is no competition, there is no exit. On the other hand, consumers may decide to opt for voice, which means to complain against the decline in the quality of the product in order to reverse it. This situation is possible only if (1) they are loyal to the product, and/or (2) they don't have alternate options available to them in the market (Hirschman, 1970).

Since this book is focused on political activism in Pakistan (2007), Egypt and Tunisia (2010/11), it interprets Hirschman's (1970) elements (exit and voice) in the context of a country's decline instead of that of a product or a corporation. Looking carefully at Hirschman's model of participation and collective action, this book highlights five basic elements that need to be considered in the context of demonstrations in the three countries under study: exit, voice, loyalty, level of choice, and level of freedom. In the following chapters of this book, further discussion of social movements in the three countries under investigation will be based upon these five elements. The element of voice, however, will be interpreted as *digital communication*. It will explore whether social media, in general, and YouTube's shareable videos of political protests, in particular, gave voice to social movements in the three countries.

Tarrow's Perspective of Contentious Social Movements

So far, the main focus of this chapter was to define social movements and collective actions and to describe the basic types of social movements that one needs to know in order to understand political activism in the 21st century. This part of the chapter goes more in depth and looks at the elements of anger and contention in confrontations between protesters and their powerful opponents. This discussion will help us understand how contentious social movements survive when powerful elites try to suppress them.

In his work on resource mobilization theorists, Tarrow (1998) argues that people "engage in contentious politics when patterns of political opportunities and constraints change and then, by strategically employing a repertoire of collective action, create new opportunities, which are used by others in widening cycles of contention" (Tarrow, 1998, p. 19). For him, the political opportunity structure, cultural and ideological frames, and structures of mobilization are the three main concepts that pave the way for the formation of a social movement. Political opportunity structure, in Tarrow's theorization of social movements, refers to the presence of five elements: (1) increasing access of individuals to participation, (2) political instability, (3) a divided elite, (4) repression and facilitation, and (5) influential allies. Tarrow purports that political opportunity structures are not static and may change with the changing circumstances. Cultural and ideological frames refer to new but familiar symbols, slogans and themes used by protesters/political activists that resonate with individuals' belief systems in order to mobilize them for participating and sustaining a social movement. Tarrow further states:

> social movements attempt to replace a dominant belief system that legitimizes the status quo with an alternative mobilizing belief system that supports collective action for change, movement leaders proffer the symbols of revolt to gain support and mark themselves off from opponents. (Tarrow, 1998, p. 106)

Structure of mobilization refers to a kind of resource or a "delicate balance between formal organization and autonomy" that brings "people together in the field, shape[s] coalitions, confront[s] opponents, and assure[s] their own future after the exhilaration of the peak of mobilization has passed" (p. 123). To put it another way, changes in the political opportunity structure create incentives for collective action, while cultural and ideological frames contribute toward sustaining protests by justifying, dignifying and animating collective action, and formal movement organizations develop only if they are able to mobilize existing dense networks of people.

Tarrow (1998) further argues that collective challenge, common purpose, social solidarity and sustained interaction with opponents and authorities are the four basic properties of a social movement. In other words, a collective action does not become a social movement unless sustained (e.g., Gandhi's nonviolent civil disobedience movement against the British rule, the Civil Rights movement in the United States, and the recent Arab Spring uprisings in the Middle East and North Africa), and a social movement involves action against powerful opponents. Tarrow took the debate on collective action and social movements beyond economic logic. His main contribution to the literature is his idea of contention in social movements. He also discussed the importance of cultural and ideological frames for the sustainability of social movements.

From the media and communication perspective, it is pertinent to mention here that Tarrow's idea of cultural and ideological frames is basically about the importance of sustained, effective and strategic communication. From his theory, we can infer that only those social movements and collective actions that have the capability to effectively communicate among the protest participants and among potential sympathizers—deploying effective cultural and ideological frames such as slogans, narratives of protest against their powerful opponent and a sense of togetherness in their struggle—will succeed in achieving their goals. In contrast, a collective action with a broken and ineffective communication network or strategy is destined to fail in the face of a powerful opponent.

The adage, "united we stand, divided we fall," is also applicable to understand the formation of social movements. According to Tarrow (1998), changes in political opportunities and constraints create incentives for people to participate in contentious politics. By strategically employing the collective action repertoire, protest participants create new opportunities, which are used by others in widening cycles of contention. Tarrow (1998) argues that when poor people originate contentious politics, they lack money and other expensive resources to support their campaigns and instead use contention as a vehicle for their collective actions. He describes three kinds of contention: (1) violence, which is visible, but has the risk of scaring off sympathizers; (2) disruptions, which involve marches and rallies and have a tendency to become violent; and (3) conventional contention, which involves protests and other conventional forms of campaigns.

In order to apply Tarrow's (1998) theorization to the cases of political uprisings in the countries under study, let's take two important elements of his theory: political opportunity structure and contention. Tarrow (1998) believes that we need to have some sort of political opportunity for political activism. Most of the time, such political opportunities appear when there is a divided elite. For example, the origin of the Arab Spring 2011 is mostly traced to an incident of December 18, 2010 when a Tunisian street vendor, Mohamed Bouazizi doused himself with gasoline and then self-immolated as a protest against police torture and corruption (Mir, 2011, Volpi, 2017). The image of the burning man spread quickly over the digital media and was seen everywhere in the world. A strong case can be made that Bouazizi's self-immolation served as a political opportunity that online activists used to form an uprising on social media and in the streets. However, in this particular case, the ruling elite was not yet divided. In the following chapters, this book explores political opportunity structures surrounding Pakistan, Egypt and Tunisia's political uprisings, which occurred even though there were no divided elites in the three countries. These chapters will explore whether the presence of traditional media (e.g., Al Jazeera) and social media tools such as Facebook, Twitter, blogs and YouTube in the three countries can be seen as providing opportunities for citizens to engage in a political activism.

Furthermore, Tarrow (1998) argues that contentious social movements are aimed at challenging the status quo, so they need new slogans to mobilize potential sympathizers. These slogans, which he terms as cultural and ideological frames, should be compatible with the people's ideologies, so that they can identify themselves with these frames. He adds that the mass media can spread these cultural and ideological frames and magnify the grievances of people in order to get potential sympathizers to act against the status quo. This book argues that Al Jazeera, YouTube protest videos and Facebook and Twitter activism helped magnify cultural and ideological frames and the messages of grievances and solidarity used by the social movements in the three countries.

Lohmann's Perspective of "Informational Cascades"

In her article, "The Dynamics of Informational Cascades: The Monday demonstrations in Leipzig, East Germany, 1989–91," Susanne Lohmann (1994) interprets political demonstrations as informational cascades. Since the mass media are not free in authoritarian regimes, people do not get accurate information about the nature of the regime. However, Lohmann believes, political demonstrations in this kind of situation serve as informational cascades by making "public some of the previously hidden information about the nature of the regime" (p. 44). Lohmann explains the dilemma of people who lack accurate information about their authoritarian regime this way:

> In their daily interactions with the regime, some people have positive experiences, others negative ones. Since these are private experiences, it is possible that the status quo regime is maintained by a sufficiently large number of people who are imperfectly informed, whereas it would collapse if some or all of the dispersed negative information were to become publicly known. (Lohmann, 1994, p. 50)

Lohmann's main contribution here is the fact that she looked at the role of information and communication in a collective action as one of the most important factors in movement development. Lohmann (1994) is sensitive to the fact that in the absence of organized tools of information such as mass media, the flow of communication is no more a simple act involving source, message, channel and receiver (Barnlund, 1970; Foulger, 2004; Katz, 1957; Shannon & Weaver, 1949), rather it involves multiple stakeholders both at the sharing and receiving ends of a communication pattern:

> There are then multiple senders and receivers. The set of senders coincides with that of the receivers, consisting of the entire population. Thus, although each sender and receiver has only imperfect information about the status quo regime, in the aggregate the population is well informed. (Lohmann, 1994, p. 50)

Put this way, in any authoritarian regime lacking meaningful freedom of expression, when a group of political activists comes out on streets against its rulers, it threatens the status quo as the observers of these political protests get the information about people's unhappiness with the regime. For example, during the Tunisian uprisings of 2010, when protesters in the Tunisian city of Siddi Bouzid started coming out on streets against President Ben Ali, other people in the rest of the country got the information that something was wrong with the regime, and so they started joining the protests in different parts of the country.

While providing an historical account of East Germany's political struggle, Lohmann (1994) reviewed different theories of mass political action, examining the suppression of mass discontent in East Germany over the period 1949–89, as well as critical events and external political changes in the late 1980s. She also analyzed the East German revolution and its aftermath and used the evidence to evaluate theories of mass political action. To build her model of informational cascade, Lohmann (1994) relies on the rational choice approach. According to the rational choice approach, people do not join a protest movement randomly, rather they decide to join a protest movement based on their participation incentive. Lohmann argues that the aggregate turnout of protesters over time serves as an informational cascade for people who extract benefit-cost information from these aggregate turnouts regarding who is turning out in these protests. She argues that the aggregate turnout—and specifically who is turning out (radicals or moderates) to protest movements—can inform the public about the negative experience of individuals under a regime. Let's take the example of the political protests commonly referred to as the Lawyers' Movement of 2007 in Pakistan and consider what signal these protests sent to middle class Pakistanis who might have been deciding whether or not to tolerate the military regime. Since lawyers represent a faction of the educated middle class in Pakistan and since they were deploying nonviolent tactics to protest the military rule in the country, these protests sent signals to potential sympathizers to join. However, if 30,000 Taliban supporters from Waziristan (a city in mountainous region in Pakistan that shares its border with Afghanistan) hold demonstrations on the streets of Islamabad and deploy violent tactics against the regime, this would ward off observers from joining such protests. Hence, the informative role of these political protests is to send a signal to potential challengers as to whether it's just radicals in large numbers (such as the Taliban) protesting against the regime, or if there are moderates (like the Pakistani Lawyers Movement) turning out for the demonstrations as well. Using the example of East German protests during the period 1989–1991 in Leipzig, Lohmann (1994) argued that the success of one protest sent signals to others who joined similar protests.

In the light of Lohmann's logic of informational cascade, this book argues that during their respective political crises in Pakistan, Egypt and Tunisia, political protests served as informational cascades. These informational cascades were sending signals not only to potential protestors, but also to the ruling elites simultaneously. After all, when political protests in the three countries started, armed forces and authoritarian regimes were not divided and acted together to curb the ongoing political unrest. However, the ever-increasing aggregate turnout of the protests under study served as signals of information to the ruling elite that they could not curb these protests by force, which later created rifts among rulers themselves. For example, in Pakistan, President Musharraf lost the support of the military when he could not curb the protests by force. As a result, Musharraf eventually had to resign. Thus, the previously undivided military elite started to show cracks, which ultimately resulted in reduced support for Musharraf's policies. The cases were similar in Egypt and Tunisia, where President Mubarak and President Ben Ali had to give up their reigns after their national armed forces withdrew their support.

Lohmann's (1994) description of the cycle of protests, i.e., that the aggregate turnout of a protest leads to the formation of another protest, also resonates with Tarrow's idea of cycle of contentions, which describes the process by which the success of a contentious collective action in a political uprising may lead to other similar protests. Simply put, both Tarrow (1998) and Lohmann (1994) look at political uprisings not as random occurrences, but as a process through which the success of one protest movement will pave the way for another. Furthermore, according to Lohmann (1994), the reaction of people to the negative information about a regime depends upon the nature of the regime. For example, if people in a democratic setting get negative information—such as revelations of governmental corruption—they may demand a change of leadership, but not of the system. However, single-party or authoritarian regimes, wherein freedom of speech and expression are prohibited, do not entertain such negative information. Once negative public opinion against such regimes is created, the status quo is destabilized.

Informational Cascades and Icons of Outrage

Lohmann's (1994) informational cascade echoes the concept of "icons of outrage" presented by Perlmutter (1998). According to Perlmutter (1998), sometimes certain images become the center of public and elite attention because of their uniqueness. To define such images, he introduced the term icons of outrage to differentiate ordinary protest images from the ones that have the tendency to generate public and elite discourse and/or upheavals.

According to Perlmutter (1998), images that have the tendency to become icons of outrage must have following elements: celebrity, prominence, frequency, profit, instantaneousness, transposability, fame of subjects, importance of events, metonymy, primordiality and/or cultural resonance, and striking composition. Out of these elements, transposability, fame of subjects, importance of events, metonymy, primordiality and/or cultural resonance seem to be most relevant to Lohmann's signals of the informational cascade model. To elaborate further, let's look at the definitions of these elements. "Transposability" in Perlmutter's (1998) icons of outrage refers to a quality of icons that "are often replicated across media" (p. 14). Both fame of subjects and importance of events correspond to the significance of an icon, which is tied to important social events or historical occurrences. Metonymy refers to an image's ability to represent a greater event because of its summing up quality. For example, the images of planes hitting the World Trade Center on September 11, 2001 can be considered metonymic. Primordiality and/or cultural resonance suggest an icon's ability to resonate with our common cultural history. In Islamic traditions and culture, the image of the Kaaba (the Holy place for Muslims in Mecca, Saudi Arabia, where they gather every year to perform pilgrimage) fulfills the quality of primordiality. When these basic conditions are met, any image (still or moving) may have the ability to fulfill Lohmann's (1994) signals of information in her informational cascade model.

Furthermore, thinking in terms of Perlmutter's (1998) conceptualization of icons of outrage, this chapter asserts that during the political uprisings in Pakistan, Egypt and Tunisia, certain images in the form of YouTube video clips and Facebook posts became icons of outrage among citizens. These helped the formation and sustainability of social movements in the three countries. One example of such images can be the self-immolation of Mohamed Bouazizi. The image travelled on social media platforms with the speed of light to the rest of the world, resulting in online and offline political activism inside and outside of Tunisia. These icons of outrage also resonate with Tarrow's (1998) idea of cultural and ideological frames. Tarrow believes that protesters deploy ideological frames to sustain their protest movements. Thus, iconic images can sometimes become so strong that they carry cultural and ideological powers with them. Whenever such images are deployed as a resource in a protest situation, they don't only send signals of people's unhappiness to a particular regime, they also attract potential sympathizers to join the protest because of the images' resonances to the cultural and political ideologies of potential sympathizers.

Conclusion

In summary, after surveying Hirschman, Tarrow and Lohmann's theories on social movements and political participation, we note that all three scholars see a role for communication in successful social movements. Where Hirschman sees the role of communication in the form of voice, Tarrow and Lohmann observe its utility in amplifying grievances by sharing cultural and ideological frames via the mass media. Likewise, Perlmutter's (1998) *icons of outrage* help us determine the iconic power of still and moving images that protesters may deploy as cultural and ideological frames in order to sustain mass political uprisings. The forthcoming chapters about the three countries, Pakistan, Egypt and Tunisia, will benefit from the influential works of these scholars while explaining the factors and circumstances that contributed to the mass political uprisings of Pakistan (2007), Egypt and Tunisia (2010–11).

References

Barnlund, D. (1970). A transactional model of communication. In K. K. Sereno, & C. D. Mortensen, *Foundations of communication theory* (pp. 83–92). New York: Harper and Row.

Berkowitz, D. A. (Ed.). (1997). *Social meanings of news: A text-reader*. Thousand Oaks, CA: Sage Publications.

Blumer, H. (1939). Critique of research in the social science, i: An appraisal of Thomas and Znaniecki's, "The Polish peasant in Europe and America." New York: Social Science Research Council. *Bulletin, 44*.

Boudreau, V. & Meyer, D. S. (2009). Social movements. In T. Landman and N. Robinson (Eds.) *The Sage handbook of comparative politics*. Thousand Oaks, CA: Sage Publications, Inc.

Dahl, R. (1971). *Polyarchy: Participation and opposition*. New Haven, CT: Yale University Press.

Dewey, J. (1954). *The public and its problems*. Chicago, IL: Swallow Press.

Edgerly, S., Vraga, E. K., Dalrymple, K. E., Macafee, T. & Fung, T. K. (2013). Directing the dialogue: The relationship between YouTube videos and the comments they spur. *Journal of Information Technology & Politics, 10*(3), 276–292.

Foulger, D. (2004). Models of the Communication Process. Brooklyn, New Jersey. Retrieved February 15, 2018, from http://davis.foulger.info/research/unifiedModelOfCommunication.htm

Gerbaudo, P. (2016). Constructing Public Space| Rousing the Facebook Crowd: Digital Enthusiasm and Emotional Contagion in the 2011 Protests in Egypt and Spain. *International Journal Of Communication, 10*, 20. Retrieved March 27, 2019, from https://ijoc.org/index.php/ijoc/article/view/3963

Ghannam, J. (2011). Social media in the Arab world: Leading up to the uprisings of 2011. *Center for International Media Assistance, 3*(1), 1–44. Retrieved April 26, 2019, from http://www.cima.ned.org/wp-content/uploads/2011/02/Ghannam-Jeffrey-Arab_Social_Media-Report-10-25-11.pdf

Gitlin, T. (2003). *The whole world is watching: Mass media in the making and unmaking of the new left*. Oakland, CA: University of California Press.

Habermas, J. (1989). *The structural transformation of the public sphere*. Cambridge, MA: MIT Press.
Harb, Z. (2011). Arab revolutions and the social media effect. *M/C Journal, 14*(2). Retrieved June 10, 2019, from http://journal.media-culture.org.au/index.php/mcjournal/article/view/364Two
Hirschman, A. O. (1970). *Exit, voice, and loyalty; responses to decline in firms, organizations, and states*. Cambridge, Mass: Harvard University Press.
Huntington, S. (1965). Political development and political decay. *World Politics, 17*(3), 386–430.
Imig, D. R., Tarrow, S., & Tarrow, S. G. (Eds.). (2001). *Contentious Europeans: Protest and politics in an emerging polity*. Lanham, MD: Rowman & Littlefield.
Jenkins, J. C. (1983). Resource mobilization theory and the study of social movements. *Annual Review of Sociology, 9*(1), 527–553.
Katz, E. (1957). The two-step flow of communication. *An Up-To-Date Report on an Hypothesis. Political Opinion Quarterly, 21* (1*)*, 61–78.
Kolb, F. (2007). *Protest and opportunities: The political outcomes of social movements*. Frankfurt, Germany: Campus Verlag.
Kousis, M. & Tilly, C. (2005). *Economic and political contention in comparative perspective*. Boulder, CO: Paradigm Publishers.
Lohmann, S. (1994). The dynamics of informational cascades: the Monday demonstrations in Leipzig, East Germany, 1989–91. *World Politics, 47*(1), 42–101.
Milan, S. (2015). From social movements to cloud protesting: the evolution of collective identity. *Information, Communication & Society, 18*(8), 887–900.
Mir, J. (2011). Political and media transitions in Tunisia: A snapshot of media policy and regulatory environment. *Internews Report*. Retrieved May 20, 2019, from https://internews.org/sites/default/files/resources/Internews_Tunisia_MediaLawReview_Aug11.pdf
Olson, M. (1965). *Logic of collective action*. Cambridge, MA: Harvard University Press.
Ostrom, E. (1998). A behavioral approach to the rational choice theory of collective action: Presidential address, American Political Science Association, 1997. *American Political Science Review, 92*(1), 1–22.
Perlmutter, D. D. (1998). *Photojournalism and foreign policy: Icons of outrage in international crises*. Westport, Conn.: Praeger.
Robinson, S. (2011). Journalism as process: The organizational implications of participatory online news. *Journalism & Communication Monographs, 13*(3), 137–210. https://doi-org.lib-e2.lib.ttu.edu/10.1177/152263791101300302
Ross, M. L. (2001). Does oil hinder democracy? *World Politics, 53*(3), 325–361.
Shannon, C. E., & Weaver, W. (1949). The mathematical theory of communication. Urbana: University of Illinois Press.
Shibutani, T. (1988). Blumer's contributions to twentieth-century sociology. *Symbolic Interaction, 11*(1), 23–31.
Singer, J. B., Hermida, A., Domingo, D., Heinonen, A., Paulussen, S., Quandt, T., … & Vujnovic, M. (2011). *Participatory journalism: Guarding open gates at online newspapers*. West Sussex, UK: Wiley-Blackwell.
Skocpol, T. (1979). *States and social revolutions: A comparative analysis of France, Russia, and China*. Cambridge, England: Cambridge University Press.

Tarrow, S. G. (1998). *Power in movement: Social movements and contentious politics.* Cambridge, England: Cambridge University Press.

Tarrow, S. G. (2012). *Strangers at the gates: Movements and states in contentious politics.* Cambridge, England: Cambridge University Press.

Tilly, C. (1992). *Coercion, capital, and European states, AD 990–1992.* Hoboken, NJ: Blackwell.

Tilly, C. & Tilly, L. (Eds.). (1981). *Class conflict and collective action.* Beverly Hills, CA: Sage Publications.

Tilly, C. & Wood, L. J. (2012). *Social movements, 1768–2012.* New York, NY: Routledge

Treré, E. (2016). The dark side of digital politics: Understanding the algorithmic manufacturing of consent and the hindering of online dissidence. *IDS Bulletin, 1*(47). Retrieved May 17, 2019, from https://opendocs.ids.ac.uk/opendocs/handle/123456789/7697

Verba, S., Nie, N. H., & Kim, J. O. (1987). *Participation and political equality: A seven-nation comparison.* Chicago, IL: University of Chicago Press.

Volpi, F. (2017). Revolution and authoritarianism in North Africa. Oxford Scholarship Online. DOI: 10.1093/oso/9780190642921.001.0001

von Stein, L. (1848). *Socialist and communist movements since the third French Revolution.* Stuttgart: Olms.

2

Creative Protests

Art is not, as the metaphysicians say, the manifestation of some mysterious idea of beauty or God; it is not, as the aesthetical physiologists say, a game in which man lets off his excess of stored-up energy; it is not the expression of man's emotions by external signs; it is not the production of pleasing objects; and, above all, it is not pleasure; but it is a means of union among men, joining them together in the same feelings, and indispensable for the life and progress toward well-being of individuals and of humanity. (Leo Tolstoy, in his essay "What is art?" as quoted by Popova, 2012)

Creative protests in media and communication studies are relatively new phenomena that has opened a unique window of opportunity for mass media scholars to better understand the political power of the arts when studying the role of communication in social movements. The rise of social media and the ability of protesters to produce, publish and share their creative messages with wide audiences has spurred the growth of creative protests in several parts of the world, including Pakistan, Egypt and Tunisia. This chapter presents three case studies, one from each of the aforementioned countries. It examines how the artists in question became a voice of protest in their respective settings, as well as how social media contributed to these artists' ability to share their messages of creative protest and thus gain more recognition.

Even though many people contributed to the creative protests of the three countries under discussion (e.g., look at the works of the following scholars: Ahmad, 2010; Foran, 2014; Habib, 2016; Kraidy, 2017; Lennon, 2014; LeVine, 2015; Nazmi, 2016; Robertson, 2015; Valassopoulos & Mostafa, 2014), this chapter focuses only on three artists who are celebrated and remembered as the most iconic creative protest artists in their respective countries. To provide a roadmap, the chapter starts with Pakistani rapper, Ali Gul Pir, and follows with Ramy Essam, an Egyptian protest singer. The third case study of the chapter sheds light on Hamada Ben Amor, a Tunisian rapper, known as the bard of the North African revolutionary wave (Walt, 2011). The chapter ends by providing a quick summary of commonalities that exist in all the three cases and examines how these common traits contribute to the sustainability of political uprisings in non-Western settings.

In order to understand the importance and relevance of creative protests in the context of social movements in Pakistan, Egypt and Tunisia, let's revisit what art actually is. As a common adage, we all know that art is a form of expression. The form of expression, however, can carry different meanings in different societies. To some, an artist's creativity is nothing more than a presentation of aesthetically appealing aspects of our society, while for others, a particular form of art might be interpreted as an emotional expression about a sensitive issue (Kraidy, 2017; Carroll, 2000; Davies, 1991; Mithen, 1999; Popova, 2012; Stecker, 1997).

In relatively closed societies, where monarchs and dictatorships leave little to no room for people to express themselves, some may turn to indirect forms of expression through creative means such as poetry, paintings, singing, music, blogging, body art, etc. (Kraidy, 2017). Put this way, in authoritarian societies, where an individual's freedom of expression is not without a price, an artistic way of expressing oneself is relatively less harmful and has the ability to become a voice of the voiceless. Our recent past is full of such examples. Creative arts played a great role in bringing down the Berlin Wall in 1989. In fact, the message of love and freedom that was delivered by song writers, artists and pianists in East Germany during the 1980s, triggered a social movement that ended up bringing down the Wall, which had separated families and friends during the cold war era. Two artists (both singers), Leonard Bernstein and Bruce Springsteen, are commended for launching a social movement through their live concerts in East Germany that changed the course of the history of the region, forever (Dring, 2018; Evans, 2014). Their songs and live performances in front of crowds consisting of hundreds and thousands of people in East Germany gave those people freedom to think, and such a sense of freedom of thought led the masses in the closed society to mobilize themselves for a collective action. It is believed that the American singer and song writer, "Bruce Springsteen delivered a message of freedom to a huge concert in East Berlin in July 1988—and the Berlin Wall fell the following year" (Evans, 2014, Para 1). Likewise, Bernstein's song 'Ode To Freedom', which he performed live for Christmas in 1989 contributed as a catalyst to mobilize and bring people together both from the East and West Germany. As a result of these artists' contributions, the era to an ideology of separation ended in November 1989 with the fall of Berlin wall after almost 30 years of its construction.

Thus, in closed societies where freedom of information, expression and communication are seen as privileges, not as rights, creative art tends to take the form of innovative protests in order to grab the attention and support of a divided, confused and distracted public. Such art is aimed at seeking change in the society. Communications and comparative politics scholars agree on the fact that the attention of people toward a common cause provides momentum to the cause, which is an asset for all kinds of collective action, protest and resistance. Social movements survive and sustain on momentum (Lohmann, 1994; Perlmutter, 1998; Shirky, 2011; Skocpol, 1979; Tarrow, 1998; Tilly, 1990). In this digital age, many forms of social media are providing more opportunities for people to express themselves to wider audiences, thanks to the Internet, smartphones and satellite communications networks. In the absence of traditional media outlets, artists are using these new communication platforms to launch creative protests expressing their unhappiness toward a particular regime. If these creative protests gain momentum, they can become revolutions carrying the power to topple regimes, as we have witnessed in the cases of political uprisings of Pakistan (2007), Tunisia (2010) and Egypt (2011).

Pakistan

Pakistan has a long history of love and appreciation for art and creativity, dating back to the prehistoric ages. The Indus Valley Civilization, which is named after the Indus river system in Pakistan, is the earliest known urban culture of the Indian subcontinent (2500–1700 BCE). The people of the Indus River Valley Civilization developed expertise in handicraft, carving, sculptures, pottery, clay toys, brick houses and well-engineered drainage system (Indus Civilization, 2018; "Indus River Valley Civilizations," n.d.; Violatti, 2013).

Founded in 1526 and ended in 1857, the Mughal Empire of the Indian Subcontinent is also known and remembered for its love for art and creativity (Mughal Dynasty, 2018). Mughal emperors who ruled the region for over 300 years promoted architecture, Quranic calligraphy on walls and poetry during their rule (KnowIndia.Gov, n.d.; Mughal Art and Architecture, n.d.). This trend to promote art continued even after the British Empire took over the South Asian region from the Mughals and kept it colonized for over 100 years (Kaul, 2011). In order to protest the British rule, several poets started using Urdu as a language of poetry against the British Empire (Siddiqui, 2016). Since such poetic verses were in Urdu, they carried deep cultural context. It was difficult for the English-speaking rulers of that time to fully understand and grasp the hidden meaning of the poetry. However, the message of resentment against the British Empire kept moving from one generation to the other through this art of poetry. In fact, poetic protest was one of the contributing factors in building resistance against the British rule that eventually resulted in the creation of Pakistan and India in 1947 (Jalil, 2017; Siddiqui, 2016).

After its inception in 1947, Pakistan's fragile democratic system was soon to be taken over by military dictatorships. Poets and literary figures such as Habib Jalib, Faiz Ahmad Faiz and Saadat Hasan Manto challenged the dictatorships using art as a tool of creative protest against military rule (Russell, 1972; Siddiqui, 2016). These artists were threatened—and in some cases jailed—by the military rulers (Siddiqui, 2016; Singh, 2016). Habib Jalib, who was known as "the people's poet [, was] jailed multiple times by Zia [a military dictator between 1977–88] for penning verses against his rule" (Asif, 2018, para. 4). Jalib expressed his dissent this way: "*Virsay mein humay yeh gham hai mila, iss gham ko naya kya likhna?* (We've inherited this sad state of affairs, why write this sadness as something new?)" (Asif, 2018, para. 4).

Even though his poetry did not always directly target the military regime, the rulers in Pakistan and the people of the country both understood the hidden or indirect voice of protest against the military dictatorship. This led to Jalib's multiple arrests, attempts to suppress his voice against the regime. However, the suppression of creative expression took a new form with the emergence of social media, because artists were finding new and innovative ways to launch creative protests, rather than just relying on poetic verses. The Internet that made its debut in Pakistan in late 1990s when there was only one state-run TV, Pakistan Television (PTV) to serve a population of around 200 million people (Arif, 2010). Since the *PTV* was directly controlled and operated by the government of Pakistan, any voice of dissent stood no chance of getting on air. The introduction of the Internet and the subsequent social media challenged and changed this hegemony of state-run television media in the country, forever. The Internet brought with it an opportunity for creative artists to express themselves on this alternative platform of communication relatively freely.

In 2007, when Pakistan was going through yet another military dictatorship, self-imposed president, General Musharraf banned the entire country's news media in an effort to discourage and stop ongoing political protests against him. Yet, some of these protests were not even taking place in streets, but rather on social media, such as in YouTube videos, which included background music and creative editing to attract more sympathizers against the regime. Even though Musharraf was ousted from his office as a result of these countrywide political protests against him, his successors in the government had already realized the power of social media as an alternative platform of communication, and thus banned YouTube in the country so as to discourage people from using YouTube as an alternative form of media in the absence of traditional broadcast media (For more details see Chapter 6 about Pakistan's Politico-Cultural situation).

Some of the Pakistani artists, particularly solo singers, used their art as a form of creative protest against the government's decision to block the access of average Pakistanis to this social media platform. One such singer, is Ali Gul Pir whose song "Kholo BC" gained national attention as "an anthem against Pakistan's … ban on YouTube" ("Viral video," 2014, para. 1).

"Kholo BC": A Movement Against Online Censorship

"Kholo BC," a music video by Ali Gul Pir and Adil Omar, was released in February 2014 as "a part of the youth initiative, 'Pakistan for All,' a movement that campaigns against state censorship," which "came together with a rap song to speak against the authorities" (Nazmi, 2016, para. 3). The music video utilizes creativity and satire to protest the government's control over the media, especially the video-sharing site YouTube (Habib, 2016). The video depicts an influential Pakistani politician who promulgates this ban on YouTube. Law enforcement agents then run to capture the YouTube mascot, which is trying to escape arrest. The song curses and mocks the government by referencing the culturally well-known phrase "kholo ban chor," "[t]he … latter two words of [which] are homophones of South Asia's most famous expletive: 'bhen chod' (sister f**er), a jibe clearly directed at the government" (Habib 2016, para. 4).

In a country like Pakistan, where simply speaking up against the powerful is considered nothing less than a crime, using such references against the ruling elite in everyday settings is almost impossible because one has to pay a price for such openness. As some have observed:

> this song is perhaps the most controversial song released by Ali till date and is almost matched to the norm breaking music that was once produced by the Beygairat Brigade, whose songs got banned in cyber space because of their mockery of the Pakistan army. (Phadnis, 2014, para. 5)

The viral music video creators, Ali Gul Pir and Adil Omar, used an extremely creative form of protest, using cultural cues to the abusive curse but never using the complete term, thus protecting themselves from any legal repercussions of being indecent or immoral. The song also warns the government that if the rulers continued blocking YouTube, Pakistani citizens can also use Facebook as an alternative form of media and share all the breaking news via that platform. In other words, the song was simultaneously offering an alternate avenue to the citizens to turn to other social media, such as Facebook, and never stop expressing their unhappiness against the powerful elites, no matter what it takes.

This perspective of being able to utilize other forms of media in the absence or control of traditional mass media is one of the most important theses of this book. Before the age of the Internet, closed societies such as Pakistan could be controlled and regulated by the ruling elites, as they had absolute control over the traditional sources of news and information. Historically, the government could single-handedly decide what the public should know and what information should be kept from the public. Alternatively, if masses were unhappy about the government's way of ruling them, they lacked any formal platform to express their unhappiness about their rulers, because the entire mass media was state-run or state-controlled. This hegemony, however, for the very first time in the history of Pakistan, was challenged when the Internet started becoming a part of the average citizen's life. As I have mentioned before, historically, a majority of Pakistani artists used poetry as a creative tool of protest to express their emotions against their rulers, yet this has also changed this time. Social media platforms such as YouTube and Facebook have enabled the emergence of creative protest songs like "Kholo BC" at a time when traditional media outlets were tightly controlled by the regime. Put this way, it was because of the emergence of social media in Pakistan that something that was once an oral tradition—and thus only shareable with a small, immediate group of people in the same physical location—could now be put online and reach a wider audience. The Internet, in general, and social media, in particular, have given Pakistani citizens a powerful alternative to express themselves when traditional media outlets were unable to perform their civic role. Artists, too, now have the ability and opportunity to get more creative than just uttering some dual-meaning poetic verses. Now they can express themselves powerfully by combining music, poetry and visuals as a form of creative protest (Robertson, 2015; Valassopoulos & Mostafa, 2014). "Kholo BC" is a powerful example of such an expression.

It is pertinent to mention here that language use plays a great role in spreading the narrative of a protest, and an artist's decision to choose a particular language for the expression of his/her art carries strong meanings behind it. In this case, half of the song was sung in Urdu in order to target the Pakistani community, while the next half is sung in English. The English version allows this message to be conveyed to not only English-speaking Pakistanis, but also to the rest of the world, through English as a global language. Through this spreading of the message on a global level, other countries could also join this movement against the ban on YouTube and exert their pressure on the Pakistani government to lift this ban. For context, the English lyrics of the second verse of the song, written and performed by Adil Omar are included:

> We storm the PTA office, bring reporters and cameras
> Rocking V for Vendetta masks like anonymous hackers
> Was going viral on the web, I was stomping some rappers
> But now I have to Hide My Ass with a proxy and password
> They shut Spotflux off and now there's boys in the street
> Dry humping everything in sight like some monsters in heat
> Pent up testosterone in men with no form of release
> And then we wonder why they're angry, obnoxious, and creeps
> —but banning YouTube?—this is a new age
> Of sleazy politicians with their comb-overs and toupees
> And scummy supervillians with control over what you play
> And who's to say they can when they burn through money you pay
> They go enforce their censorship, but ignore the bigger threats
> I doubt these pricks can even grasp the f**king internet
> Let alone be in charge of important decisions
> Blatant hypocrisy with bullshit moral convictions
> And how we're blind, we face their machine with no rage
> While they rape us and take us back to the stone age
> So if the government don't like the venom this man spits
> You can be a silly bitch and tell em to ban this
>
> (Omar, 2013)

Grateful acknowledgement is made to the following for permission to reproduce copyrighted material: Adil Omar, Singer/Songwriter, 2013. Reprinted by permission of the publisher.

In summary, "Kholo BC" represents not only a viral music video, but an example of new ways and forms of protests that artists in Pakistan are utilizing to seek attention of their fellow citizens in order to gain momentum and support for ongoing social movements for change in their society. Also, these new forms of creative art are geared toward a wider audience because of social media's ability to spread the narrative of protests across the globe with the velocity of light, which had never been the case in the history of this region.

Egypt

The political uprisings of 2011 in Egypt changed the country forever in multiple ways, one of which remains the political influence of creative art that has continued reshaping the country, even during the post-revolution era. As protesters began growing in numbers, so did the methods of protest. Protest anthems began spreading, poets wrote prose, and visual artists placed their work on walls and posters around Cairo and Egypt as a whole (Robertson, 2015; Valassopoulos & Mostafa, 2014). All of this Do It Yourself (DIY) creative arts represents a fundamental shift in power dynamics as the people of Egypt now started to realize that they don't need the government's permission to do things. In other words:

> [i]n the 100 days since one of the world's most entrenched dictatorships was toppled, Egypt has borne witness to an explosion of creative energy seeking to memorialise, critique and carry forward the country's moment of revolutionary fervour, a process which has itself revolutionised the country's long-stagnant cultural landscape; buskers can perform without police permits. (Shenker, 2011, para. 7)

This section will highlight one of the most prominent examples of creative artists who became a part and parcel of Egypt's political uprisings, which resulted in the removal of the country's most powerful dictator, Hosni Mubarak.

Ramy Essam: The Singer of the Egyptian Revolution

"I will not stop singing 'til Hosni Mubarak goes' " was the courageous response of Ramy in a video message soon after he was badly beaten by the Egyptian military (Anghel, 2011, 4:01). Ramy was an Egyptian singer, not known before the protests (Valassopoulos & Mostafa, 2014). He originally joined the crowds in Tahrir Square, but soon turned into a hero when he wrote the protest anthem "Irhal" (Leave), directed at Mubarak. It was because of its creativity and timeliness, "[t]he song took on a life of its own. This, during a movement that saw two million protestors, hundreds of deaths, thousands of injuries and countless arrests. 'Irhal' was named one of *Time Out's* 100 Songs That Changed History" (Hamad, 2017, para. 27).

The song "Irhal" was based on the protest chants by his fellow Egyptians at Tahrir Square (Inskeep, 2011). As Ramy describes it, " 'People were saying the same things over and over, and it got old … I thought if it were in music it would be better' " (McTighe, 2011, para. 6). His point here reinforces the claim of this book chapter that creativity and art can give new life to boring or repetitive slogans and chants, thus attracting more protesters to join a cause. Creative art is not only a form for expressing anger and unhappiness toward a regime during critical circumstances, but also an opportunity for people to reunite and celebrate their togetherness, despite of all the hardships that they are going through. In this context, some believe that it's not only the mood of protesters that a protest artist like Ramy was able to capture, but also "Mr. Essam's music offered an artistic reprieve from the violence and hardship in Tahrir Square and became a rallying point that emboldened protesters to continue their fight" (McTighe, 2011, para. 12).

Another aspect that needs to be acknowledged here is the fact that Ramy Essam's fame as a protest artist is also tied directly with his sacrifice for the cause. He was badly beaten during the Battle of the Camel but returned to the stage to perform. This can be seen as a case of a protester performing for the protesters. In other words, Ramy was not only an artist who was writing for a revolutionary cause, but, in fact, he himself was an active participant of the ongoing social movement against the regime. And this aspect gave more power and credibility to his words. In the wake the of Egyptian revolution, after Mubarak stepped down, Ramy's anthem "Irhal" was redirected toward the military after the country's armed forces stepped in to replace Mubarak. In other words, the Egyptian military tried to reap the fruit of revolution by taking over the reins of the country. Protestors did not give up and returned to the Square with a new purpose: to take the military out of the country's democratic offices. This did not go well, as the Egyptian military forces broke up a sit-in, and Essam was arrested, beaten and tortured (Inskeep, 2011; McTighe, 2011). It was only after protesters began chanting outside the museum where he was being tortured that the military released him. From that experience, he wrote another song, "Hit Me," which also became a hit (McTighe, 2011; Hamad, 2017). As protests began to die down due to government crackdowns, Essam accepted asylum in Sweden. He continued to write protest and socially conscious music and is now considering returning to Egypt (Crowcroft, 2017; Hamad, 2017).

Tunisia

Creative protests on social media and in the streets gave witnesses a sense of the potential impact of actions, such as sustaining and spreading messages of resistance. The Tunisian uprisings, which are commonly referred to as the Jasmine revolution of 2010/11 resulted in the removal of the Ben Ali regime. The creative works of two artists, Hamada Ben Amor and el Seed, stand out while revisiting the memories of Tunisian revolution of 2010/11. While Hamada chose music and singing as his tool to protest the regime, el Seed blended the "historic art of Arabic calligraphy with graffti" ("eL Seed: Can the Beauty of Arabic Calligraphy Shift Perspectives?", 2017, Para 2) as his weapon of resistance. For this chapter, however, I will focus on Hamada Ben Amor because of his comparative similarities to that of Pakistani and Egyptian singers who have been discussed previously.

Hamada Ben Amor: *Rais Lebled*—the Anthem of the Mideast revolution

Like the previous two examples, Tunisian artist, Hamada Ben Amor, better known as El Général, was an unknown artist until 2011 when his song, "Mr. President Your People Are Dying," went viral. El Général's song was based on the "words [that] were sung by demonstrators. The lyrics include: Mr. President, your people are dying/People are eating rubbish/Look at what is happening/Miseries everywhere Mr. President/I talk with no fear/Although I know I will only get troubles/I see injustice everywhere' " (Walt, 2011, para. 5).

Since traditional mass media were under state control, El Général had to turn to social media, which offered an alternative platform to disseminate his message against the regime (Morgan, 2011). El Général recalls during an interview with *Time* magazine, "I just used my personal Facebook page to become known. I had two friends, one filmed my songs on a small video camera, and the other edited the videos and put them up on YouTube" (Walt, 2011, para. 4). Soon after his music video went viral on Facebook and YouTube, El Général was arrested in his home and taken for interrogation by President Zine El Abidine Ben Ali's security forces. Since El Général's song was a representative of the voice of Tunisian protests (Morgan, 2011), people came out in the streets demanding his release from the government and security forces. This led to his freedom on the condition that he would not write any more songs against the president (LeVine, 2015). This did not stop El Général (Bohn, 2011). When Mohamed Bouazizi, a young vegetable vendor, doused himself with gasoline and set himself alight on Dec. 17, 2010, as a mark of protest against police corruption and brutality, it was a turning point for El Général (LeVine, 2015). In response to this incident, he "wrote a new song called 'Tunisia Our Country' on Dec. 22, about the accelerating protest movement" (Walt, 2011, para. 5).

Putting things in perspective, it is imperative to note here that El Général's popularity as a protest singer/rapper did not end with the fall of President Zine El Abidine Ben Ali's regime. His narrative via his creative arts moved on to Egypt and inspired protesters there (Foran, 2014; LeVine, 2015). His music video, "Rais Lebled" (meaning Head of State) became the anthem on the streets in Tunisia. In early 2011, "the song was picked up in Cairo and sung in Tahrir Square" (Walt, 2011, para. 9). Perhaps this is the reason that El Général's song is also known as the anthem of the Mideast revolution. A vivid connection can be observed between the Tunisian political uprisings and the Egyptian political unrests, not only in terms of geographic proximity, but also how artists in these countries got inspiration from each other and launched their own versions of creative protests. Thus, a strong case can be made that the success of one creative protest may inspire others to utilize similar tools and resources in order to sustain their social movements.

Finally, we cannot ignore the fact that mass media sources in these countries were already banned and/or barred from covering the protests and protesters' demands, and these artists were not allowed to hold their concerts in public. This means that in such a scenario when the traditional media was completely absent from the scene, there must be a more powerful and effective means of communication taking place to carry the narrative of protests from one country to another. This alternative platform of communication was, in fact, social media such as Facebook and YouTube, which were readily available in the hands of a majority of youth in these countries. These protesters were not only able to communicate and promote their message of dissent, they also were able to regroup and reorganize on a common platform and inspire other nations to join hands in their struggle against the powerful and exploitative elite.

Applying a more academic lens to this debate, I would like us to rethink Lohmann's (1994) model of informational cascade. As explained in Chapter 1, Lohmann (1994) suggested that communication and information carry the most important role when it comes to protest politics. She calls political demonstrations an "informational cascade." These political demonstrations take the place of alternate media as observers of these protests extract benefit-cost information from turnout members. Based on this information regarding who is turning out (extremists or moderates), sympathizers decide to join or leave a protest movement (Lohmann, 1994).

In this context, a strong case can be made that creative arts in certain situations can serve as powerful "signals" in an informational cascade. Such signals not only serve the purpose to disseminate the message of grievances against the regime, but also inspire others to join a collective action both on digital platforms and on streets. Further academic research is needed to explore this connection so that media and communication scholars can better understand how the deployment of creative arts can serve as an integral resource in bringing people together for a collective action and the sustainability of a social movement.[1]

Conclusion

While talking about creative protests and the artists who used their arts to protest the powerful elite, several commonalities exist. For example, all the artists discussed in this chapter come from middle class families and were relatively young when they rose to fame. Ali Gul Pir was 28 years old when he launched his protest song "Kholo BC".; Ramy Essam was 24 years old when he rose to fame because of his song "Irhal"; and Hamada Ben Amor was only 21 when he was hailed as the bard of the North African revolutionary wave because of his song, "Mr. President Your People Are Dying." After looking at the case studies of the three countries, it can be observed that the artists who used their creative arts to protest against their respective regimes were relatively unknown figures/artists before the political unrests of Pakistan, Egypt and Tunisia. Their fame is not associated with people's appreciation of their art, but is directly related to the context in which these artists came forward to unite protesters for a common cause by using their creative means.

Also, in all the three cases, these artists used their creative arts in an utterly direct and blunt way when it came to challenge the powerful elite of their respective countries. Their messages of protest, regardless of how they were delivered (music videos, calligraphy, graffiti, etc.) resonated directly with people's demands and their feelings. Put this way, all three artists used their creative art as not only a way of creative protest, but also to amplify the grievances of their fellow citizens both via street and online platforms, such as YouTube. Thus, art in extraordinary situations can be an extremely powerful tool to sustain a social movement by keeping up the momentum of protest participants to achieve a particular goal.

Note

1. To better understand my argument here, look at my discussion about Lohmann (1994) and Tarrow's (1998) works on social movements in Chapter 1 of this book.

References

Ahmad, S. (2010). *Rock & roll jihad: A Muslim rock star's revolution.* Free Press. New York.

Anghel, I. (2011, February 15). Ramy Essam- The real revolution song of Tahrir square [video file]. Retrieved May 01, 2019, from https://www.youtube.com/watch?time_continue=262&v=-rEKmTBKiBM

Arif, R. (2010). How Terrorism Killed the News: Pakistani Journalism after 9/11. Saarbrucken, Germany: Lambert Academic Publishing. http://www.amazon.com/How-Terrorism-Killed-News-journalism/dp/3838335791

Asif, H. (2018, October 8). General Ziaul Haq: The man to answer for a lot that went wrong with Pakistan. *Herald.* Retrieved March 12, 2019, from https://herald.dawn.com/news/1398686

Bohn, L. (July 22, 2011). Rapping the revolution. *Foreign Policy.* Retrieved February 09, 2018, from https://foreignpolicy.com/2011/07/22/rapping-the-revolution/

Carroll, N. (Ed.). (2000). *Theories of art today.* Madison, WI: University of Wisconsin Press.

Crowcroft, O. (2017, September 1). Years after Egypt's revolution, Tahrir Square singer Ramy Essam wants to return home. *NewsWeek.* Retrieved March 28, 2019, from https://www.newsweek.com/cairo-calling-tahrir-square-singer-ramy-essam-eyes-return-egypt-658200

Davies, S. (1991). *Definitions of art.* Ithaca, NY: Cornell University Press.

Dring, C. (2018, August 16). Leonard Bernstein Marked The Fall Of The Berlin Wall With 'Ode To Freedom'. Retrieved April 03, 2019, from https://radio.wosu.org/post/leonard-bernstein-marked-fall-berlin-wall-ode-freedom#stream/0

Evans, S. (2014, October 21). How Bruce Springsteen rocked the Berlin Wall. BBC. Retrieved June 12, 2019, from http://www.bbc.com/culture/story/20130626-how-springsteen-rocked-the-wall

Foran, J. (2014). Beyond insurgency to radical social change: The new situation. *Studies in Social Justice, 8*(1), 5–25.

Habib, A.H. (2016, February 9). Pulling the plug on art. *Norient.* Retrieved March 11, 2019, from https://norient.com/video/kholo-bc-first/

Hamad, M. (2017, July 3). The journey of Tahrir Square singer Ramy Essam: The Egyptian rock star, who rose to fame with his song 'Irhal', releases a new album. *Gulf News*. Retrieved July 22, 2018, from https://gulfnews.com/entertainment/music/the-journey-of-tahrir-square-singer-ramy-essam-1.2052537

Indus civilization. (2018). *Encyclopaedia Britannica*. Retrieved April 13, 2019, from https://www.britannica.com/topic/Indus-civilization

Indus river valley civilizations. (n.d.). *Khan Academy*. Retrieved April 13, 2019, from https://www.khanacademy.org/humanities/world-history/world-history-beginnings/ancient-india/a/the-indus-river-valley-civilizations

Inskeep, S. (2011, March 15). Ramy Essam: The singer of the Egyptian revolution. *NPR*. Retrieved July 22, 2018, from https://www.npr.org/2011/03/15/134538629/ramy-esam-the-singer-of-the-egyptian-revolution

Jalil, R. (2017, August 15). Why it is impossible to think of Urdu poetry without thinking of India's journey to (and after) 1947. *Scroll.In*. Retrieved March 11, 2019, from https://scroll.in/article/846902/why-it-is-impossible-to-think-of-urdu-poetry-without-thinking-of-indias-journey-to-and-after-1947

Kaul, C. (2011, March 3). From empire to independence: The British Raj in India 1858–1947. *BBC History*. Retrieved April 13, 2019, from http://www.bbc.co.uk/history/british/modern/independence1947_01.shtml

KnowIndia.gov. (n.d.). Medieval history: The Mughal Empire. Retrieved April 13, 2019, from http://knowindia.gov.in/culture-and-heritage/medieval-history/the-mughal-empire.php

Kraidy, M. (2017). *The naked blogger of Cairo: Creative insurgency in the Arab world*. Cambridge, MA: Harvard University Press.

Lennon, J. (2014). Assembling a revolution: Graffiti, Cairo and the Arab spring. *Cultural Studies Review*, *20*(1), 237–75.

LeVine, M. (2015). When art is the weapon: Culture and resistance confronting violence in the post-uprisings Arab world. *Religions*, *6*(4), 1277–1313.

Lohmann, S. (1994). The dynamics of informational cascades: the Monday demonstrations in Leipzig, East Germany, 1989–91. *World Politics*, *47*(1), 42–101.

McTighe, K. (2011, December 7). Out of protest, an anthem for Egypt's Revolution. *New York Times*. Retrieved June 17, 2019, from (https://www.nytimes.com/2011/12/08/world/middleeast/out-of-protest-an-anthem-for-egypts-revolution.html

Mithen, S. (1999). *The prehistory of the mind: The cognitive origins of art, religion and science* (1st ed.). London, England: Thames & Hudson.

Morgan, A. (2011, February 26). From fear to fury: how the Arab world found its voice. *The Guardian*. Retrieved April 09, 2019, from https://www.theguardian.com/music/2011/feb/27/egypt-tunisia-music-protests

Mughal art and architecture. (n.d.) *The Columbia Encyclopedia* (6th ed.). Retrieved April 13, 2019, from https://www.encyclopedia.com/reference/encyclopedias-almanacs-transcripts-and-maps/mughal-art-and-architecture

Mughal Dynasty. (2018, September 20). *Encyclopedia Britannica*. Retrieved April 13, 2019, from https://www.britannica.com/topic/Mughal-dynasty

Nazmi, S. (2016, January 19). How #KholoBC video forced Pakistan to lift YouTube ban. *Daily O*. Retrieved April 28, 2019, from https://www.dailyo.in/variety/pakistan-kholo-bc-youtube-ban-innocence-of-muslims-islam-blasphemy/story/1/8544.html

eL Seed: Can The Beauty Of Arabic Calligraphy Shift Perspectives? (November 10, 2017). NPR.Org. *eL Seed: Can The Beauty of Arabic Calligraphy Shift Perspectives?* Retrieved October 24, 2019, from https://www.npr.org/2017/11/10/562880267/el-seed-can-the-beauty-of-arabic-calligraphy-shift-perspectives

Omar, A. (2013). Kholo BC (English lyrics). Retrieved April 28, 2019, from https://genius.com/Ali-gul-pir-kholobc-lyrics

Perlmutter, D. D. (1998). *Photojournalism and foreign policy: Icons of outrage in international crises*. Westport, Conn.: Praeger.

Phadnis, A. (2014, March 25). Pakistanis aren't too keen on censorship-free Internet. *The Express Tribune*. Retrieved April 27, 2019, from https://tribune.com.pk/story/687112/pakistanis-arent-too-keen-on-censorship-free-internet/

Popova, M. (2012, June 22). What is art? A few famous definitions, from antiquity to today. *The Atlantic*. Retrieved May 16, 2019, from https://www.theatlantic.com/entertainment/archive/2012/06/what-is-art-a-few-famous-definitions-from-antiquity-to-today/258871/

Robertson, C. (2015). Whose music, whose country? Music, mobilization, and social change in North Africa. *African Conflict and Peace building Review*, *5*(1), 66–87.

Russell, R. (1972). Poetry and politics in Pakistan. *Modern Asian Studies*, *6*(3), 353–357.

Shenker, J. (2011, May 19). Egypt's uprising brings DIY spirit out on to the streets. *The Guardian*. Retrieved February 09, 2018, from https://www.theguardian.com/world/2011/may/19/egypts-uprising-diy-art-cairo-streets

Shirky, C. (2011). The political power of social media. *Foreign Affairs*. Retrieved April 05, 2019, from http://www.foreignaffairs.com/articles/67038/clay-shirky/the-political-power-of-social-media

Siddiqui, S. (2016, September 5). Resistance literature and the British Raj. *The News International*. Retrieved April 13, 2019, from https://www.thenews.com.pk/print/147794-Resistance-literature-and-the-British-Raj

Singh, R. (2016, December 5). Why we need revolutionary poet Faiz Ahmed Faiz more than ever. *Literary Hub*. Retrieved April 13, 2019, from https://lithub.com/why-we-need-revolutionary-poet-faiz-ahmed-faiz-more-than-ever/

Skocpol, T. (1979). *States and social revolutions: A comparative analysis of France, Russia, and China*. Cambridge, England: Cambridge University Press.

Stecker, R. (1997). *Artworks: Definition, meaning, value*. University Park, PN: Pennsylvania State University Press

Tarrow, S. G. (1998). *Power in movement: Social movements and contentious politics*. Cambridge, Mass: Cambridge University Press.

Tilly, C. (1990). Coercion, capital, and European states, AD 990–1990. In C. Calhoun, J. Gerteis, J. Moody, S. Pfaff & I. Virk (Eds.) *Contemporary Sociological Theory*, (3rd ed.). Cambridge, Mass: Wiley-Blackwell.

Valassopoulos, A., & Mostafa, D. S. (2014). Popular protest music and the 2011 Egyptian revolution. *Popular Music & Society*, *37*(5), 638–659.

Violatti, C. (2013, October 30). Indus valley civilization. *Ancient History Encyclopedia.* Retrieved April 27, 2019, from https://www.ancient.eu/Indus_Valley_Civilization/

Viral video reignites fight to end Pakistan's YouTube ban. (2014, February 27). *Al Jazeera.* Retrieved May 02, 2019, from http://stream.aljazeera.com/story/201402271640-0023515

Walt, V. (2011, February 15). El Général and the rap anthem of the mideast revolution. *Time.* Retrieved April 15, 2019, from http://content.time.com/time/printout/0,8816,2049456,00.html

3

The Pivotal Role of Al Jazeera

Al Jazeera: A Channel of Revolutions

The Qatar-based television network, Al Jazeera, meaning "The Island" in English, emerged as the most credible non-western media source in the Arabic world in November 1996 (Abdelmoula, 2015; El-Nawawy & Iskandar, 2003; El-Nawawy & Khamis 2009; Hafez, 2007; Lynch, 2006; Pintak, 2006). With over 70 bureaus across the globe, "Al Jazeera Network has more than 3,000 staff members … including more than 400 journalists from more than 60 countries" ("About Us," n.d.). The channel, which was originally established as Arabic news and current affairs TV, now has multiple operations in several languages, including English. Just like many other Western news media organizations, Al Jazeera was also quick to embrace the Internet as an avenue to reach the global audiences. The network launched its free Arabic website in 2001, followed by Al Jazeera Mubasher in 2005 and Al Jazeera Global English Services in 2006. Al Jazeera Mubasher is known for its unedited political programs and opinions.

According to the organization's website (www.aljazeera.com), the Al Jazeera network, which is representative of 70 nationalities, consists of: a) Al Jazeera Satellite channel (Arabic); b) Al Jazeera English; c) Al Jazeera Documentary; d) Al Jazeera Sport; e) Al Jazeera Mubasher (Live); f) Al Jazeera Media Training and Development Centre; g) Al Jazeera Centre for Studies; h) Al Jazeera Mobile; i) Al Jazeera.net (Arabic website); and j) Al Jazeera English Online (English website).

Based on the data provided by the Al Jazeera website, the TV network's English channel is broadcasting to more than 310 million households in more than 100 countries ("About Us.," n.d.; Zayani & Sahraoui, 2017). Not only this, Al Jazeera continues to maintain its strong presence on social media, as the TV network is the most watched news channel on YouTube and has 3.1 million subscribers in "over 140 countries across the globe" ("About Us," n.d.). It may be mentioned here that Al Jazeera, which was originally launched in Arabic language to target the Middle Eastern audience, maintains its global presence by making its content available in the English language as well (Seib, 2016). Since the English language continues to dominate the social media landscape, Al Jazeera's decision to launch its English version can be seen as a strategic move by this news outlet so as to benefit from social media platforms like YouTube (Bebawi, 2016).

Al Jazeera and Pakistan

Even though Al Jazeera provided comprehensive coverage of the political crisis of 2007 in Pakistan both in English and Arabic languages, academic archives provide little to no discussion on the role of the Al Jazeera network in Pakistan's political uprisings. On the contrary, the news network's role in the political transformations has been well documented and acknowledged by the academic and news media archives in the cases of the Arab Spring uprisings—including Egypt and Tunisia—of 2010–11 and the aftermath of these political unrests (Abdelmoula, 2015; Alalawi, 2015; Bebawi, 2016; Khosrokhavar, 2016; Lynch, 2015; Seib, 2016; Zayani & Sahraoui, 2017). There could be multiple factors for the lack of debate on Al Jazeera's role in Pakistan that range from a global misunderstanding that clumps the entire Muslim world into the Middle East, to treating Arabic language as the only default language of Muslims, to looking at Al Jazeera as a news network representing only the Middle East, and not the rest of the Muslim-majority countries such as Indonesia, Pakistan, Bangladesh and so on. Let us discuss these possibilities in further detail.

For mass media scholars who are interested in expanding their research horizons beyond the geographical boundaries of the Western world, it is imperative to understand why they should refrain from treating the Arabic region as the entire Muslim world. Most of the scholarship on the Muslim-majority countries intentionally or unintentionally interprets the Middle East as the Muslim world and discusses the Arab media landscape as Muslim media landscape. In fact, the most densely populated Muslim-majority countries (Pakistan, India, Bangladesh, and Indonesia) are located outside the Middle East. Since Pakistan is not an

Arabic speaking country and is not located inside the Middle East, it is hard for Western media scholars to understand and establish a direct connection between Al Jazeera and Pakistan.

Furthermore, since Al Jazeera originates from Qatar, located in the Arabian Peninsula, many Western media scholars associate the TV network with the Arab world. This misperception limits the scope of Al Jazeera as the network, which serves 310 million households in more than 100 countries ("About Us," n.d.). Al Jazeera was launched in Arabic and then during the later years, the network started its services in other languages including English, yet it is generally believed that the TV network has its outreach only in Arabic speaking countries. This impression needs to be changed to better understand the global role of Al Jazeera.

Unlike the Middle East, Pakistan's national language is Urdu, but English is also widely understood and is used as an official language both for military and civil bureaucracy. However, an overwhelming majority of the country cannot understand and speak Arabic. So far, Al Jazeera does not offer its services in Urdu. This may be another reason that the existing scholarship on Al Jazeera's presence in the Muslim world does not even recognize the TV network's role in Pakistan, particularly during the political uprisings of 2007, when thousands of protesters came out in the streets against the military dictator, General Musharraf, and demanded the regime change. Yet Al Jazeera widely covered and broadcasted these protests. It may be noted that Al Jazeera was already present in Pakistan (since 2001 when the U.S. went to war in Afghanistan) and had established its bureaus in all the major cities of Pakistan, including the federal capital, Islamabad. When President Musharraf banned all the privately-owned national TV networks, Al Jazeera was still covering the political protests and airing them to the rest of the world. For example, in 2007, after the assassination of Pakistan's former prime minister, Benazir Bhutto, when Pakistani authorities decided to ban all political processions, Al Jazeera was quick to jump in and interviewed the then prime minister, Shaukat Aziz, for its program, *Talk to Al Jazeera* ("Shaukat Aziz," 2007). In summary, Al Jazeera's informational cascade role had already begun from Pakistan's political uprisings of 2007/08. More discussion about Al Jazeera's informational cascade will be provided later in this chapter.

Al Jazeera and the Middle East

In the immediate aftermath of 2010/11 political unrests in the Arab world, most of the literature on the political uprisings of Tunisia and Egypt celebrated the role of Al Jazeera as an activist network before and during the Arab Spring revolutions (Abdelmoula, 2015; Eko, 2012; El-Nawawy & Iskandar, 2003; Ghannam, 2011; Harb 2011; Khosrokhavar, 2016; Lynch, 2006; Lynch, 2015; Pintak, 2006). Therefore, most of the literature reviewed in this section will be Arab-culture specific. However, this chapter argues that the Al Jazeera factor was not specific to the Arab region, rather it should be seen in the context of the broader Muslim world. More discussion on this important aspect will be provided in detail in later sections. Also, since the existing scholarship used the term "Arab world" to discuss the role of Al Jazeera, this book will interchangeably use the terminologies such as "Arab world," "Muslim world" and "Muslim-majority countries" in this section, depending upon the context. However, it is important to clarify here that I disagree with the term "Arab world" because, as stated earlier, Al Jazeera's role was even more prominent and controversial during the war on terror in Afghanistan and Pakistan than in the cases of the Egyptian and Tunisian political crises (Gerhards & Schäfer, 2014; Abdullah & Elareshi, 2015). One such example can be seen in the *Control Room*, a controversial documentary released in 2004 on Al Jazeera's role in the coverage of the U.S. invasion of Afghanistan and Iraq, commonly referred to in the U.S. as the war on terror (Inskeep, 2004). This documentary created ripples in and outside of the Muslim-majority countries because of its ability to successfully provide a different narrative on the war on terror that did not comply with the Western narrative regarding the Afghanistan and Iraq invasions. This was probably the first time that the global media started to recognize Al Jazeera as a powerful non-Western medium, able to counter and challenge the Western view of the world.

In the context of the Arab Spring, this chapter argues that Al Jazeera actively used social media, particularly YouTube, to cover, disseminate and promote narratives of political uprising in the Arab world. Because of the iconic importance of Al Jazeera, we need to review the literature on this TV network to help us better understand, contextualize, and explain the role of media and communications in the political uprisings of the three countries under investigation. Furthermore, a discussion on the emergence and popularity of the Qatar-based TV network will help answer whether any connection exists between social media and Al Jazeera during the recent political uprisings.

In order to discuss Al Jazeera, let's revisit Marshall McLuhan's claim (and title to his book), *The Medium is the Message* (McLuhan & Fiore, 1967). Although he made this claim in the 1960s before satellite TVs and digital media, the claim has started making more sense to media and communication scholars in this information age. Through his claim, McLuhan emphasizes that the medium itself, not the message, should be the focus of a study to understand change in a society. People tend to go for obvious (news) and ignore the structural realities (medium) that bring change in the society. Thus, the claim, "The medium is the message," refers to understanding the changes in audience attitudes that result from the introduction of new media.

Looking at the literature—and particularly news coverage of recent political uprisings in the Muslim world—it is clear that a majority of claims and studies have focused on the obvious (Arab Spring) and ignored how and why the Arab Spring took place. Thus, an understanding of the medium, which is Al Jazeera and the Internet in this case, will be helpful in finding out the root causes and ground realities that might have contributed to the social movements and revolutions across the Muslim world. This discussion will help us contextualize the overall media landscape in the Muslim-majority countries, and explain why social media were welcomed so quickly in most of these authoritarian countries (Gerbaudo, 2018; Rød & Weidmann, 2015).

To an average viewer, Al Jazeera is just a satellite TV network based in Doha, Qatar. However, if we look at the history and context of this Arab-based satellite TV network, we realize that it is more than that. To some, Al Jazeera is a phenomenon; to others it is a channel of revolutions (Abdelmoula, 2015; Khosrokhavar, 2016; Zayani & Sahraoui, 2017). Whereas some celebrate Al Jazeera as an independent Arabic lens to view the world, others see it as a "mouthpiece" of Al-Qaeda (El-Nawawy & Iskandar, 2003; Gerhards & Schäfer, 2014; Lynch 2006; Lynch 2015; Pintak 2006). Launched in November 1996, after the collapse of BBC Arabic TV, Al Jazeera continues to dominate the Arab and Muslim media landscape even today. The BBC's Arabic channel collapsed when its major funder, Saudi Arabia, backed off because of the channel's decision to air a controversial documentary on Sharia law (El-Nawawy & Iskandar, 2003). The Emir of Qatar, Al-Thani, hired the entire BBC Arabic staff and pledged the first five years of financial support to Al Jazeera to help it survive (El-Nawawy & Iskandar, 2003; Miles, 2006). The TV network launched a special Al Jazeera Mubasher Misr website exclusively for Egypt during the 2011 Arab Spring revolution (Haschke, 2013). This specific version of Mubasher, dedicated just to Egypt, played a significant role during the Egyptian Arab Spring, and thus was seen as a threat by the military-backed government of al-Sisi ("Al Jazeera Suspends," 2014). In fact, Al Jazeera Mubasher Misr became a prime point of animosity between Qatar and Egypt, resulting in Al Jazeera taking down its Egypt version of Al Jazeera Mubasher in order to mend the relationship between the two states ("Al Jazeera Suspends," 2014).

Al Jazeera as Politico-Cultural Catalyst

Al Jazeera is known as a platform for change, a channel of revolutions, a counter-hegemonic channel and the medium that changed the Muslim world's private sphere into a public sphere (Abdelmoula, 2015; El-Nawawy & Iskandar, 2003; Harb, 2011; Khosrokhavar, 2016; Lynch, 2006; Lynch 2013; Pintak, 2006). In their landmark study on Al Jazeera, El-Nawawy and Iskandar (2003) looked at multiple sides of Al Jazeera's contributions to Arab society. The authors claimed that the most important politico-cultural change in the Arab region was because of Al Jazeera's ability to break the spell of the private Arab sphere, which then provided a level-playing field for networked social media (Abdelmoula, 2015; Eko, 2012; El-Nawawy & Iskandar, 2003; Ghannam, 2011; Hafez 2007).

For decades, citizens in the Muslim world had been oppressed by their authoritarian regimes; they did not enjoy individual or media freedom; and they had no right to express their political opinions and take part in the political process (El-Nawawy & Iskandar, 2003; El- Nawawy & Khamis, 2009). The only place where citizens in a majority of Muslim countries could express their opinions was in the private sphere (Abdelmoula, 2015). In other words, citizens in authoritarian regimes in the Muslim world engaged in political discussions in their private rooms and parlors with their friends (Wheeler, 2006), and this private sphere ensured their anonymity and safety so long as it did not become public. The practice of private sphere discourse also fits well with the idea of collectivistic culture, wherein people value and cherish their collective space rather than demanding individual spaces for themselves.

However, the launch of Al Jazeera broke this spell by providing people a platform for expressing and shaping their opinions and taking part in the political discussions. Now the citizens in these oppressive countries had their own TV channel in the Arabic language that allowed them to listen and speak on matters of important political issues of their everyday lives (El-Nawawy & Iskandar, 2003). Pintak (2006) describes such a change in the Arab culture as a "political and psychological watershed" (pg. 156). After the launch and popularity of Al Jazeera, it is now common for Arab citizens to say, "I am going out for a cup of coffee and Al Jazeera" (pg. 156).

Unification of Arab Citizens

Another major contribution of Al Jazeera was its unification of the global Arab audience. Using the example of the Canadian immigrant Helal family in their book, El-Nawawy and Iskandar (2003) make the case that regardless of their physical location, Arab citizens now feel united by watching Al Jazeera. For this reason, the channel is successful in creating public opinion in the Arab world. Arab immigrants in the U.S. and Canada who used to rely on Western news sources such as CNN have now shifted to Al Jazeera because of its coverage of controversial issues such as the Palestinian conflict, which was largely missing or underreported on Western news outlets (Pintak, 2006; Youmans & Youmans, 2017). Such a shift and unification had already started taking place well before the political uprisings of Egypt and Tunisia in 2010 and 2011. Thus, Al Jazeera had started to provide a level playing field of ideas and information not only for the citizens of the Arab region, but also for the immigrants from the Middle East who were now residing in Europe, Canada and the United States. Because of their exposure to the Western world where freedom of media is cherished as a basic human right, these immigrants were more sensitive and receptive to a relatively independent and indigenous voice from the Arab world, such as Al Jazeera.

Controversial News from the Arab Regions

Another important change in the Arab culture was Al Jazeera's decision to cover controversial issues in the Arab world. For centuries, the Muslim world in general—and the Arab world in particular—was known for its triangle of taboos: religion, sex and politics (Hafez, 2007). Mass media outlets in the Arab world were not allowed to discuss these three issues. However, Al Jazeera challenged and changed this practice. This decision appalled not only the rulers in the Middle East, but also audience members themselves, who were not prepared to listen to and watch controversial news and programs on their indigenous news media, particularly when these programs were being aired in Arabic. It also came as a surprise to the West as Al Jazeera broke the one-way flow of communication by providing the Arab perspective on controversial news stories. The satellite channel provided coverage on controversial issues such as AIDS, the demolition of statues of Buddha in Afghanistan, military regimes and their negative effects on society and why Arabs are treated as a joke in the Western world—all examples of controversial content discussed on the famous Al Jazeera program, *The Opposite Direction* by Ahmad Mansour (Lynch, 2006).

Al Jazeera and the "Other" Opinion

This section deals with the Arab audience's ability and patience to listen to controversial points of views. To understand this point, it is imperative to understand the political and social culture of the Arab region. Muslim-majority countries in the Middle East have been living under dictatorship for decades: Hosni Mubarak ruled Egypt for 29 years (1981–2011); Ben Ali ruled Tunisia for 23 years (1987–2010). Likewise, Saudi Arabia, one of the most politically and economically influential countries in the Middle East, has been formally ruled by the Al-Saud family since 1932, but their informal rule extends much further back (Ochsenwald & Philby, 2019). In order to extend and strengthen their powers over the people, these kingdoms and monarchies exerted absolute control over the freedom of expression and freedom of media of their citizens. Thus, over the years, it became an embedded cultural norm for the citizens of such countries not to complain about their rulers. Likewise, these citizens were exposed only to the versions of reality that their rulers deemed necessary for them to know. Being a state-run entity, mass media in these dictatorial countries were at the center of maintaining a status quo of opinions and ideas. Simply put, a majority of people in the Arab region were not used to of listening and digesting "other" opinions that did not match their political, cultural and religious beliefs (Ciftci, 2018).

Keeping in view Al Jazeera's motto, "The opinion and the other opinion," scholars including El-Nawawy and Iskandar (2003), Lynch (2006; 2015), Harb (2011), and Pintak (2006) looked at how Al Jazeera prepared the Arab audience to have the patience to listen to other opinions that do not conform to their ideologies. One of Al Jazeera's talk shows, *The Opposite Direction* by Ahmad Mansour, can be seen as an example of this strategy. As El-Nawawy and Iskandar (2003) describe in their book, Mansour invited not only Palestinian leaders to discuss the Palestine-Israel conflict, he also invited the Israeli leadership, which generated a lot of anger and frustration among Arab audiences and leadership. In other words, Arab media scholars claim that Al Jazeera prepared the stage for revolution and change in the Arab world by preparing the audience to not only express their opinions, but to have the patience to listen to and respect others' opinions.

Al Jazeera, a Counter-hegemonic Channel

Al Jazeera's ability to generate, promote and sustain other opinions among its viewership, in fact, made this platform less of a channel and more of a challenge to the hegemonic elite in the Arab world. Simultaneously, the pan-Arabic network "broke the hegemony of the western networks and reversed the flow of information from east to west for the first time since the middle ages" (Miles, 2017, para. 1). According to Harb (2011), Al Jazeera's ability to criticize and challenge oppressive regimes and leadership in the Muslim world makes the satellite network a counter-hegemonic channel. Throughout the history of the Arab world, mass media has either been under direct control of these regimes or was in service of the leadership. This was the very first time that an independent channel started airing programs in their indigenous language (Arabic) and dared to openly criticize the oppressive regimes and foster public opinion against oppression.

Another scholar, Lynch (2006), observed that Al Jazeera's independence from Saudi Arabia and its decision to report on politics and controversial issues created an entirely new and radical Arab media environment that will continue to redefine and reshape the Arab media landscape. Al Jazeera's decision to challenge and criticize Arab leaders and raise political awareness across the Middle East, however, came with many challenges that the TV network had to face. In the wake of the political uprisings in 2010/11 when Al Jazeera emerged as a powerful medium of communication and information to mobilize the protesters, it dawned upon the Arab leadership that they could not continue to ignore this strong political actor in the region, and that they must put an end to it. Thus, in June of 2017:

> Saudi Arabia, the United Arab Emirates, Bahrain and Egypt subjected Qatar to unprecedented diplomatic and economic sanctions, followed by an aggressive blockade and threats of further action if Qatar fail[ed] to meet a list of 13 demands, one of which [was] to shut down the Al Jazeera network. (Miles, 2017, para. 3)

The current situation is no better for Al Jazeera and Qatar, as the channel continues to struggle for its survival, giving more and more concessions to its coverage on controversial issues and trying to appease the ruling elites of the Arab world. One such concession was Al Jazeera's decision to shut down its Mubasher Misr services for Egypt to placate the country's new military-backed leadership ("Egypt's military shuts down," 2013). Only another episode of powerful political uprisings in the Muslim world will determine the fate of Al Jazeera in the future, which is directly associated with its potential decisions on whether to cover such political uprisings against the ruling elite of the Middle East region.

In summary, a majority of Arab media scholars believe that the channel not only created ripples in the status quo in the Arab world, but also changed the Arab media landscape forever. In fact, Saudi Arabia launched Al-Arabiya TV as a direct response to Al Jazeera (Harb, 2011; Haschke, 2013), to not only compete for news, but also to protect and promote the national ideology (Harb, 2011). This sense of competition in Arab media is something extraordinary. No one could have imagined that the Arab world would now have its own independent media, let alone that the society would be redefined and reshaped because of the competing media landscape. This competitive media environment has entered a new phase since Al-Arabiya has started to explore new markets in the non-Arabic world, where Al Jazeera has already been present for decades. In early 2019, Al-Arabiya launched its multimedia news network in Urdu for Pakistani audiences as an attempt to counter the presence and narrative of Al Jazeera in Pakistan (Al-Arabiya.net, 2019; Haschke, 2013). This move on the part of Al-Arabiya will give Saudi Arabian ideology in the region a boost, particularly because Al Jazeera has yet to offer any Urdu language services for the region.

Similarly, other Arab countries could not remain indifferent in the presence of Al Jazeera's aggressive programs and growing popularity. In response, other Muslim-majority countries including Pakistan, Egypt, Saudi Arabia and the United Arab Emirates (U.A.E.) started investing more in mass media and opened up new satellite channels, generating a new era of competition and difference of opinions (Arif, 2010; Miles, 2006). According to Arabic media scholars, what used to be the news and journalism in the Middle East is no more because of the Al Jazeera factor (Abdelmoula, 2015; Eko, 2012; El-Nawawy & Iskandar, 2003; Ghannam, 2011; Hafez 2007). This pan-Arabic news network has changed the balance of political and communication power in the Middle East. Either countries will engage more and more in media wars, or they will attempt to squelch existing media freedoms to re-exert their control over the narrative. In other words, now the voice of monopoly (Lynch, 2006) has been challenged and changed in ways that cannot be reversed.

Arab Governments and the Arab League

As stated earlier, Al Jazeera's decision to challenge and criticize Arab governments was not without a price. The channel's aggressive programming and open criticism of the Arab world's leadership infuriated the political elites, especially in Saudi Arabia, Kuwait, Egypt and Tunisia. Saudi Arabia, which plays a leading role in the oil producing Gulf region (which includes Saudi Arabia, Kuwait, Oman, Qatar, U.A.E., and Bahrain) has forced member countries (Gulf states) not to give advertising to Al Jazeera. Thus, despite having more than 300 million viewers worldwide, Al Jazeera is dependent on funding from Qatar ("About Us," n.d.; Harb, 2011; Lynch, 2006; Miles, 2006). The Arabic TV network could not grow revenues from advertising, but this did not change its commitment to challenging the voice of monopoly and criticizing Arab leadership (El-Nawawy & Iskandar, 2003), which continues into the present day.

Apart from depriving the Qatar-based TV network from advertising revenue, Arab governments and particularly the Arab League used another tactic to contain Al Jazeera. In 2008, they introduced the Arab Satellite Broadcasting Charter. In response to Al Jazeera's critical programing and open criticism of their policies, information ministers from countries in the Arab League proposed "Principles for regulating broadcasting satellite transmission in the Arab World." All the Arab League countries, except Qatar, signed the Arab Satellite Broadcasting Charter (Amin, 2008). According to this charter, all satellite TV channels in the Arab world are bound to an "Arab Media Code of Ethics." No channel can air any program or content that defames Arab leadership and/or religious symbols. The charter also bans any kind of content that jeopardizes the national peace and solidarity of Arab nations. It pledges nations to maintain and protect the Arab culture in a globalized world and encourages fair competition among satellite channels that promote understanding between different cultures.

If we look at the charter carefully, it clearly shows the frustration and fear of Arab governments because of Al Jazeera. This charter can be seen as another attempt by the oppressive regimes to maintain their voice of monopoly and hegemony over the mass media and individuals' freedom of expression. Qatar, for which Al Jazeera is the biggest export after liquified natural gas and oil, understood the potential threat to Al Jazeera's media freedom and thus decided not to sign the charter. This factor of not being a signatory of the charter makes Al Jazeera an independent and free satellite TV network that continues to challenge and criticize the status quo and power monopoly in the Arab world (Abdelmoula, 2015; "Changing the Channel," 2017; Lynch, 2006).

Despite their frustration and fear, Arab governments must deal with Al Jazeera. For example, in 1999, Kuwait banned Al Jazeera and asked its staff to leave the country (El-Nawawy & Iskandar, 2003). Similarly, in 2009, two years before the revolution, Tunisia cancelled Al Jazeera's license when the channel hosted opposition party leaders during the Tunisian presidential elections. In 2017, six years after the Egyptian Arab Spring, the country blocked access to Al Jazeera, accusing the channel of supporting terrorism ("Egypt Blocks Access," 2017). Also, in 2017, Saudi Arabia "banned hotels and tourist facilities from airing Al Jazeera news channels and threatened to punish violators with the closure of their facility and a fine of up to $26,000" ("Saudi Arabia Bans," 2017, para. 1). It is pertinent to mention here that the hostile relationship of the ruling elite with Al Jazeera continues even in early 2019 when this book was being written. For example, in order to curb the coverage of pro-democracy demonstrations in Sudan, the military government of the country was quick to shut down Al Jazeera's Khartoum bureau on May 31, 2019 (The Guardian, 2019). Despite the repeated attempts to completely ban this Qatar-based news network, Arab governments including Kuwait, Saudi Arabia, Tunisia, Bahrain and Egypt had to reissue licenses to Al Jazeera. This consequence could be the result of the fact that people from these countries love to watch Al Jazeera, or there might be some other factors that future researchers need to explore. For instance, a complete ban on Al Jazeera may disconnect the Arab world from the rest of the globe as, so far, this channel has proven itself as the only strong voice representing the non-Western media perspective for the Arab region.

The "Arab Street"

It is also important to look at how the average Arab citizen reacted to Al Jazeera's relatively independent approach toward social and political issues in the Muslim world. Reviewing the literature, it becomes clear that Arab governments and their citizens had opposite reactions to Al Jazeera. While Al Jazeera was challenged by Arab governments, the people of the Arab world welcomed Al Jazeera, which for them is connected to their sense of identity (El-Nawawy & Iskandar, 2003).

In the Middle East, people have a history of trusting foreign and Western news channels instead of their own mass media. The reason for this distrust of their own media is the fact that the mass media in the Arab world are not free and serve as the propaganda machine of the state (Harb, 2011; Mir, 2011; Pintak, 2006). For example, in Tunisia almost all the mass media belonged to former President Zain-el-Abidine Ben Ali, and so people in Tunisia trusted Al Jazeera and France 24 more to shape their public opinions on certain issues (Mir, 2011). As we discussed earlier, Al Jazeera united Arab citizens across the globe, and this factor of unification is based on the element of trust that people in the Middle East value the most (Fandy, 1999; Wheeler, 2006). In other words, the Arab street (the common people of the Middle East region) trusts Al Jazeera and its programs. They understand that it is an independent channel, with the audacity to challenge regimes in the Arab world.

Furthermore, as El-Nawawy and Iskandar (2003) put it, Al Jazeera contextualized the aspect of journalistic objectivity in the Arab perspective. This refers to the interpretation of so-called objective facts and figures of news in the Arab perspective, rather than a Western interpretation and contextualization of such facts dedicated toward Western audiences. For example, when Al Jazeera covers the Palestinian conflict, it uses the word "martyr" for Palestinians who die during the conflict, whereas CNN does not use such words while reporting on the conflict. Thus, this element of contextualizing objectivity in the Arab perspective provides an opportunity to the Arab audience to connect themselves with Al Jazeera. Pintak (2006) viewed Al Jazeera as the Arab people's own independent lens to view the world. It is because of the element of trust that Al Jazeera is known as the most influential TV network in shaping and creating public opinion in the Arab world. And perhaps this is the reason that Arab regimes are frustrated and afraid of Al Jazeera's extraordinary power and popularity across the Muslim world.

Al Jazeera's Role as Informational Cascade

Another important aspect that needs some discussion here is the fact that Al Jazeera's success on the forefronts of the Arab and global media landscape cannot be measured and understood by applying only a traditional media lens to this news network. In fact, Al Jazeera should be seen and studied in the context of social media as well. During the literature review for this study, it was observed that Al Jazeera disseminated amateur video clips of political protests in Tunisia and Egypt via its Mubasher website. The news network was also relying on YouTube to disseminate the narrative of protests in the three countries under investigation. Given this, an important question needs to be explored further: Was Al Jazeera a major player in the informational cascade that took place on YouTube during the political uprisings in Pakistan, Egypt and Tunisia?

A political science scholar, Lohmann (1994) suggests that communication and information carry the most important role when it comes to protest politics. She calls political demonstrations an informational cascade. According to the informational cascade model, individual participants' decisions to join a political protest may depend on changes in aggregate turnout over time, because people extract benefit-cost information from turnout numbers. This chapter looked at the informational role of Al Jazeera during the political crises of the three countries. The rationale for exploring Al Jazeera's role as an informational cascade is that the scholarship on the political uprisings in the Muslim world treats Al Jazeera as the channel of revolutions, a channel that played an activist role by spreading narratives of political protests to its viewers (Eko, 2012; Harb, 2011; Lynch, 2013). Before we further discuss this aspect of Al Jazeera's videos of protests posted on YouTube, let's have a contextual understanding of this pan-Arabic TV channel's reach into social media platforms.

Al Jazeera's English YouTube channel boasts 2.9 million subscribers and claims to reach around 300 million households in 140 countries (Al Jazeera English, n.d.), and averages about 800,000 views per day (Social Blade, 2019). Launched on April 16, 2007, the Al Jazeera English YouTube channel, as of early 2019 has more than 77,000 uploaded videos and more than 1.2 billion views (Statsheep, 2019).

Many scholars believe that the Arab Spring revolution was not an overnight phenomenon (Eko, 2012; Ghannam, 2011; Harb, 2011). Hence, this chapter argues that we should look at the role of Al Jazeera in the revolutions to determine whether this platform had any role in the informational cascade of political protests during the Arab Spring revolution. Harb (2011) terms the Qatar-based satellite channel as the channel of revolutions and claims that Al Jazeera started creating an environment for change long before the Arab Spring. Once Arab audiences were connected and ready for change, social media took over and the message of revolution spread across the region. In this context, Bouazizi's protest suicide got national and global attention when someone posted the cellphone-recorded video of the "Tunisian burning man" on Facebook. Al Jazeera, "picked up Ali Bouazizi's footage from the man's Facebook page, and transmitted it to its transnational Arabic satellite audience that same evening" (Eko, 2012, p. 130). Harb (2011) adds it was because of social media that the message of the Tunisian revolution spread everywhere and was supported by non-Tunisians (e.g., Egyptians) as well. The images of the Tunisian burning man spread everywhere because of social media and served as a catalyst for the Arab Spring uprising (Mir, 2011).

Let's put things in perspective. On January 25, 2011, when protesters gathered at Tahrir Square, the Mubarak regime blocked the Internet in Egypt to suppress the protests. However, Al Jazeera quickly jumped in and started providing coverage of the protests in Egypt (Eko, 2012; Ghannam, 2011). When the Mubarak regime banned Al Jazeera, the channel launched a version of the Al Jazeera Mubasher website exclusively for Egypt (Haschke, 2013). The website allowed protestors and citizens to upload their amateur videos of demonstrations on the website. Al Jazeera used these amateur videos and unedited content for its own satellite news programming. The Mubasher Misr (meaning Egypt) was also available and accessible via Al Jazeera's YouTube channel during that time. In other words, a traditional news network had found a way to utilize social media tools such as YouTube in order to maintain the informational cascade of political protests aimed at the regime. Thus, social media and mass media collaborated to promote democratic change in the society (Ghannam, 2011).

Put differently, the channel encouraged average citizens to perform a journalistic role in crisis situations such as the political upheavals in the three countries under investigation. Al Jazeera gained more trust from average citizens of the Arab world when it started airing unedited amateur content. In this way, the network not only kept the rest of the world informed about what was happening in Egypt, but it also bridged the digital divide. People who were unable to use social media (such as senior citizens and less educated people) still had a chance to watch the traditional broadcast version of Al Jazeera to keep themselves informed on what was happening in the Arab world.

Conclusion

In light of this discussion, this book argues that social media in general and YouTube in particular should be investigated as tools that both protesters and Al Jazeera used to disseminate the narratives of political uprisings in the Muslim world. However, using another lens, we can look at the informational cascade role of Al Jazeera that started much earlier than the so-called Arab Spring. As I have discussed earlier, Al Jazeera's main contribution was to unify the Arab audiences by amplifying their voices through its platform. It has been argued that Al Jazeera paved the way for another medium to penetrate the Arab world: the Internet. As is evident from reviewing the literature on the Arab Spring, the revolution in Egypt that started on January 25, 2011 within just 10 days of the success of the Tunisian revolution is mostly celebrated as an exclusive achievement of social media without even acknowledging the role of Al Jazeera. Also, Al Jazeera has opened a new battlefield for a competing media environment in the region. Besides Qatar, media privatization is being witnessed in Pakistan, Egypt, Saudi Arabia and the U.A.E., which is a step forward in breaking the private sphere and initiating the creation of a Muslim public sphere in the Middle East and beyond. The credit goes to Al Jazeera for such a change.

References

Abdelmoula, E. (2015). *Al Jazeera and democratization: The rise of the Arab public sphere*. New York, NY: Routledge.

Abdullah, S., & Elareshi, M. (2015). Building narratives: A study of terrorism framing by Al Jazeera and Al Arabiya TV networks. *Arab Media & Society*, 21, 1–14. Retrieved February 25, 2018, from https://s3.amazonaws.com/academia.edu.documents/38269568/20150625122309_Elareshi_Spring2015_Final.pdf?AWSAccessKeyId=AKIAIWOWYYGZ2Y53UL3A&Expires=1547654954&Signature=fgNZxULg30W7h80p%2BTLPNvf6q64%3D&response-contentdisposition=inline%3B%20filename%3DBuilding_Narratives_A_Study_of_Terrorism.pdf

About us. (n.d.). About us: Facts and figures. *Al Jazeera*. Retrieved June 11, 2019, from https://www.aljazeera.com/aboutus/

Al-Arabiya.net (2019). Pakistan. Retrieved June 10, 2019, from https://urdu.alarabiya.net/

Alalawi, N. (2015). How Media Covered "Arab Spring" Movement: Comparison between the American Fox NEWS and the Middle Eastern Al Jazeera. *Cross-Cultural Communication*, *11*(10), 44–49.

Al Jazeera English (n.d.). About Al Jazeera English. Retrieved June 10, 2019, from https://www.youtube.com/user/AlJazeeraEnglish/about

Al Jazeera suspends Egyptian channel Mubasher Misr. (2014, December 23). *BBC News*. Retrieved April 13, 2018, from https://www.bbc.com/news/world-middle-east-30585551

Amin, H. (2008). The Arab states charter for satellite television: A quest for regulation. *Arab Media & Society*. Retrieved February 10, 2018, from https://www.arabmediasociety.com/the-arab-states-charter-for-satellite-television-a-quest-for-regulation/

Arif, R. (2010). How Terrorism Killed the News: Pakistani Journalism after 9/11. Saarbrücken, Germany: Lambert Academic Publishing. http://www.amazon.com/How-Terrorism-Killed-News-journalism/dp/3838335791

Bebawi, S. (2016). *Media Power and Global Television News: The Role of Al Jazeera English*. London, U.K.: IB Tauris.

Changing the Channel (2017, July 1). *The Economist*. Retrieved January 15, 2019, from https://www.economist.com/middle-east-and-africa/2017/07/01/why-al-jazeera-is-under-threat

Ciftci, S. (2018). Self-expression values, loyalty generation, and support for authoritarianism: Evidence from the Arab world. *Democratization*, *25*(7), 1132–1152. doi: https://doi.org/10.1080/13510347.2018.1450388

Egypt blocks access. (2017, May 25). *The Guardian*. Retrieved June 14, 2019, from https://www.theguardian.com/world/2017/may/25/egypt-blocks-access-news-websites-al-jazeera-mada-masr-press-freedom

Egypt's military shuts down news channels. (2013, July 3). *Al Jazeera*. Retrieved June 14, 2019, from https://www.aljazeera.com/news/middleeast/2013/07/2013740531685326.html

Eko, L. (2012). *New media, old regimes: Case studies in comparative communication law and policy*. Lanham, MD: Lexington Books.

El-Nawawy, M. & Iskandar, A. (2003). *Al-Jazeera: The story of the network that is rattling governments and redefining modern journalism*. Boulder, CO: Westview.

El-Nawawy, M. & Khamis, S. (2009). *Islam dot com: Contemporary Islamic discourses in cyberspace*. New York, NY: Palgrave Macmillan.

Fandy, M. (1999). *Saudi Arabia and the politics of dissent*. New York, NY: St. Martin's.

Gerbaudo, P. (2018). *Tweets and the streets: Social media and contemporary activism*. London, England: Pluto Press.

Gerhards, J., & Schäfer, M. S. (2014). International terrorism, domestic coverage? How terrorist attacks are presented in the news of CNN, Al Jazeera, the BBC, and ARD. International Communication Gazette, 76(1), 3–26. Retrieved June 28, 2019, from https://journals.sagepub.com/doi/pdf/10.1177/1748048513504158

Ghannam, J. (2011). Social media in the Arab world: Leading up to the uprisings of 2011. *Center for International Media Assistance*, *3*(1), 1–44. Retrieved June 14, 2019, from http://www.cima.ned.org/wp-content/uploads/2011/02/Ghannam-Jeffrey-Arab_Social_Media-Report-10-25-11.pdf

Hafez, K. (2007). *The myth of media globalization*. Cambridge, UK: Polity Press.

Harb, Z. (2011). Arab revolutions and the social media effect. *M/C Journal*, *14*(2). Retrieved October 21, 2019, from http://journal.media-culture.org.au/index.php/mcjournal/article/view/364Two

Haschke, P. (2013, April 12). Al Jazeera: When politics hijack journalism. *INA Global*. Retrieved May 22, 2019, from https://www.inaglobal.fr/en/television/article/al-jazeera-when-politics-hijack-journalism

Inskeep, S. (2004, June 18). 'Control Room': Inside *Al-Jazeera*. *NPR*. Retrieved March 16, 2018, from https://www.npr.org/templates/story/story.php?storyId=1963788

Khosrokhavar, F. (2016). *New Arab Revolutions That Shook the World*. London, U.K.: Routledge.

Lohmann, S. (1994). The dynamics of informational cascades: the Monday demonstrations in Leipzig, East Germany, 1989–91. *World Politics*, *47*(1), 42–101.

Lynch, M. (2006). *Voices of the new Arab public: Iraq, Al-Jazeera, and Middle East politics today*. New York, NY: Columbia University Press.

Lynch, M. (2013). *The Arab uprising: The unfinished revolutions of the new Middle East*. New York, NY: Public Affairs.

Lynch, M. (2015). How the media trashed the transitions. *Journal of Democracy*, *26*(4), 90–99. doi: 10.1353/jod.2015.0070

McLuhan, M. & Fiore, Q. (1967). *The medium is the message*. New York, NY: Bantam Books.

Miles, H. (2006). *Al-Jazeera: The inside story of the Arab news channel that is challenging the West*. New York, NY: Grove Press.

Miles, H. (July 1, 2017). Al-Jazeera, insurgent TV station that divides the Arab world, faces closure. Retrieved January 26, 2019, from https://www.theguardian.com/media/2017/jul/01/demand-al-jazeera-closure-shows-how-much-enemies-fear-it

Mir, J. (2011). Political and media transitions in Tunisia: A snapshot of media policy and regulatory environment. *Internews Report*.

Ochsenwald, W. & Philby, H. (2019). Saudi Arabia. In *Encyclopedia Britannica Online*. Retrieved July 26, 2019, from https://www.britannica.com/place/Saudi-Arabia/The-Kingdom-of-Saudi-Arabia

Pintak, L. (2006). *Reflections in a bloodshot lens: America, Islam and the war of ideas*. London, England: Pluto Press.

Rød, E. G., & Weidmann, N. B. (2015). Empowering activists or autocrats? The Internet in authoritarian regimes. *Journal of Peace Research*, *52*(3), 338–351. Retrieved June 29, 2019, from https://www.jstor.org/stable/pdf/24557404.pdf

Saudi Arabia bans Al Jazeera. (2017, June 9). *Al Jazeera News*. Retrieved January 25, 2019, from https://www.aljazeera.com/news/2017/06/saudi-arabia-bans-al-jazeera-channels-hotels-170609141041079.html

Seib, P. (2016). *Al Jazeera English: Global news in a changing world*. New York City, N.Y.: Springer.

Shaukat Aziz. The Prime Minister of Pakistan talks to Al Jazeera. (2007, November 27). Al Jazeera. Retrieved August 04, 2018, from https://www.aljazeera.com/programmes/talktojazeera/2007/10/2008525173717468863.html

Social Blade. (2019) Al Jazeera English Statistics. Retrieved June 10, 2019, from https://socialblade.com/youtube/user/aljazeeraenglish

Statsheep (2019). Al-Jazeera English. Retrieved June 10, 2019, from https://www.statsheep.com/AlJazeeraEnglish

The Guardian. (May 31, 2019). Sudan bans Al-Jazeera as pro-democracy demonstrations continue. Retrieved August 04, 2019, from https://www.theguardian.com/world/2019/may/31/sudan-bans-al-jazeera-as-pro-democracy-demonstrations-continue

Wheeler, D. L. (2006). *The Internet in the Middle East: Global expectations and local imaginations in Kuwait*. Albany, New York: SUNY Press.

Youmans, W., & Youmans, W. L. (2017). *An unlikely audience: Al Jazeera's struggle in America*. Oxford, England: Oxford University Press.

Zayani, M., & Sahraoui, S. (2017). *The culture of Al Jazeera: Inside an Arab media giant*. Jefferson, NC: McFarland.

Part II

Pakistan

With a population of 208 million people, Pakistan is the world's second largest Muslim-majority country. Located in Southern Asia, Pakistan borders the Arabian Sea, "between India on the east and Iran and Afghanistan on the west and China in the north" (CIA, 2019, para. 3). The country's literacy rate is 57.9%, with 29.5% of the population living below the poverty line (CIA, 2019).

Since the country witnessed online political activism long before the so-called Arab Spring of 2010–11, this case should be taken into context while studying political uprisings in the Muslim world. In November 2007, when President Musharraf imposed a state of emergency in the country and blocked the entire broadcast media, "[o]nline media were used as an organizing tool during the Lawyer's Movement and protests against President Musharraf in 2007 and 2008. Information about demonstrations was disseminated through email lists, SMS, and YouTube" (Ricchiardi, 2012, p. 15). The more than 10-year rule of Musharraf, the military dictator who had toppled former Prime Minister Nawaz Sharif's government in a bloodless military coup, could not withstand online and offline (street) political protests that erupted in response to President Musharraf's decision to sack Chief Justice Iftikhar Chaudhry (Arif, 2010; Lieven, 2011; Rashid, 2008). The independent-minded chief justice was removed from office after he refused to support President Musharraf's re-election (Hashim, 2012). Furthermore,

Chaudhry had "irked the government by pressing it to provide information on the whereabouts of 400 'disappeared' people, who [had] been secretly held by Pakistan's intelligence agencies" (Wilkinson, 2007, para. 13). These factors led to the dismissal of Iftikhar Chaudhry, which subsequently resulted in a "series of bloody protests [all over the country, especially, in front of the President House, Islamabad] and edged the country toward a constitutional crisis" (Wilkinson, 2007, para. 2). These protests against President Musharraf were joined by thousands of lawyers, civil society organizations, political and religious parties, and other people from all walks of life (Arif, 2018). Despite the government's crackdown on these protesters, President Musharraf could not contain the ongoing protests in front of the President's House. Besides providing 24/7 news coverage to the protesters, the newly born private media—particularly TV news channels—started becoming more critical of the military regime and demanded the restoration of the Constitution and democracy in the country (Ricchiardi, 2012). This led President Musharraf to take the extreme measures of shutting down the entire broadcast media in the country (Masood, 2007). Thus, to control the content of private television channels, the government banned all the private news channels for more than a month in November 2007 (Freedom House, 2011). Journalists were also threatened with arrests and punishment if they tried to cover any political protests against the government or the military establishment (Freedom House, 2011).

It is pertinent to mention here that military interventions and bans on media freedom were not something unusual for Pakistan, as the country has witnessed many such examples since its inception in 1947. However, the only factor that made a difference in people's struggle against the dictatorship is that they now had an alternative medium—the Internet—to express their disapproval of the regime. Therefore, in the absence of traditional media, people started using networked social media including blogs, Facebook, Twitter and YouTube to provide informational activism to online and offline (street protests) for the first time in the country's history (Khalid, 2008; "Pakistan Blocks Access," 2010). Even a decade after the political uprisings of the 2007–08, the country continues to witness communication activism on digital media platforms.

References

Arif, R. (2010). *How terrorism killed the news: Pakistani journalism after 9/11.* Saarbrucken, Germany: Lambert Academic Publishing.

Arif, R. (2018). Social Networks, Social Movements and Politico-Cultural Situation of Pakistani Media. In Julie Dee (Ed.), *From Tahrir Square to Gezi Park: Social Networks as Facilitators of Social Movements*. New York, NY: Peter Lang Publishing.

Central Intelligence Agency (CIA). (2019). Pakistan. In *The World Factbook*. Retrieved May 21, 2019 from https://www.cia.gov/library/publications/the-world-factbook/geos/pk.html

Freedom House (2011). *Pakistan freedom report*. Retrieved May 23, 2019, from https://freedomhouse.org/report/freedom-world/2011/pakistan

Hashim, A. (2012, April 30). Pakistan: A political timeline. *Al Jazeera*. Retrieved August 21, 2017, from https://www.aljazeera.com/indepth/interactive/2012/01/20121181235768904.html

Khalid, K. (2008). *The face of media freedom in Pakistan*. Lahore, Pakistan: Asia Media.

Lieven, A. (2011). *Pakistan: A hard country*. London, England: Allen Lane

Masood, S. (2007, June 5). Musharraf issues decree cracking down on news media. *The New York Times*. Retrieved May 08, 2019, from https://www.nytimes.com/2007/06/05/world/asia/05pakistan.html

Pakistan blocks access to YouTube in Internet crackdown. (2010, May 20). *BBC News*. Retrieved July 19, 2018, from https://www.bbc.com/news/10130195

Rashid, A. (2008). *Descent into chaos: The United States and the failure of nation building in Pakistan, Afghanistan, and Central Asia*. New York, NY: Viking.

Ricchiardi, S. (2012). *Challenges for independent news media in Pakistan: A report to the Center for International Media Assistance*. Washington, DC, National Endowment for Democracy. Retrieved May 27, 2018, from http://www.centerforinternationalmediaassistance.org/wp-content/uploads/2015/01/Challenges-for-Independent-News-Media-in-Pakistan_Ricchiardi-updated.pdf

Wilkinson, I. (2007, March 17). Crisis for Musharraf over justice chief's sacking. *The Telegraph*. Retrieved September 23, 2017, from https://www.telegraph.co.uk/news/worldnews/1545843/Crisis-for-Musharraf-over-justice-chiefs-sacking.html

4 Supreme Court Chief Justice Iftikhar Muhammad Chaudhry

Pakistani former Chief Justice, Iftikhar Chaudhry, has been called an icon of outrage, serving as a catalyst to the political uprisings of 2007–08, later to be known as the Lawyers' Movement. This movement resulted in the removal of President Musharraf and the institution of a new government (Ahmed & Stephan, 2010; Arif, 2011; Ghias, 2010; Hashim, 2013; Mufti, 2007; Wilkinson, 2007). The Lawyers' Movement, which was also referred to as "[t]he 'men in black' ", was a movement "whose insistence on the rule of law and embrace of nonviolent struggle captured the hearts and minds of millions of Pakistanis. [The movement] helped transform the country's political landscape in unexpected ways" (Ahmed & Stephan, 2010, p.492).

This chapter provides a contextual framework in order to understand why the deposed chief justice's act of resistance to a dictator sparked a social movement in the country and how this phenomenon relates to Egypt and Tunisia's iconic examples of outrage. It then discusses how the images of Chief Justice Iftikhar Muhammad Chaudhry being arrested and abused by Pakistani security forces served as a catalyst to bring people to action, and how the population used social media platforms to continually share and spread both the original images of Chaudhry as well as images and videos of the resulting military crackdown to build the social momentum that eventually brought down the military dictator.

Judiciary & Military Coups of Pakistan

Pakistan has historically submissive judicial system that has rarely stood against the will of the military establishment (Ahmed & Stephan, 2010; Iqbal, 2007; Zaman, 2011). It is a prevalent view that the "judiciary in Pakistan has traditionally been viewed as a rubber stamp for coup-makers who intrude into politics" (Mustafa, 2018, para. 1). The double-standards of Pakistan's judiciary treats the country's elected leaders and generals differently:

> Since August 1947, in seventy years of Pakistan's existence, prime ministers have been overthrown in military coups, removed by high courts, murdered, and executed. Not a single prime minister has been able to complete the constitutional tenure. By contrast, not a single military general has been successfully prosecuted for overthrowing the Constitution or subverting the institutions. (Khan, 2017, paras. 1 & 2)

One such most recent example is of prime minister Nawaz Sharif, who the Supreme Court disqualified "under the 'Sadiq and Amin' [dishonest and untrustworthy] clause of the 1973 Constitution" (Khan, 2017, para. 1). On the other hand, General Pervez Musharraf, who is facing "cases of treason, murder, [and] unlawful detention of Supreme Court justices" (Khan, 2017, para. 2), has never been brought to justice as the "Supreme Court did little to assure that the General [was] prosecuted under the laws of Pakistan" (Khan, 2017, para. 2).

It can be argued that weak judiciary is one of the prime factors that has led to three dictatorial regimes during the 72-year history of this relatively young country (Ahmed & Stephan, 2010; Mustafa, 2018; Rao, 2018). The three dictators who ruled the country for around 33 cumulative years—General Ayub Khan (1958–69), General Zia-ul-Haq (1977–1988), and General Pervez Musharraf (1999–2008)—found it extremely convenient to topple elected governments and take over the reins of Pakistan's political system, even though it was in direct violation of the Constitution of the country (Hashim, 2013). As stated earlier, none of these military dictators in the little over 70 years history of Pakistan was tried or punished for their acts, because Pakistan's Supreme Court has always sided with the authority of military establishment rather than with protecting and upholding constitutional provisions, which clearly term such an involvement in Pakistan's political system as an act of treason. For reference, Article 6 of Pakistan's Constitution defines the act of high treason as following:

1. Any person who abrogates or subverts or suspends or holds in abeyance, or attempts or conspires to abrogate or subvert or suspend or hold in abeyance, the Constitution by use of force or show of force or by any other unconstitutional means shall be guilty of high treason.
2. Any person aiding or abetting or collaborating the acts mentioned in clause (1) shall likewise be guilty of high treason.

   2A. An act of high treason mentioned in clause (1) or clause (2) shall not be validated by any court including the Supreme Court and a High Court.

3. Majlis-e-Shoora (Parliament) shall by law provide for the punishment of persons found guilty of high treason. (Pakistan Constitutional Law.com, n.d.)

One such occurrence, which can be referred to as the darkest period of Pakistan's judicial history, was when the Supreme Court ordered death by hanging for the ninth elected prime minister of Pakistan, Zulfiqar Ali Bhutto (1973–1977), who the military establishment of that time did not like. In a successful military coup, the then Chief of the Army Staff, General Zia-ul-Haq, toppled prime minister Bhutto's government and took over the reins of the country, ruling for a little over 10 years (1977–1988) until his death on August 17, 1988 (Asif, 2018; Sciolino, 1988). On the directives of Zia-ul-Haq, Prime Minister Bhutto was jailed and tried for his alleged involvement in a murder. After a controversial Supreme Court ruling, the elected premier was hanged in Rawalpindi, a city in Punjab that headquartered the Pakistan Army and is adjacent to the federal capital of Pakistan, Islamabad. The Supreme Court's ruling was widely criticized as carrying out a political murder of an elected prime minister of the country (Niesewand, 2016). The proceedings of the highest court of Pakistan "revealed murky aspects in the background of the case against Mr. Bhutto. It was noted that General Zia, using his supreme power under martial law, had changed chief justices before the appeal" ("Sentence of Death," 1979, para. 18). Appeals to Zia to lift the death sentence penalty against the deposed prime minister were many:

> As time began running out for Mr. Bhutto, pleas for clemency poured in from around the world to President Mohammad Zia ul-Haq. Among those who appealed on Mr. Bhutto's behalf were President Carter of the United States, President Leonid I. Brezhnev of the Soviet Union, Chairman Hua Guofeng of China, King Khalid of Saudi Arabia, Pope John Paul II, and organizations

> such as Amnesty International and the International Commission of Jurists. ("Sentence of Death," 1979, para. 13)

Despite national and international outcry, prime minister Bhutto was hanged on April 4, 1979 (Niesewand, 2016; "Sentence of Death," 1979; "Zulfikar Ali Bhutto," 2019).

Almost two decades later, in 2005, the people of Pakistan who were not accustomed to seeing top judiciary members taking a stance in the interests of ordinary citizens, witnessed a short-lived period of judicial activism (Rao, 2018). Iftikhar Chaudhry, who was appointed as Chief Justice by General Musharraf in 2005, started to become "an advocate of ordinary Pakistanis, challenging anti-terrorist measures, taking on individual human rights cases and exposing corruption" (Ahmed & Stephan, 2010, p.494). Out of these controversial issues that Chaudhry had started to intervene in as a Chief Justice, the most sensitive one was about the mysterious disappearances of some people in Pakistan. These "cases included those of approximately 563 missing Pakistanis believed to have been rounded up without charge by intelligence agencies, whose heads Chaudhry summoned to the Supreme Court, and cases of women gang raped while in police custody" (Ahmed & Stephan, 2010, p. 494). Not only this, but "[i]n early 2007, the Supreme Court ruled against the improper privatization of Pakistan Steel Mills to a Musharraf crony—a huge embarrassment for the military ruler" (Ahmed & Stephan, 2010, p. 494). While Chaudhry gained much praise from the common citizens of Pakistan, this kind of judicial activism was neither appreciated nor supported by the ruling elite in the country, who had already started looking at ways to get rid of the independent-minded Chief Justice, particularly since Iftikhar Chaudhry himself was direct beneficiary of General Musharraf (Ghias, 2010; Mustafa, 2018). After all, why would an appointee of a military dictator turn against his boss?

Iftikhar Chaudhry: Pakistan's Icon of Outrage

In a stark contradiction to what has been the tradition of Pakistan's judiciary under a dictatorial regime, the independent-minded approach of Chief Justice Iftikhar Chaudhry became the reason for his removal from office after he refused to support President Musharraf's re-election (Ghias, 2010; Hashim, 2013). Furthermore, Chaudhry had "irked the government by pressing it to provide information on the whereabouts of 400 [the number rose to 563 during the later months] 'disappeared' people, who [had] been secretly held by Pakistan's intelligence agencies" (Wilkinson, 2007, pg. 1). These factors that led to the dismissal of Iftikhar Chaudhry resulted in a "series of bloody protests [all over the country, especially, in front of the President House, Islamabad] and edged the country toward a constitutional crisis" (Wilkinson, 2007, pg. 2). The nonviolent protests against President Musharraf were joined by thousands of lawyers, civil society organizations, political and religious parties, and other people from all walks of life (Arif, 2011; Zaidi, 2008).

On March 09, 2007, Pakistani media aired the news about the dismissal of the Chief Justice by the self-appointed military ruler, Musharraf (Mufti, 2007). A majority of the news channels and print newspapers showed an image of General Musharraf in uniform at his military residence and Iftikhar Chaudhry helplessly sitting in front of him (Iqbal, 2007). Ironically, this image that the Pakistani media kept airing was the official image provided by President Musharraf's own media cell. It ultimately backfired as the image sparked anger across the country. In the context of the historically weak judiciary of Pakistan, Justice Iftikhar Chaudhry's refusal to resign and his decision to go against the will of a military dictator, General Musharraf, was not only seen as an act of bravery, but an attempt to uphold the supremacy of the country's highest court. Put this way, this moment in history was seen as a new dawn for Pakistan's judicial system. The Supreme Court had openly resisted to bow in front of a military dictator in uniform (Iqbal, 2007; Wilkinson, 2007; Zaidi, 2008). On the other hand, "[t]he former Pakistani president, accustomed to a compliant and submissive judiciary, was unprepared for the organized resistance that followed his politically-motivated sacking of the nation's top judge" (Ahmed & Stephan, 2010, p. 493).

A second image that achieved iconic status in this case was the image of the Chief Justice's brutal arrest outside his official Islamabad residence, where security officials and policemen are seen humiliating and arresting him ("Profile," n.d.). The image shows "[a]n agent is holding Chaudhry's hair as he is being pushed into a car" ("Profile," n.d., para. 1) during the arrest. Social media activists on YouTube repeatedly used this image to gain the support and sympathy of others. This strategy worked, and these two images served as catalysts for the protesters who soon stormed the streets.

In the absence of traditional media outlets, participants in the Lawyers' Movement started to get innovative so as to attract potential sympathizers to join these protests. Ahmed and Stephan (2010), describe the movement as "a home-grown nonviolent movement that was both self-sufficient and innovative" (pg. 502). One of the innovative aspects of this movement was related to the use of the Internet. Activists in Pakistan used social media to promote their narrative of protest in new ways. They started uploading amateur and edited videos of protests to platforms such as YouTube and Facebook. Some of these videos showed the images of the Chief Justice's humiliation and arrest. They were frequently juxtaposed with Musharraf's images of pride in his military uniform. The plotline showed Musharraf as the criminal who attacked Pakistan's independent judiciary by sacking the Chief Justice, whereas, Iftikhar Chaudhry became a hero who decided not to bow in front of the dictator even when facing arrest and humiliation at the hands of country's law enforcement agencies. In other words, the protesters utilized both the "icons of outrage" and the "icons of arrogance" (Perlmutter, 1998) to motive potential sympathizers to join their cause. More discussion on these icons is provided in the following section of this chapter.

Icons of Outrage

This phenomenon, which makes certain images stand out among others in terms of their power and transposability, is referred to as the icons of outrage (Perlmutter, 1998). According to Perlmutter (1998), sometimes certain images (still or moving) become the center of public and elite attention because of their uniqueness. Perlmutter's (1998) "icons of outrage" idea differentiates ordinary images from the ones that have the tendency to generate public and elite discourses and/or upheavals. Thus, Chief Justice Iftikhar Chaudhry's image of arrest and humiliation can be seen as a powerful example of an iconic image that outraged the Pakistani society at large. It was not only the average citizens who came forward on streets to protest against such a treatment of their Chief Justice, but, in fact, the image also sparked anger among lawyers and other civil society organizations in the country, prompting them to join the movement, which gave it more credibility.

It is imperative to highlight that on social media platforms, the images of the Chief Justice's arrest and humiliation were not only being shared, replicated, and reproduced, but also re-interpreted in various ways. Some people interpreted this image as a disgrace to the judicial system of Pakistan at the hands of the military because General Musharraf had secured his office by force and was still serving as the chief of staff of the army while holding the office of president. Others saw President Musharraf as a man in military uniform who had absolutely no respect for the Supreme Court/judiciary and for the Constitution of Pakistan, which he had suspended soon after toppling Prime Minister Nawaz Sharif's government.

According to Perlmutter (1998), sometimes an image becomes so powerful that it does not require any caption or explanation. In other words, the image itself gains the "summing up" quality. By looking at it, people can relate themselves to a bigger picture. The image of Chief Justice's arrest and humiliation thus served as a metonymic image, which reminded the protesters of the fact that they were living under a dictatorship and that the military institution had no respect for civil institutions.

Conclusion

The discussion provided in this chapter leads us to three important conclusions that need to be summarized here. The first conclusion is about the outcome of the Lawyers' Movement of 2007–08. The second conclusion sheds light on a thoughtful connection between traditional media outlets and social media in order to achieve a common goal. The third conclusion is about looking at the common themes that might exist between the iconic images of the three countries, Pakistan, Egypt and Tunisia during their respective political uprisings.

First, the icons of outrage (arrest images of Iftikhar Chaudhry) triggered a Lawyers' Movement that began as an effort to reinstate the deposed Chief Justice. As a reaction to the military ruler's decision to overthrow the Chief Justice to gain control of the country's judicial system, Pakistani protesters used the arrest of Chaudhry as an iconic example to sustain their protests of the military regime. Thus, the image itself became a powerful resource that protesters and social media activists deployed to gain the attention of potential sympathizers and mobilize them for a collective action against the regime. This anger triggered flash mobs in the streets of Islamabad, the federal capital of Pakistan. Several other sympathizers, including civil society organizations and random and unorganized protesters, later joined these protests, which eventually resulted in the overthrow of President Musharraf and led to Iftikhar Chaudhry being reinstated as the Chief Justice of the country.

Second, during the Lawyers' Movement, despite the government's crackdown on protesters, President Musharraf could neither contain the ongoing protests in front of the Presidential House, nor was he able to control the media narrative against him. In other words, the decade-long rule of the military dictator who had already suspended the Constitution and was enjoying the powers of the two highest offices (President and Army Chief) could not withstand the will of the common people protesting to support the deposed Chief Justice Iftikhar Chaudhry

(Arif, 2010; Lieven, 2011; Rashid, 2008). The situation was becoming more troublesome for the military-led government as the newly privatized television news networks were providing uninterrupted coverage of the protests (Mufti, 2007). Besides providing 24/7 news coverage to the protesters, the newly born private media, particularly TV news channels, started becoming more critical of the military regime and demanded the restoration of the Constitution and democracy in the country (Mufti, 2007; Ricchiardi, 2012). This led President Musharraf to take extreme measures by shutting down the entire broadcast media in the country (Pirzada, 2007). Thus, to control the content of private television channels, the government banned all the private news channels for more than a month in November 2007 (Freedom House, 2018; Mufti, 2007). The journalists were also threatened with arrests and punishment if they tried to cover any political protests against the government or the military establishment (Freedom House, 2018). Historically, such a strategy to gag the media's freedom used to work in Pakistan, but this time it was different.

Despite the absolute control over the traditional media outlets, the narrative of protests against the military dictator was still spreading fast on alternative platforms via the Internet. Knowing that they may no longer be heard by the traditional media outlets, people with their smartphone cameras kept recording videos of these protests and uploading them on YouTube. Such videos of protests kept utilizing the iconic images of the Chief Justice on social media platforms. Also, it is pertinent to mention here that military interventions and bans on media freedom were not something unusual for Pakistan, as the country has witnessed many such examples since its inception in 1947. However, the only factor that made a difference in people's struggle against the dictatorship is that they now had an alternative medium—the Internet—to express their disapproval of the regime. Hence, in the absence of traditional media, people started using networked social media, including blogs, Facebook and YouTube as online and offline (street protests) informational cascades for the first time in the country's history (Ahmed, 2012; Khalid, 2008;). In short, a movement that was first reported on traditional media outlets of Pakistan was now being carried forward on alternate platforms of media. This was a unique moment in the history of controversial media freedom in Pakistan. In fact, this unique moment—which took place two years prior to the Arab Spring of 2010–11, was the stepping-stone for what was about to come in the form of political uprisings in the Muslim-majority countries.

Finally, even though this chapter was about the iconic images of Pakistani Chief Justice—the iconic images in the cases of Egypt and Tunisia will be discussed in the later chapters of this book—it may be noted that among all the iconic images from the three countries, the element of humiliation of citizens at the hands of security forces was found to be common. The disfigured face of an Egyptian man, the immolation of Tunisian street vendor, and the humiliation of Pakistan's Chief Justice at the hands of security forces are all examples that contributed to the political uprisings in these countries.

References

Ahmed, Z. S. (2012). The role of the Pakistani mass media in the Lawyers' Resistance against the Musharraf dictatorship, 2007–2009. *Pakistaniaat: A Journal of Pakistan Studies*, *4*(3), 61–77). Retrieved May 26, 2019, from http://pakistaniaat.org/index.php/pak/article/view/177/177

Ahmed, Z. S., & Stephan, M. J. (2010). Fighting for the rule of law: Civil resistance and the lawyers' movement in Pakistan. *Democratization*, *17*(3), 492–513. Retrieved August 14, 2018, from https://www.tandfonline.com/doi/full/10.1080/13510341003700360

Arif, R. (2010). *How terrorism killed the news: Pakistani journalism after 9/11*. Saarbrucken, Germany: Lambert Academic Publishing.

Arif, R. (2011, August). *The Emergence of social edia & the political crisis in Pakistan*. Paper presented at the meeting of AEJMC, St. Louis, Mo.

Asif, H. (2018, October 8). General Ziaul Haq: The man to answer for a lot that went wrong with Pakistan. *Herald*. Retrieved May 29, 2019, from https://herald.dawn.com/news/1398686

Freedom House (2018). *Pakistan Freedom Report*. Retrieved May 02, 2019, from https://freedomhouse.org/report/freedom-world/2018/pakistan

Ghias, S. A. (2010). Miscarriage of chief justice: Judicial power and the legal complex in Pakistan under Musharraf. *Law & Social Inquiry*, *35*(4), 985–1022. Retrieved August 16, 2019, from https://www.jstor.org/stable/pdf/40926291.pdf

Hashim, A. (2013, April 30). Pakistan: a political timeline. *Al Jazeera*. Retrieved February 21, 2019, from https://www.aljazeera.com/indepth/interactive/2012/01/20121181235768904.html

Iqbal, N. (2007, March 10). CJ suspended, escorted home: Justice Iftikhar summoned by SJC on 13th for reference hearing. *Dawn*. Retrieved February 05, 2019, from https://www.dawn.com/news/236769

Khalid, K. (2008). *The face of media freedom in Pakistan*. Lahore, Pakistan: Asia Media.

Khan, L. A. (2017, July 28). Pakistan punishes Prime Ministers but not military generals. *Huffington Post*. Retrieved April 08, 2019, from https://www.huffingtonpost.com/entry/pakistan-punishes-prime-ministers-but-not-military_us_597b65f7e4b0c69ef70527a5

Lieven, A. (2011). *Pakistan: A hard country*. London, England: Allen Lane

Mufti, S. (2007). Musharraf's monster. *Columbia Journalism Review*, *46*(4), 46–51. Retrieved May 07, 2018, from http://www.shahanmufti.com/cjr/NOVDEC_2007_Musharrafs_monster.pdf

Mustafa, Z. (2018, April 27). Justice for all. *Dawn*. Retrieved July 01, 2019, from https://www.dawn.com/news/1404169/justice-for-all

Niesewand, P. (2016, April 5). Pakistan's Zulfikar Ail Bhutto executed- archive. *The Guardian*. (Republished online from "A vain autocrat who gave his nation confidence," 1979, April 5. *The*

Guardian). Retrieved August 05, 2019, from https://www.theguardian.com/world/2016/apr/05/pakistan-zulfikar-ali-bhutto-executed-1979

Pakistan Constitutional Law.com. (n.d) Article 6: High treason. Retrieved May 30, 2019 from https://pakistanconstitutionlaw.com/article-6-high-treason/

Perlmutter, D. D. (1998). *Photojournalism and foreign policy: Icons of outrage in international crises.* Westport, Conn.: Praeger.

Pirzada, M. (2007, November 19). Musharraf and the media. *The Guardian.* Retrieved October 18, 2019, from https://www.theguardian.com/commentisfree/2007/nov/19/musharrafandthemedia

Profile: Iftikhar Chaudhry (n.d.). *History Commons.* Retrieved May 26, 2019, from http://www.historycommons.org/entity.jsp?entity=iftikhar_chaudhry_1

Rao, B. Z. (2018, April 12). Perils of the judiciary's populist rhetoric. *Daily Times.* Retrieved November 03, 2019, from https://dailytimes.com.pk/226754/perils-of-the-judiciarys-populist-rhetoric/

Rashid, A. (2008). *Descent into chaos: The United States and the failure of nation building in Pakistan, Afghanistan, and Central Asia.* New York, NY: Viking.

Ricchiardi, S. (2012). Challenges for independent news media in Pakistan: A report to the Center for International Media Assistance. Washington, DC, National Endowment for Democracy. Retrieved December 01, 2018, from http://www.centerforinternationalmediaassistance.org/wp-content/uploads/2015/01/Challenges-for-Independent-News-Media-in-Pakistan_Ricchiardi-updated.pdf

Sciolino, E. (1988, August 18). Zia of Pakistan kills as blast downs plane. *The New York Times.* Retrieved May 28, 2019, from https://www.nytimes.com/1988/08/18/world/zia-of-pakistan-killed-as-blast-downs-plane-us-envoy-28-others-die.html

Sentence of death for Bhutto upheld. (1979, March 24). *New York Times.* (Republished online, n.d.) Retrieved July 23, 2019, from https://www.nytimes.com/1979/03/24/archives/sentence-of-death-for-bhutto-upheld-pakistani-court-refuses-a.html

Wilkinson, I. (2007, March 17). Crisis for Musharraf over justice chief's sacking. *The Telegraph.* Retrieved July 21, 2019, from https://www.telegraph.co.uk/news/worldnews/1545843/Crisis-for-Musharraf-over-justice-chiefs-sacking.html

Zaidi, S. A. (2008). An emerging civil society? *Journal of Democracy, 19*(4), 38–40. doi: https://doi.org/10.1353/jod.0.0042

Zaman, M. (2011). Social movements, conflicts and rise of extremism in Pakistan. *Academic Journal of the Institute of Social Prevention and Resocialisation of the University of Warsaw (Prace Instytutu Profilaktyki Społecznej i Resocjalizacji), 17,* 154–173. Retrieved May 18, 2019, from https://www.academia.edu/3882751/Social_Movements_Conflicts_and_Rise_of_Extremism_in_Pakistan

Zulfikar Ali Bhutto. (2019, January 1). *Encyclopedia Britannica.* Retrieved July 24, 2019, from https://www.britannica.com/biography/Zulfikar-Ali-Bhutto

5 Social Movements in Pakistan

Since its independence in 1947, Pakistan has witnessed the rise of numerous religious, political and secular social movements (Fair, Littman, Malhotra, & Shapiro, 2016; Gregg, 2016; Rashid, 2008). In fact, the creation of Pakistan itself was the result of a contentious social movement, led by *The All-India Muslim League*, against British rule (Jalal, 1994). The movement started under the leadership of Mohammed Ali Jinnah, who would later be the founder of Pakistan. As part of its fight against British rule, the League demanded a separate state for the Muslims of British-India (Ahmed, 1997). The movement realized its dream on August 14, 1947, when the British decided to divide the Indian subcontinent into two countries, Pakistan and India (Malik, 2008). In order to better understand the social fabric of the country and its deep-rooted history of resistance and collective actions, let's explore the pre-partition resistance movements of the British controlled subcontinent.

Rebellion of 1857 (Indian Subcontinent's First War of Independence)

A major and frequently referenced political uprising on the Indian subcontinent was the mutiny against the British Empire in 1857. The British East India Company, which had originally entered the Indian subcontinent in 1600s with the purpose of trade with the Mughal Empire, controlled "two thirds of the subcontinent" by 1857 ("Indian Mutiny," n.d., para. 2). Cracks and divisions in the ranks of the Bengal Army based on discrimination and British officers' lack of respect and understanding for locals' culture contributed to the revolt (Dash, 2012; "Indian Mutiny," n.d.; "Indian Mutiny," 2019; "India's First War," 2016). Feelings of discontent were eventually ignited by rapidly circulating rumors "that the cartridges for the new rifle [Enfield Rifle] were greased with pig and cow fat. This made them offensive to both Muslims and Hindus" ("Indian Mutiny," n.d., para. 13). In utter disregard for their religious and cultural beliefs, the high-ranking British soldiers started to arrest and punish Muslim and Hindu soldiers who refused to use these cartridges (Alavi, 1996; Anderson, 2007). Such circumstances started to pave the way for a rebellion inside the military ranks.

> The Mutiny proper began at Meerut on 10 May 1857 when 85 members of the 3rd Bengal Light Cavalry, who had been jailed for refusing to use the new cartridges, were broken out of prison by their comrades. They ransacked the nearby military station and killed any Europeans they could find. ("Indian Mutiny," n.d., para. 17)

When the news about the local soldiers revolting against their British rulers broke out, common people and local rulers also joined the revolt to set their region free from British rule (Alavi, 1996; Anderson, 2007; Dash, 2012). The participation of common people and local rulers took the revolt further away from protesting against the controversial use of cartridges to demanding the overthrow of the British rule. "Many wanted to destroy the system by which the Company collected taxes. Peasants, who had been forced to switch from subsistence farming to export crops in order to meet increasing tax demands, needed little encouragement to rebel" ("Indian Mutiny," n.d., paras. 23–24). In a way, the division in military ranks served as a political opportunity for the oppressed factions of the society, who were quick to join the resistance against their foreign ruler.

Another important aspect of this revolt was the factor of unity among the protesters, despite of their different religious beliefs. With a population of over

250 million people in 1857 (Dash, 2012), the undivided subcontinent was represented by a majority of Hindus, followed by Muslims, Sikhs and other religions. In terms of language, Hindi was the major spoken language of locals, followed by Urdu, Punjabi and Bengali. Regardless of their identities, all of these religious and ethnic groups joined the collective action against the British Empire that had colonized the South Asian subcontinent for over 200 years (Alavi, 1996; Marshall, 2011). Despite its endless internal divisions based on caste system, ethnicity, economic status and religion, these divisions did not prevent people from joining their fellow Indians in the collective action aimed at getting rid of their common enemy, the East India British Company. Local people's decision to join this collective action against the British East India Company was a result of the rulers' blatant disregard for the subcontinent's culture, religion and economy. Under the Company, people were being stripped of their lands and forced to pay heavy taxes on their crops. They were also facing religious discrimination from the British. Such factors collectively provided an opportunity for common citizens to join a group action against the ruling elite, particularly when the news about mutiny in the army ranks broke out.

Even though the 1857 War of Independence would not be a successful one, it created ripples in the stagnant society of the subcontinent region, which was eventually followed by successive social movements against British rule. One of the prime factors that contributed to the failure of this independence movement was poor (or non-existent) communication networks between the epicenters of the protests. Because of the geographical vastness of the region, many of the protests during the 1857 revolt were taking place in cities that were located pretty far from each other. For example, "[s]ome epicentres of the revolt were Kanpur, Lucknow, Aligarh, Agra, Arrah, Delhi, and Jhansi. Due to all the epicentres being far from each other, there was a communication gap between the leaders of different parts of India" ("India's First War," 2016, para. 4). The participants in these social movements did not have a mechanism to evaluate the outcome of their revolt. They could not judge the reaction of the regime or whether other parts of the subcontinent were standing by the movement's demands. This factor speaks volumes about the importance and power of effective communication in any social movement. If the communication aspect is compromised, a social movement, regardless of how many people join it, may not realize its dream, as was witnessed in the case of the subcontinent's rebellion of 1857.

Although this contentious social movement failed, it changed the political landscape of the region for good. This element of change can be connected to Tarrow's (1998) claim that social movements, even if defeated, trigger a change in the society. Subsequently, the regime has no choice but to re-adjust itself according to the new circumstances. For example, even if it succeeded, a regime will have to go tougher on its people so as to make sure that such revolts never take place again (Tarrow, 1998). This was the case with the outcome of the 1857 revolt. The British Empire got tougher on its colonized land and people and continued to rule the Indian subcontinent for another 90 years, until 1947. As a revised and new strategy, British colonizers deployed a divide and rule policy on the subcontinent to ensure locals could not find unity within their ranks and join forces against the British as their common enemy again.

Second Wave of Resistance Movements in British Controlled Subcontinent

By the 1940s, another wave of social movements took to the streets of the subcontinent under the leadership of Mohandas Karamchand Gandhi and Muhammad Ali Jinnah. Unlike the resistance movement of 1857, this new wave of social movements for independence from British rule marked an era of nonviolent collective actions such as Nonviolent Civil Disobedience of 1930, Khilafat Movement of 1919 (the movement to protect the Ottoman Empire), the Non-Cooperation Movement, the Muslim League of the 1940s (a movement to acquire a separate homeland for Muslims), and the Quit India Movement ("Gandhi Leads," 2010; BBC, 2011). In August 1947, these social movements realized their dreams with the creation of two independent nation-states, India and Pakistan (Kaul, 2011; "Pakistan Movement," n.d.).

Social Movements after the Inception of Pakistan

Ironically, the creation of Pakistan did not put an end to the era of resistance and protests. Soon after getting independence from British rule on August 14, 1947, the country witnessed the emergence of a number of social movements and political uprisings, some successful and some unsuccessful. Today, Pakistan continues to go through cycles of contentious and nonviolent social movements. It is worth noting that during the post-partition phases of Pakistan's history, "a majority of nonviolent movements including civil disobedience, movements of art and literature, women's struggle for their rights, and movements for freedom of press and expression had been waged against General Zia-ul-Haq" in the 1980s (Abbas, 2018, para. 3).

Ethnicity, religion and politics continue to dominate as the prime motives for these social movements in this relatively young country (Gregg, 2016). Some of these social movements have included: the 1969 political uprising in former East Pakistan (Bangladesh) to seek independence from West Pakistan; the Islamic Movement known as *Jama'ati Islami Pakistan* to transform the country into an Islamic state; the Lawyers' Movement of 2007; the Movement for the Restoration of Democracy of 2007; the struggle for the rights of peasants, which could never be acknowledged at national level because of poor communication networks among peasants; the Movement for the Freedom of Media and Expression, which continues its struggle regardless of military or civilian government set up in the country; the Balochistan Liberation Movement; and *Tehreek-e-Taliban*, Pakistan, which started after 9/11 and is still a major threat to the country's existence (Abbas, 2018; Arif, 2010; Fair, Littman, Malhotra, & Shapiro, 2016; Gregg, 2016; Haqqani, 2005; Lieven, 2011; Nasr, 1996; Rashid, 2008; Tehranian, 1990).

Some scholars classify these social movements in Pakistan under three ideological categories: Traditionalism, Islamism and Constitutionalism, where traditionalism and Islamism represent violent social movements. Providing further explanation to this classification, Zaman (2011) says:

> The traditionalist social movement argues that tribal values are an important base for social justice and should be given supremacy. Islamists see the divine rules as the panacea of justice. However, constitutionalists (or modernists) are pushing for modernization and the rule of law. (Zaman, 2011, p. 156)

In this context, the Balochistan Liberation Movement and *Tehreek-e-Taliban*, Pakistan can fit into the categories of traditionalism and Islamism, respectively. Among others, the Lawyers' Movement and the Movement for the Restoration of Democracy, initiated simultaneously in 2007 (Traub, 2008), can be categorized as examples of Constitutionalism. These latter nonviolent movements eventually merged into one when the Lawyers' Movement gained momentum in its efforts to restore the deposed Chief Justice of Pakistan (Hashim, 2013).

The Lawyers' Movement

The Lawyers' Movement was later joined by protesters and civil society organizations (NGOs), and thus turned into mass political protests throughout the country. This collective movement used social media (YouTube) as an alternative to the traditional media because President Musharraf had banned the entire broadcast media from covering any political protests against his regime (Ricchiardi, 2012). Unable to withstand the ever-increasing protests against his regime, President Musharraf transferred powers to a democratically elected government in 2008 and fled the country to avoid prosecution (Leiby, 2013). If we observe the tactics deployed in the Pakistani Lawyers' Movement, it is remarkable to see how smartly other relatively smaller movements (civil society; freedom of media; alliance for the restoration of democracy) decided to merge into one in order to have a bigger impact on a national and international scale. This tactic contributed not only to the success of the Lawyers' Movement, but also paved the way for smaller groups' collective actions to join the larger group so as to benefit from the outcome of such a collective action. This strategy relates to Olson's (1965) economic logic of group actions, discussed in Chapter 1 of this book. Olson (1965) believes that people participate in a collective action based on their evaluation of the outcome of a group action. He argues that the potential outcome or reward of a group action motivates individuals to participate in a particular collective action. Keeping this economic logic in perspective, it can be argued that if during the political uprisings of Pakistan these smaller social movements had decided to continue their struggle independently, they would have died down or been suppressed by the regime much earlier. Another lesson that can be learned here is that all these social movements could merge into one because they were nonviolent in nature. We can infer that nonviolent social movements not only tend to gain more sympathizers, but also stand a better chance of succeeding in their struggle against the powerful opponent. Thus, Tilly's (1990) idea of contention as a resource for the sustainability of a movement may need to be revisited when it comes to the study of scenarios of non-Western social movements such as Pakistan. It is imperative to note that in certain situations, the element of nonviolence can actually replace the element of contention and, thus, be used as a powerful resource to sustain a social movement. I invite future researchers to study the element of nonviolence as a resource to sustain a collective action while looking into Tilly & Tarrow's (2007) theorization of "contention" as a resource for social movements.

Azadi March (Freedom March)

The biggest contribution of the political uprisings of the 2007 Lawyers' Movement was not the regime change, but it was, in fact, the ability of people to realize the power and potential of social media and how to use these new tools of information and communication as alternative to traditional media sources. Once they had realized the true power of social media, Pakistani people did not stop there, rather they kept using these tools for the promotion of political dialogue in the country.

A 2014 social movement commonly referred to as the Azadi March can be seen as another example of political activism that took place within seven years of "Pakistan's Spring" (Nasr, 2013). The leader of the March was Imran Khan, who was elected prime minister of Pakistan in 2018 (Hashim, 2018). The cricketer-turned-politician started his largest public protest march against former Prime Minister Nawaz Sharif's government on August 14, 2014, claiming that the government rigged the 2013 general elections (Hussain, 2014). These countrywide protests that lasted just over four months were later joined by Sufi cleric Muhammad Tahrir-ul-Qadri, the leader of Pakistan Awami Tehreek (PAT). Even though these protests did not topple Nawaz Sharif's government at that time, they were a powerful example of the common man's ability to influence change through active participation in the country's politics. Protesters in the Azadi March actively used social media such as Facebook, Twitter and blogs to spread their narrative of protests and to unite people against the government (Arif, 2018).

The Balochistan Liberation Army (BLA), A Militant Movement in Balochistan

Another ongoing violent social movement that has received relatively little coverage on Pakistan's traditional media outlets is the Balochistan Liberation Army (BLA). This violent separatist movement was formed in 2000 "in response to growing resentment in Balochistan over the perceived government monopoly of Balochistan's natural resources and unequal allocation of jobs to Punjabis over Balochi natives" ("Balochistan Liberation Army," 2015, para. 2). The Ethnonationalist separatist movement, which is still active in Pakistan's geographically largest province of Balochistan (Gates & Roy, 2011), "seeks greater regional autonomy of Balochistan from Pakistan" (Stanford University, 2015, para. 13). Furthermore, BLA challenges the creation of the country on the basis of religion as the "group believes that the foundation that Pakistan was built on, that all Muslims are created equal, is wrong and that, instead, ethnic identity takes precedence over religious identity" ("Balochistan Liberation Army," 2015, para. 13). Because of its violent tactics and involvement in violent attacks including a series of bombings that has killed several people so far, the BLA has been labelled a terrorist organization by Pakistan and the United Kingdom ("Balochistan Liberation Army," 2015; Home Office, 2019).

Women's Action Forum (WAF), A Social Movement for Pakistani Women

A relatively less studied, and the least acknowledged, social movement in Pakistan is women's rights activism. Women's movements took to the stage during 1980s and 1990s. In 1980s, the movement started against the suppression of women by the then military dictator, Zia-ul-Haq. With the support of religious leaders, the military ruler tried "to push women back within the strict confines of 'home and hearth' or *chador aur chardiwari* (veil and four walls of a homestead), rescind their rights, and curtail their liberties" (Shaheed, 2016, p. 100). In an effort to resist the controversial legislations against women, such as the Hudood Ordinance, the educated middle-class urban women of Pakistan initiated the "Khawateen-Mahaz-e-Amal, better known by its English name, Women's Action Forum, as a platform for women and women's organizations to defend women's rights" (Shaheed, 2016, p. 100). Although it is hard to judge the success of this movement of resistance during the 1980s because of strict military control and suppression, one outcome is undeniable: such a political and collective action purely initiated by women served as "signals" of the cascade of information (Lohmann, 1994) for other women to come out and take part in more broad, collective actions in society, such as demanding women's quota in the parliament of Pakistan's National and Provincial Assemblies. Women's activism continues to grow in Pakistan. Now there is more awareness about female representation in political party manifestos and people are being educated about issues of domestic violence against women, among other issues. Furthermore, the country has started to witness more organized platforms to support women's activism such as the Aurat Foundation (Women's Foundation), *Shirkat Gah* for Women's Rights, the Women's Rights Association, the Simorgh-Women's Resource and Publication Center, the Women's Association Struggle For Development (WASFD) and the All Pakistan Women's Association, among others ("Women Rights," 2013).

Also, the recent social movements, such as the Lawyers' Movement, the movement for the restoration of democracy and the Azadi March by Imran Khan, have witnessed overwhelming representation of women as equal partners and stakeholders along with men. Future researchers interested in studying political activism in non-Western scenarios should look at the participation aspect of women in such marches in societies like Pakistan where the female faction of the society has been historically undermined and discriminated. Even though women's social movements in a male dominated society like Pakistan are doing a marvelous job by mobilizing their fellow citizens to take action and demand their rights, this social and political action still has a long road to walk in order to realize the dream of equality in all walks of life.

Conclusion

To recap, social movements in Pakistan are not a new phenomenon. The country has a history of collective action that goes back to the Indian subcontinent's struggle for independence, beginning in 1857. Communication is the most important factor that has distinguished the recent social movements in Pakistan from the previous ones. This chapter argues that in nonviolent social movements, where contention is not an option to be deployed as a resource, communication assumes the role of being the most important resource for a social movement to survive. Thus, nonviolent social movements of the digital age in Pakistan assured an effective and sustained mechanism of communication between and among protesters regardless of their geographical limitations. Such a sustained communication pattern, even when interrupted by the ruling elites, moved to alternate platforms of information and communication such as YouTube, Facebook and Twitter, making sure that the narrative of protests continued to spread among the potential sympathizers. Also, social movements that are originating entirely on digital platforms such as #MeToo movement (which originated from the United States and has spread to more than 80 countries, including Pakistan, India and China) were only possible because of a much stronger, independent and efficient communication network among digital activists, who continue to use social media as a tool of collective action about social issues of importance. Thus, it can be argued that sustained and effective communication is the most important factor in the formation and sustainability of a collective action to achieve its goals as we had witnessed in the case of the Lawyers' Movement of Pakistan.

References

Abbas, K. (2018, April 5). 'People's movements in Pakistan' –An account of political struggle. *Daily Times*. Retrieved May 12, 2019, from https://dailytimes.com.pk/224155/peoples-movements-in-pakistan-an-account-of-political-struggle/

Ahmed, A. (1997). *Jinnah, Pakistan, and Islamic identity: The search for Saladin.* London, England: Routledge.

Alavi, S. (1996). *The sepoys and the company: Tradition and transition in northern India 1770–1830.* Oxford, England: Oxford University Press.

Anderson, C. (2007). *Indian uprising of 1857–8: Prisons, prisoners and rebellion.* New York, NY: Anthem Press.

Arif, R. (2010). *How terrorism killed the news: Pakistani journalism after 9/11.* Saarbrucken, Germany: Lambert Academic Publishing.

Arif, R. (2018). Social networks, social movements and politico-cultural situation of Pakistani media. In Julie Dee (Ed.), *From Tahrir Square to Gezi Park: Social networks as facilitators of social movements.* New York, NY: Peter Lang Publishing.

Balochistan Liberation Army. (2015). *Mapping Militants Project.* Retrieved June 02, 21, 2019, from http://web.stanford.edu/group/mappingmilitants/cgi-bin/groups/view/297?highlight=baloch

Dash, M. (2012, May 24). Pass it on: The Secret that preceded the Indian Rebellion of 1857. *Smithsonian Magazine.* Retrieved June 03, 2019, from https://www.smithsonianmag.com/history/pass-it-on-the-secret-that-preceded-the-indian-rebellion-of-1857-105066360/

Fair, C. C., Littman, R., Malhotra, N., & Shapiro, J. N. (2016). Relative poverty, perceived violence, and support for militant politics: Evidence from Pakistan. *Political Science Research and Methods, 6*(1), 57–81.

Gandhi leads civil disobedience. (2010, February 9). *History.* Retrieved May 11, 2019, from https://www.history.com/this-day-in-history/gandhi-leads-civil-disobedience

Gates, S. & Roy, K. (2011). *Unconventional warfare in South Asia: Shadow warriors and counterinsurgency.* London, England: Routledge Publishers.

Gregg, H. S. (2016). Three theories of religious activism and violence: Social movements, fundamentalists, and apocalyptic warriors. *Terrorism and Political Violence, 28*(2), 338–360.

Haqqani, H. (2005). *Pakistan: Between mosque and military.* Washington, D.C: Carnegie Endowment for International Peace.

Hashim, A. (2013, April 30). Pakistan: A political timeline. *Al Jazeera.* Retrieved February 21, 2019, from https://www.aljazeera.com/indepth/interactive/2012/01/20121181235768904.html

Hashim, A. (2018, August 17). Imran Khan elected as Pakistan's Prime Minister. *Al Jazeera.* Retrieved June 30, 2019, from https://www.aljazeera.com/news/2018/08/imran-khan-elected-pakistan-prime-minister-180817074849200.html

Home Office (2019, March 1). Proscribed terrorist organizations. *Gov. UK.* Retrieved June 04, 2019], from https://www.gov.uk/government/publications/proscribed-terror-groups-or-organisations--2

Hussain, A. (2014, June 13). Were Pakistan's 2013 elections really rigged? *The Express Tribune Blogs.* Retrieved from https://blogs.tribune.com.pk/story/22678/were-pakistans-2013-elections-really-rigged/

Indian Mutiny (n.d.) *National Army Museum.* Retrieved from https://www.nam.ac.uk/explore/why-did-indian-mutiny-happen

Indian Mutiny. (2019, February 22). *Encyclopedia Britannica.* Retrieved July 03, 2019, from https://www.britannica.com/event/Indian-Mutiny

India's first war of independence. (2016, May 10). *India Today*. Retrieved July 03, 2019, from https://www.indiatoday.in/education-today/gk-current-affairs/story/indias-first-war-of-independence-322576-2016-05-10

Jalal, A. (1994). *The sole spokesman: Jinnah, the Muslim League and the demand for Pakistan*. Cambridge, England: Cambridge University Press.

Kaul, C. (2011, March 3). From empire to independence: The British Raj in India 1858–1947. *BBC History*. Retrieved July 03, 2019, from http://www.bbc.co.uk/history/british/modern/independence1947_01.shtml

Leiby, R. (2013, April 19). Musharraf arrest risks clash of powers. *The Washington Post*. Retrieved June 08, 2019, from https://www.washingtonpost.com/world/musharraf-arrest-tempts-clash-of-powers/2013/04/19/6b1e78c6-a8dc-11e2-9e1c-bb0fb0c2edd9_story.html?noredirect=on&utm_term=.5ca7a9522024

Lieven, A. (2011). *Pakistan: A hard country*. London, England: Allen Lane

Lohmann, S. (1994). The dynamics of informational cascades: the Monday demonstrations in Leipzig, East Germany, 1989–91. *World Politics*, *47*(1), 42–101.

Malik, I. (2008). *The history of Pakistan*. Westport, Conn.: Greenwood Press.

Marshall, P. (2011, February 17). The British presence in India in the 18th century. *BBC History*. Retrieved June 05, 2019, from http://www.bbc.co.uk/history/british/empire_seapower/east_india_01.shtml

Nasr, V. (1996). *Mawdudi and the making of Islamic revivalism*. Oxford, England: Oxford University Press.

Nasr, V. (2013). *The dispensable nation: American foreign policy in retreat*. New York, NY: Doubleday.

Olson, M. (1965). *Logic of collective action*. Cambridge, MA: Harvard University Press.

Pakistan movement, The. (n.d.). *Story of Pakistan: A Multimedia Journey*. Retrieved March 03, 2018, from https://storyofpakistan.com/events/the-pakistan-movement

Rashid, A. (2008). *Descent into chaos: The United States and the failure of nation building in Pakistan, Afghanistan, and Central Asia*. New York, NY: Viking.

Ricchiardi, S. (2012). Challenges for independent news media in Pakistan: A report to the Center for International Media Assistance. Washington, DC, National Endowment for Democracy. Retrieved July 10, 2019, from http://www.centerforinternationalmediaassistance.org/wp-content/uploads/2015/01/Challenges-for-Independent-News-Media-in-Pakistan_Ricchiardi-updated.pdf

Shaheed, F. (2016). Pakistan's women's movement: Protests, programming, and revitalization. In A. Basu (ed.) *Women's Movements in the Global Era: The Power of Local Feminisms* (2nd ed., pp. 95–128). London, England: Routledge.

Tarrow, S. G. (1998). *Power in movement: Social movements and contentious politics*. Cambridge, Mass: Cambridge University Press.

Tehranian, M. (1990). Communication and revolution in the Islamic World: An essay in interpretation. *Asian Journal of Communication*, *1*(1), 1–33.

Tilly, C. (1990). Coercion, capital, and European states, AD 990–1990. In C. Calhoun, J. Gerteis, J. Moody, S. Pfaff & I. Virk (Eds.) *Contemporary Sociological Theory* (3rd ed.). Cambridge, Mass: Wiley-Blackwell.

Tilly, C., & Tarrow, S. (2007). Contentious politics. Boulder, Colo.: Paradigm.

Traub, J. (2008, June 1). The lawyers' crusade. *The New York Times*. Retrieved July 28, 2019, from https://www.nytimes.com/2008/06/01/magazine/01PAKISTAN-t.html

Women Rights NGOs in Pakistan. (2013). *Pakistan NGOs Directory & Guide*. Retrieved July 03, 2019, from http://www.ngo.com.pk/rights/women_rights_ngos_pakistan.htm

Zaman, M. (2011). Social movements, conflicts and rise of extremism in Pakistan. *Academic Journal of the Institute of Social Prevention and Resocialisation of the University of Warsaw (Prace Instytutu Profilaktyki Społecznej i Resocjalizacji), 17*, 154–173. Retrieved July 07, 2019, from https://www.academia.edu/3882751/Social_Movements_Conflicts_and_Rise_of_Extremism_in_Pakistan

6 Politico-Cultural Context of Pakistan

Pakistan, which means, "Land of the Pure," got its independence from British rule on August 14, 1947 (Lieven, 2011; Rashid, 2008). Even though the formal independence date of Pakistan is 1947, the country's culture and traditions are deep-rooted in the human history of civilization. The "Indus Valley civilization, one of the oldest in the world and dating back at least 5,000 years, spread over much of what is presently Pakistan" (CIA, 2019, para. 1). Located in the Indian subcontinent, the area has a long history of successive invasions "from the Persians, Greeks, Scythians, Arabs (who brought Islam), Afghans, and Turks" (CIA, 2019, para. 1) and, most recently, the British.

The country, slightly less than twice the size of California, with a population of more than 200 million people, has a number of historical and contemporary problems including repeated military interventions, poor economic conditions, emergency crises, unfriendly relations with neighboring states (including India, Iran and Afghanistan), rising inflation, unemployment among educated youth and the challenges of media freedom (Al-Mujahid, 1982; Arif, 2010; CIA, 2019; Lieven, 2011; "Pakistan Blocks Access," 2010). According to World Bank (2018), more than 24% of the population of Pakistan is currently living below the poverty line. More than 96% of the country's population is Muslim (Sunni 90%, Shia 10%), while Christian and Hindus constitute 4% of the country's total population. The CIA's World Factbook (2019) summarizes Pakistan's challenges this way:

> Decades of internal political disputes and low levels of foreign investment have led to underdevelopment in Pakistan. Pakistan has a large English-speaking population, with English-language skills less prevalent outside urban centers. Despite some progress in recent years in both security and energy, a challenging security environment, electricity shortages, and a burdensome investment climate have traditionally deterred investors. Official unemployment was 6% in 2017, but this fails to capture the true picture, because much of the economy is informal and underemployment remains high. Human development continues to lag behind most of the region … The Pakistani rupee has remained relatively stable against the US dollar since 2015, though it declined about 10% between November 2017 and March 2018 … Pakistan must continue to address several longstanding issues, including expanding investment in education, healthcare, and sanitation; adapting to the effects of climate change and natural disasters; improving the country's business environment; and widening the country's tax base. Given demographic challenges, Pakistan's leadership will be pressed to implement economic reforms, promote further development of the energy sector, and attract foreign investment to support sufficient economic growth necessary to employ its growing and rapidly urbanizing population, much of which is under the age of 25.

While this book was being written, the previously mentioned challenges to Pakistan became more complicated. For example, the government of Nawaz Sharif was overthrown after his party fell out of favor with the country's armed forces. As in the past, the Supreme Court of Pakistan was used once again to push the elected premier out of office (Masood, 2017). Sharif was replaced by Imran Khan during the general elections of 2018. Several independent and media reports have claimed military interference in the outcome of the elections as, this time, Imran Khan was seen as the apple of Pakistan military eye (Fair, 2018; Shackle, 2018; Siddiqui, 2018).

During this process of political change, some of the most influential Pakistani media personalities, including news anchors and political analysts, started to question the military's role in Pakistani politics. As in the past, such a criticism of the military establishment was not welcomed by the ruling elite (military and civilian), which paved the way for another era of censorship on Pakistani print and electronic media. This time, the government did not wait to include censorship on social media profiles of its critics. There are new laws in place, such as the Prevention of Electronic Crimes Act (PECA), which allow Pakistan's security and law enforcement agencies to arrest anyone who share their political opinions, particularly against the military's role in politics (Aziz, 2018). Such controversial laws are directly interfering with the freedom of media in Pakistan. "Journalists and press freedom advocates say the military and its agencies are pressuring media outlets to quash critical coverage" ("Lawyer: Pakistani journalist," 2019, para. 4). Journalists were arrested for writing critical articles and given the choice of jail time or silence ("Pakistani journalist arrested," 2019). Also, journalists are being punished by other tactics such as economic consequences for the ones who refuse to comply with the desires of the ruling elite. In this regard, "[t]he government also is coming heavy on social media, pressuring newspapers and TV stations by slashing their advertising revenue, squeezing a key source of income for local media" ("Lawyer: Pakistani journalist," 2019, para. 4). Since this newly-formed and military-backed government took over, around 2000 journalists have lost their jobs (Hasan, 2018; "Over two thousand journalists," 2018). In order to better understand the level of freedom of speech and expression, let's revisit the constitutional frame of the country.

Constitutional Framework of Free Speech in Pakistan

Prior to discussing the media situation in Pakistan, let's look at the *Constitution of Pakistan* and whether it provides any liberties for the freedom of speech and expression to the citizens of Pakistan. Article 19 and 19A of Pakistan's constitution guarantee the right to freedom of speech and expression and the right to freedom of the press in the country (Naqvi, 2013). According to Article 19 of the constitution:

- *Article 19*: Every citizen shall have the right to freedom of speech and expression, and there shall be freedom of the press, subject to any reasonable restrictions imposed by law in the interest of the glory of Islam or the integrity, security or defense of Pakistan or any part thereof, friendly relations with foreign States, public order, decency or morality, or in relation to contempt of court, commission of or incitement to an offence.
- *Article 19A*: Right to information– Every citizen shall have the right to have access to information in all matters of public importance subject to regulation and reasonable restrictions imposed by law (Constitution, 1973).

It may be noted that the more than 130 page-long constitution of Pakistan is comprised of 280 articles that cover subjects ranging from religion, to definition of the state, to ensuring justice and equality to all the citizens of the country. Some of the articles such as the "Protection of Property Rights" (Article 24) and "Promotion of Social Justice and Eradication of Social Evils" (Article 37) take up most of the space in the constitution because they are described in detail. On the contrary, the articles related to the freedom of speech and expression carry very limited space in the constitution. This limited explanation to the freedom of speech and expression in the constitution provides an opportunity for the rulers to benefit from all the existing grey areas when it comes to free expression. It also speaks volumes to the evidence that freedom of speech and expression are consistently the first victims of dictatorships and military interventions.

On the contrary, religion, particularly Islam, takes up most of the discussion in the constitution. For example, Article 2, and Article 31 of the Constitution focus on Islam as the state religion and mandate the country's responsibility to promote an Islamic way of life (Constitution, 1973). This focus on religion in Pakistan's constitution leads us to another important aspect of the controversial laws in the country that hinder free speech and freedom of expression. Time and again, Pakistan's ruling elite has played the religion card to suppress media freedom in the country.

Anti-blasphemy Laws in Pakistan

Among all countries with a Muslim-majority, Pakistan is known for having the harshest anti-blasphemy laws ("Pakistani Girl Accused of Blasphemy, 2013; "What are Pakistan's Blasphemy Laws," 2019). It is ironic that the former colonial rulers of the region introduced such controversial laws, which remain in place even though the previous masters have already left the subcontinent. According to the British Broadcasting Corporation (BBC), Pakistan inherited anti-blasphemy laws from its British rulers. Within three years of suppressing the rebellion of 1857, British rulers felt the need to exploit religion as a tool to suppress any future rebellious movements against the empire. In this regard, "[t]he offences relating to religion were first codified by India's British rulers in 1860 and were expanded in 1927. Pakistan inherited these laws after the partition of India in 1947" ("What are Pakistan's Blasphemy Laws," 2019, para. 1). Even though the country had inherited these controversial religious laws from the British rulers, no one used them as a whip against the citizens of Pakistan until 1980s:

> Between 1980 and 1986, a number of clauses were added to the laws by the military government of General Zia-ul Haq. He wanted to "Islamicise" them and also legally to separate the Ahmadi community, declared non-Muslim in 1973, from the main body of Pakistan's overwhelmingly Muslim population. ("What are Pakistan's Blasphemy Laws," 2019, para. 2)

According to the Pakistan Penal Code (Article 295-B, Article 295-C, Article 298-A, Article 298-B, and Article 298-C), any blasphemous act—defiling of a copy of the Holy Quran, use of derogatory remarks toward the Holy Prophet Mohammed (Peace Be Upon Him), use of derogatory remarks in respect of holy personages by words, either spoken or written, or by visible representation, or by any imputation—"shall be punished with death, or imprisonment for life, and shall also be liable to fine" (Pakistan Penal Code, 1860).

It may be mentioned here that in September of 2012 the Pakistani government had blocked YouTube, accusing the site of containing a blasphemous and anti-Islam video, *Innocence of Muslims* (Wilkes, 2016). Unlike Saudi Arabia and some other Muslim-majority countries, YouTube services were not localized in Pakistan at that time, which meant that the country did not have the legal authority to ask the Google-owned video sharing website to block any controversial content in Pakistan. Thus, in order to gain more control over this powerful social media site, the Pakistani government had started negotiating "with the administration of YouTube [Google] regarding a local version of the YouTube service similar to Saudi Arabia module" ("In Consideration: Saudi-style YouTube mulled," 2014, para. 3). In 2016, the three-year ban on YouTube was lifted once Google agreed to comply with the demands of Pakistani government. As a result of this agreement, a new version of YouTube was launched in the country, and "[u]under the new version of YouTube, the Pakistan Telecommunication Authority (PTA) can ask for access to offending material to be blocked." (Wilkes, 2016, para. 3).

This book, however, argues that the Pakistani government used anti-blasphemy laws as a tool to block the ever-growing influence of YouTube as an alternative medium for sharing political discourse on the country's political stage. In other words, "[t]hough most such bans are currently for blasphemous and pornographic sites, they are increasingly used to remove content that contain criticism of the military, secessionist sentiments, and expressions of sexual freedoms" (Sethi, 2013, p. 3). YouTube's role as an alternate medium was witnessed during the political crisis of 2007/08 when President Musharraf blocked the transmission of the entire country's broadcast media (Arif, 2011; 2018; Hashim, 2013).

Political & Cultural Landscape of Pakistani Media

In order to explore the role of social media in Pakistan, it is imperative to discuss the politico-cultural context of the Pakistani media. The news media in Pakistan have a long history of resistance to the authoritarian rulers—both before and after the founding of the modern country. The resistant role of media in the region is much older than the birth of the country itself. In other words, the birth of the Pakistani press is rooted in sub-continental journalism (Al-Mujahid, 1982), and that is why it is important to study the history of the Muslim press before the inception of Pakistan. Pakistani media scholars identified three principal strands of the press in colonial India—the Anglo-Indian press, the nationalist press, and the Muslim press (Ali & Gunaratne, 2000). The emergence of the Muslim press in British India in 1836 was part of a long history of resistance against the British rule:

> The subcontinent's Muslim press, which marks the origin of the Pakistani press, emerged in 1836, with the publication of Maulvi Muhammed Baqar's *Urdu Akhbar*. It began as a literary paper in Delhi, but as relations between the local population and the British deteriorated, it became political and highly critical of British rule (Ali & Gunaratne, 2000, p. 157).

Soon after gaining independence from the British in 1947, Pakistan inherited a number of internal and external conflicts. A constitutional crisis, unequal distribution of resources among the four provinces, military interventions, and Indo-Pakistani tension over Kashmir (Paul, 2005) paved the way for all the consecutive military and so-called democratic regimes in Pakistan to hamper the freedom of the press (Freedom House, 2019).

In Pakistan, media freedom remains a dream, and almost every government (democratic or military) has attempted to suppress the media, introducing new laws and regulations, and putting economic sanctions on non-compliance media outlets in the forms of blocking advertising, reducing paper quota, and pressuring cable companies to not air a particular news network. According to a global survey of media independence, Pakistan is ranked 139th on the table of global press freedom rankings of 195 countries (Freedom House, 2019; Marchant, 2008; Ricchiardi, 2012). It is not only the press freedom ranking that puts Pakistan among one of the lowest on the list, according to several reports by international media monitors, the country has been ranked as the most dangerous place on earth for journalists (Ricchiardi, 2012). The military and religion remain the two sacred cows in Pakistan when it comes to the freedom of media, speech and expression. In Pakistan, "[m]edia workers have been kidnapped, tortured, and beaten to death for delving into the nation's potent military apparatus and spy agencies. Bodies have been found with throats slit and flesh punctured with electric drills by Islamic militants, political extremists, and gangsters who take umbrage at what they write" (Ricchiardi, 2012, p. 4).

Privatization of Electronic Media in the Wake of 9/11

Up until 2001, state-run television (Pakistan Television Corporation) and Radio Pakistan were the only electronic media sources of news for Pakistani audiences (Arif, 2010; Khalid, 2008). However, after the 9/11 attacks in the United States and the subsequent war on terror in the northern areas of Pakistan, the whole environment changed dramatically. The state-run media could no longer satisfy the increasing demands of national and international audiences, who wanted to know more about the war on terror along the borders of Pakistan and in Afghanistan (Arif, 2010). As oxymoronic as it may sound, the "renaissance began in 2002 when then-President Pervez Musharraf [military dictator] freed up the broadcast laws and set in motion a media market boom that revolutionized how news was reported" (Ricchiardi, 2012, p. 4). In order to facilitate and regulate the private electronic media and the Internet, President Musharraf established the Pakistan Electronic Media Regulatory Authority (PEMRA) (PEMRA, 2018) through an Ordinance on March 1, 2002. PEMRA was given complete authority over the operation of private media, including online media. Taking advantage of the situation, local investors, particularly print media owners, started investing in the opening of private news channels and sophisticated websites (Freedom House, 2019). By 2012, there were approximately 90 private TV channels, including national and local ones ("Pakistan Blocks Access," 2010; Ricchiardi, 2012) for approximately 86 million television viewers in the country (Internews, 2012). Besides domestic television networks, 69 foreign satellite channels are now operational in Pakistan (CIA, 2019). A majority of these channels focus on hard news coverage, particularly politics, terrorism and war-related news stories (Arif, 2010). Along with providing news and entertainment, political discussion programs on private televisions are becoming popular among Pakistani audiences. Part of the reason for the popularity of political talk shows could be the fact that the country did not witness any such political and analytical news and current affairs programs before the privatization of the electronic media. Hence, it was only natural for

Pakistani audiences to enjoy this new media freedom and for them to be able to benefit from a variety of perspectives about their country's political landscape in their own language (Urdu).

Mobile Communication as Another Avenue of Freedom of Speech

Cellphones are another significant growth in the country's communication system. According to the most recent data provided by the CIA, the country's "mobile-cellular subscribership has skyrocketed; more than 90% of Pakistanis live within areas that have cell phone coverage" and approximately 71% of Pakistanis have active cell phones. (CIA, 2019). Also, by 2012, "[t]he average Pakistani mobile phone subscriber [used to] [send] 128 SMS messages per month, compared to a global average of 105. That high number [existed] even though the country's illiteracy rate [was] 50 percent" at that time (Ricchiardi, 2012, p. 14). By 2015, this number increased to 187 SMS messages per month, as "[i]n terms of SMS statistics, total of 393 billion SMS were exchange[d] during FY 2014–15, as compared to 301.7 billion SMS during the same period [the previous year], showing a whopping 30.3% increase" (Attaa, 2015, Para 10). Additionally, in 2018 it was observed that more than 50% of Pakistanis accessed the Internet every day, and that Pakistan's mobile Internet connection speed is faster than fixed-line broadband, pushing the population more and more towards mobile Internet access (Farooq, 2018).

In November 2007, when President Musharraf imposed a state of emergency in the country (Reeves, 2007), the newly privatized electronic media became more critical of the military regime and demanded the restoration of the constitution and democracy in the country. Ricchiardi (2012) describes these circumstances this way:

In March 2007 Musharraf fired Supreme Court Chief Justice Iftikhar Muhammad Chaudhry, sparking the Lawyer's Movement and grassroots protests that brought tens of thousands into the streets to oppose his interference with the judiciary. TV's non-stop coverage, political commentary, and raucous call-in programs helped fuel public opinion, posing a public relations nightmare for the regime (p. 8).

Even before the military regime could realize it, the genie of broadcast media was already out of the bottle. In order to put this genie back into its bottle and to control the content of private television channels, the government banned all the private news channels for more than a month around November 2007 (Freedom House, 2008). Pakistani journalists were also threatened with arrests and punishment if they tried to cover any political protests against the government or the military establishment (Freedom House, 2008). This ban on the traditional media in Pakistan left journalists and audiences with no option but to rely on the Internet to meet their news and information needs and keep them updated about the ongoing political crisis in different parts of the country (Arif, 2011). By 2018, 44.6 million Internet users were documented in Pakistan (AlphaPro, 2018). In order of usage, the most popular websites among Pakistanis are Facebook, YouTube, Twitter, Pinterest, Instagram, and Google+ (AlphaPro, 2018). It is pertinent to mention here that turning their attention to alternate media sources is not a new phenomenon for Pakistani audiences. Well before the introduction of social media in the early 1990s, because "the state-owned channel Pakistan Television (PTV) dominated the media scene [in the country,] Pakistanis turned to illegal satellite dishes and illegal channels to circumvent censorship and religious repression" (Ricchiardi, 2012, p. 7).

PEMRA Ordinance

The Pakistan Electronic Media Regulatory Authority (PEMRA) was established on March 1, 2002 through an Ordinance to facilitate and regulate private electronic media. PEMRA was given complete authority over the operation of private media, including online media. All the licensing related to FM radio, satellite television, cable TV, and teleport came under PEMRA, which could cancel the license of these electronic media outlets at any time (PEMRA, 2018). For the past several years, PEMRA did not hesitate to use its authority over the private media in Pakistan. They used different tactics, including canceling licenses, banning broadcasts or imposing monetary punishments whenever media tried to exercise their freedom of expression.

It is pertinent to mention here that based on the definition of constitutional freedom of speech and expression that was discussed previously under the constitutional freedoms of Pakistan, it is evident that PEMRA, established by a military dictator, violated the constitution by imposing bans on newly emerging Pakistani private TV channels. However, it is important to keep in mind that throughout his stay in power, President Musharraf had suspended the constitution and so PEMRA's unconstitutional treatment could not be challenged in court, because Pakistan was being governed under Martial law, not the constitution.

Despite the fact that PEMRA could intervene and cancel any licenses of the broadcast media companies, PEMRA still lacked direct control over social media content. Thus, in order to have a stronger grasp over all kinds of media outlets in Pakistan—including both traditional and alternative forms of media—Imran Khan's government announced plans to replace PEMRA with PMRA (Pakistan Media Regulatory Authority). According to Pakistani Minister for Information and Broadcasting, Chaudhry Fawad Hussain, "[t]he role of regulatory bodies Pemra, Press Council of Pakistan (PCP) and Pakistan Telecommunication Authority (PTA) would be given to the new authority, which would regulate electronic, print and social media" ("Pemra to be replaced," 2019, Para 2). At the time of compiling this book, the draft bill was still under review in the parliament of Pakistan. Once it is approved by the legislative branches of the country (National Assembly & Senate), PMRA is predicted to have more oversight over people's social media profiles, in addition to exerting its power over the traditional media outlets in the country.

The Emergence of Social Media in Pakistan

Though the Internet only made its debut in 1995 in Pakistan, the country ranks 8th on the list of top 10 Internet-consumer countries in Asia (Internet World Stats, 2018). YouTube, Facebook, Twitter, Instagram, Snapchat and political blogs are gaining popularity, particularly among Pakistani youth and the educated community. In June 2010, the number of Internet users was at 20 million in the country, an 11.5% penetration rate, but that number has now more than doubled, with more than 44 million people having access to the Internet, a 22% penetration rate (Internet World Stats, 2018). This penetration contrasts sharply with the enrollment rate for higher education, which is only 9.7% (World Bank, 2019). The Internet adoption rate in Pakistan is almost double the size of the higher education rate. English language ability is the main reason for comparing Internet penetration with higher education in Pakistan. Since English is the dominant language on the Internet, the educated elite in Pakistan are benefiting the most from this communication tool. Unlike the rest of the population, the elite can communicate easily in the English language (Arif, 2011).

Founded in February 2005, YouTube—*Broadcast Yourself* is one of the most popular social networking sites in Pakistan (AlphaPro, 2018; X, 2016). In just five years, countless videos related to Pakistani politics, culture and music have been uploaded either by individuals or institutions. The growing popularity of YouTube is posing new challenges to the government's control over the flow of information in the country. In May 2010, Pakistan Telecommunications Authority (PTA) blocked access to YouTube, blaming it for disseminating sacrilegious content in the country ("Pakistan Blocks Access," 2010). PTA took this step a "day after a court order to block Facebook over 'Everybody Draw Mohammed Day,' an online competition that encouraged users to post images of Islam's Prophet" (Ricchiardi, 2012, p. 14). The directive to ban YouTube in Pakistan (later removed by the Authority's website) issued by the PTA on May 21, 2010 reads:

> PTA has directed all concerned operators to shut down website www.youtube.com in view of growing sacrilegious contents on it. It may be mentioned that PTA after all possible avenues were used within its jurisdiction, including using regular channels available on the FACEBOOK and YOUTUBE to launch protest, to avoid appearances of derogatory material available on their websites—which increased in numbers as time passed by, that PTA decided to completely shut down these sites from being viewed within Pakistan. PTA has so far blocked more than 450 links on Internet containing derogatory material. It was not only in line with the Constitution of Pakistan, the wishes of the people of Pakistan but also an extension of the court orders passed by the honorable High Court of Pakistan and directions of the Government of Pakistan. PTA has already announced a phone number and a complaint number to receive complaints on the issue. The attitude of administrators at FACEBOOK and YOUTUBE was in contravention to the WSIS Resolutions and their own policies advertised on the web for general public. PTA would welcome the concerned authorities of FACEBOOK and YOUTUBE to contact the PTA for resolving the issue at the earliest, which ensures religious harmony and respect. (Shahid, 2010)

PTA's ban included Facebook, YouTube and Wikipedia, along with other websites and Blackberry mobile services (Shahid, 2010). All of these websites and social media—except YouTube—were restored shortly after the ban. Since May 2010, YouTube remained banned in the country for six years, and the government of then newly elected Prime Minister, Nawaz Sharif, did not show any interest in lifting this ban ("YouTube Ban," 2013). This showed an example of the growing frustration of the political elite over the popularity of social media in Pakistan. YouTube was finally made available in the country in 2016 when Google agreed to Pakistan's demand of launching a localized version of the site (Wilkes, 2016).

Like YouTube, Facebook has developed into another popular social network all over the world. In 2010, Facebook had more than 500 million active users, of which 70% were outside of the United States ("You want an interactive map,"

2010). According to the most recent statistics, "Worldwide, there are over 2.32 billion monthly active users (MAU) as of December 31, 2018. This is a 9 percent increase in Facebook MAUs year over year" (Zephoria.com, 2019, para. 3). This trend also speaks to the case of social media's popularity statistics in Pakistan's case. For example, by the end of 2009, there were more than 1.3 million active Facebook users in Pakistan (Burcher, 2009). However, by late 2018, "the number of active Pakistani users monthly on Facebook [were] 35 million which has increased by 17% annually in 2017" (AlphaPro, 2018, para. 1), and the number continues to rise rapidly. The report also provides some other interesting statistics, specifically that "91% of users access Facebook by mobile. The users when classified based on gender shows that 23% profiles were identified as females and 77% as males" (AlphaPro, 2018, para. 1).

Anonymity is another element that has contributed to the popularity of social media sites such as YouTube. Because of some of the social media tool's ability to keep the consumers' identities hidden (Rohlinger & Brown, 2009), the government is finding it difficult to arrest and punish the violators of existing media laws in Pakistan. Nevertheless, the Pakistani government routinely bans Facebook and YouTube whenever controversial and blasphemous content like the Mohammed cartoons and the recent "Innocence of Muslims" videos are uploaded to these social media.

As I have mentioned somewhere else, by 2009, Pakistan had an estimated 20.4 million Internet users, with an 11.3% penetration rate (OpenNet Initiative, 2012), which has now climbed up to 44.6 million Internet users, with a penetration rate of 22 per cent (AlphaPro, 2018). Currently, approximately 130 Internet service providers (ISPs) are serving the ever-increasing demands of Internet users:

> Some of the leading ISPs include Wateen, Paknet, Linkdotnet, Comsats, and Cybernet. In 2007, Wateen Telecom, a subsidiary of Warid Telecom, introduced Worldwide Interoperability for Microwave Access (WiMAX), a telecommunications technology that provides a third-generation (3G) wireless alternative to cable and DSL. Pakistan is the first country in the world to implement such technology, which is designed to provide high-performance, high-speed Internet access over a larger area than other wireless technologies that offer either greater coverage or greater bandwidth can provide. (OpenNet Initiative, 2012)

On the one hand, Pakistan is regarded as among those few countries in the world that are grasping the latest high-end Internet technology with greater bandwidth. On the other hand, the ruling elite in Pakistan continues to implement the most controversial laws regarding the use of online media by its citizens. To understand this oxymoronic phenomenon, let's take a quick look at the existing rules and regulations that control Internet traffic in Pakistan.

Laws That Regulate the Internet in Pakistan

Ironically, there is no specific legal framework to regulate Internet filtering in Pakistan. Four governmental institutions—including the Pakistan Telecommunications Authority (PTA), the Federal Investigation Agency (FIA), the Supreme Court of Pakistan and the Ministry of Information Technology (MoIT)—are involved in regulating Internet filtering, which makes things even more complicated. This hierarchy of multiple institutions function this way:

> On September 2, 2006, the MoIT announced the creation of the Inter-Ministerial Committee for the Evaluation of Web sites (IMCEW), responsible for monitoring and blocking Web sites containing blasphemous, pornographic, or anti-state material. The IMCEW is administered by the secretary of the MoIT and is composed of representatives from the MoIT, the PTA, the Ministry of the Interior, the cabinet, and other security agencies. Directives to block content are typically handled by the government or the Supreme Court through the IMCEW to the MoIT and PTA, who then pass the orders to individual ISPs. However, because there is no specific legal framework, directives can be given directly to the PTA and ISPs to block material without going through the IMCEW. (OpenNet Initiative, 2012)

To provide some examples of how Internet filtering continues to affect people's access to social media, the *ONI* (Open Net Initiative) in its recent report provided three examples of when the Supreme Court (2006), the government (2008) and PTA (2010) censored YouTube, Wikipedia and several other social media sites:

- In 2006, the Supreme Court issued a directive that ordered the PTA to block access to 12 websites that included 'blasphemous' cartoons depicting the Prophet Mohammad [PBUH]. Among this banned content was a website that was hosted on a Blogspot domain. Rather than blocking the offending Blogspot website, the PTA blocked access to the entire domain for approximately two months. At the same time, the Supreme Court ordered police to register cases of publishing or posting of blasphemous images under article 295-C of the Pakistan Penal Code, under which blasphemy or defamation of the Prophet Mohammad [PBUH] is punishable by death.

- In 2008, the government issued an order to ISPs to block a URL and three IP addresses associated with a YouTube video clip of Geert Wilders, the Dutch lawmaker, considered "blasphemous" by the Pakistani government. Because the PIE was unable to conduct a URL-specific block, it performed an IP-wide block, which had the unanticipated consequence of rendering the entire YouTube domain inaccessible to much of the world for approximately two hours.
- In May 2010, the PTA ordered ISPs to block Facebook, YouTube and certain Flickr and Wikipedia pages when an Internet user created a Facebook page entitled 'Post Drawings of the Prophet Mohammad Day.' The ban was ordered as a result of the Islamic Lawyers Association's request for a court injunction to ban Facebook, while the other websites were later banned because of 'objectionable material.' The blanket Facebook ban was lifted after the page in question was removed; however, the government stated that it would continue to block other websites that contained "blasphemous content." In the following month, the government also ordered the PTA to monitor "offensive content" on Amazon, Bing, Google, Hotmail, MSN, Yahoo, and YouTube. (Open Net Initiative, 2012)

Conclusion

Despite the recent changes on Pakistan's political landscape (transition of power from military to democratic governments), there is no improvement in ensuring the freedom of media in the country. Regardless of the fact that YouTube has been finally made available to the people of Pakistan, social media accounts are increasingly being monitored by secret state agencies. There is a new Cyber Crime Wing of the Federal Investigation Agency (FIA), which is mostly targeting journalists and media personnel who are critical of the military policies. The Wing actively monitors social media profiles of citizens and has exclusive powers to arrest anyone on grounds of cybercrimes (Aziz, 2018). In other words, one's expression of opinions can easily be considered a cybercrime in Pakistan. This factor is contributing to a new era of fear among citizens of the country. Likewise, PTA and PEMRA continue to curb constitutional freedoms of mass media, using different tactics every day. The government is planning to merge all of these media regulatory authorities into one, PMRA (Pakistan Media Authority), so as to further centralize its control over the traditional and alternative media platforms of communication, including social media profiles of individuals ("Pemra to be replaced," 2019). Such a scenario does not portray a brighter future of media and individual freedoms in Pakistan. Social media tools that once served as a hope for the freedom of expression and speech will now become the prime targets of suppression by state agencies.

References

Ali, O. A. & Gunaratne, S. A. (2000). *Pakistan: Handbook of the media in Asia*. Thousand Oaks, Calif.: Sage Publications

Al-Mujahid, S. (1982). Pakistan. In J.A. Lent (Ed.) *Newspapers in Asia: Contemporary trends and problems* (pp. 480–502). Hong Kong: Heinemann Asia.

AlphaPro (2018, June 1). Pakistan social media stats 2018. Retrieved July 08, 2019, from http://alphapro.pk/pakistan-social-media-stats-2018/

Arif, R. (2010). *How terrorism killed the news: Pakistani journalism after 9/11*. Saarbrucken, Germany: Lambert Academic Publishing.

Arif, R. (2011, August). The emergence of social media & the political crisis in Pakistan. Paper presented at the meeting of AEJMC, St. Louis, Mo.

Arif, R. (2018). Social networks, social movements and politico-cultural situation of Pakistani media. In Julie Dee (Ed.), *From Tahrir Square to Gezi Park: Social networks as facilitators of social movements*. New York, NY: Peter Lang Publishing.

Attaa, A. (2016). 2015 in Review: Cellular voice and SMS traffic in numbers. Retrieved July 16, 2019, from https://propakistani.pk/2016/01/01/2015-in-review-cellular-voice-and-sms-traffic-in-numbers/

Aziz, F. (2018, February 14). Pakistan's cybercrime law: Boon or bane? *Heinrich Böll Stiftung: The Green Political Foundation*. Retrieved June 27, 2019, from https://www.boell.de/en/2018/02/07/pakistans-cybercrime-law-boon-or-bane

Burcher, N. (2009). *Facebook usage statistics by country- Dec 31st 2009*. Retrieved February 10, 2018, from http://www.nickburcher.com/2009/12/facebook-usage-statistics-by-country.html

Central Intelligence Agency (CIA). (2019, May 6) Pakistan: Country Overview. *The World Factbook*. Retrieved May 13, 2019 from https://www.cia.gov/library/publications/the-world-factbook/geos/print_pk.html

Constitution. (1973). The Constitution ff the Islamic Republic of Pakistan. Retrieved July 14, 2019, from Punjab Code website http://www.punjabcode.punjab.gov.pk/index/showarticle/ref/511c262b-4b3a-42ae-9286-1f8dba1bef0e

Fair, C. (2018, July 27). Pakistan's sham election: How the army chose Imran Khan. *Foreign Affairs*. Retrieved July 13, 2019, from https://www.foreignaffairs.com/articles/pakistan/2018-07-27/pakistans-sham-election

Farooq, M. (2018, April 21). Pakistan's mobile Internet stands at 21 percent of the population: Report. *Pakistan Today*. Retrieved July 15, 2019, from https://profit.pakistantoday.com.pk/2018/04/21/pakistans-mobile-internet-stand-at-21-percent-of-the-population-report/

Freedom House. (2019). Freedom in the World: Pakistan. Retrieved October 23, 2019, from https://freedomhouse.org/report/freedom-world/2019/pakistan

Freedom House. (2008). *Pakistan Freedom Report*. Retrieved December 14, 2016, from https://freedomhouse.org/report/freedom-world/2008/pakistan

Hasan, S. (2018, November 30). Why are so many Pakistani journalists losing their jobs? *TRT World*. Retrieved October 23, 2019, from https://www.trtworld.com/magazine/why-are-so-many-pakistani-journalists-losing-their-jobs-22094

Hashim, A. (2013, April 30). Pakistan: a political timeline. *Al Jazeera*. Retrieved May 18, 2017, from https://www.aljazeera.com/indepth/interactive/2012/01/20121181235768904.html

Internet World Stats (2018, April 21). Usage and population statistics: Pakistan. Retrieved May 11, 28, 2019, from https://www.internetworldstats.com/asia/pk.htm

Internews (2012, June). Pakistan media and telecoms landscape guide: Reports & surveys. Retrieved August 12, 2017, from https://www.internews.org/resource/pakistan-media-and-telecoms-landscape-guide

Khalid, K. (2008). *The face of media freedom in Pakistan*. Lahore, Pakistan: Asia Media.

Lawyer: Pakistani journalist arrested by feds out on bail. (2019, February 10). *Associated Press*. Retrieved July 29, 2019, from https://www.apnews.com/4c1d1e1a769f46a1abd4c3ec3a742a38

Lieven, A. (2011). *Pakistan: A hard country*. London, England: Allen Lane

Marchant, K. (2008). *Freedom of the press 2007: A global survey of media independence*. New York, NY: Rowman & Littlefield Publishers, Inc.

Masood, S. (2017, July 28). Nawaz Sharif, Pakistan's Prime Minister, is toppled by corruption case. *The New York Times*. Retrieved September 27, 2019, from https://www.nytimes.com/2017/07/28/world/asia/pakistan-prime-minister-nawaz-sharif-removed.html

Naqvi, H. (2013, July 20). Article 19: Freedom of speech. *The Express Tribune*. Retrieved March 24, 2018, from https://tribune.com.pk/story/579466/article-19-freedom-of-speech/

Open Net Initiative. (2012, August 6). Pakistan. Retrieved January 18, 2016, from https://opennet.net/research/profiles/pakistan

Over two thousand journalists jobless after newspapers shut in Pakistan. (2018, December 18). *International Federation of Journalists*. Retrieved July 28, 2019, from https://www.ifj.org/media-centre/news/detail/category/press-releases/article/over-two-thousand-journalists-jobless-after-newspapers-shut-in-pakistan.html

Pakistan blocks access to YouTube in Internet crackdown. (2010, May 20). *BBC News*. Retrieved May 28, 2017, from https://www.bbc.com/news/10130195

Pakistani girl accused of blasphemy (2013, June 30). *The Guardian*. Retrieved May 09, 2019, from https://www.theguardian.com/world/2013/jul/01/pakistan-girl-accused-blasphemy-canada

Pakistani journalist arrested over social media posts. (2019, February 11). *International Federation of Journalists*. Retrieved August 10, 2019, from https://www.ifj.org/media-centre/news/detail/category/press-releases/article/pakistani-journalist-arrested-over-social-media-posts.html

Pakistan Penal Code (1860). *Act SLV of 1860*. Retrieved May 15, 2019, from http://www.pakistani.org/pakistan/legislation/1860/actXLVof1860.html

What are Pakistan's blasphemy laws? (2019, May 08). BBC News. Retrieved October 23, 2019, from https://www.bbc.com/news/world-asia-48204815

Paul, T. V. (2005). *The India-Pakistan conflict: An enduring rivalry*. Cambridge, England: Cambridge University Press.

PEMRA (2018). Pakistan Electronic Media Regulatory Authority. Retrieved May 15, 2019, from http://www.pemra.gov.pk/

Pemra to be replaced by new authority: Fawad. (2019, February 26). *The News*. Retrieved May 18, 2019, from https://www.thenews.com.pk/print/382610-pemra-to-be-replaced-by-new-authority-fawad

Rashid, A. (2008). *Descent into chaos: The United States and the failure of nation building in Pakistan, Afghanistan, and Central Asia*. New York, NY: Viking.

Reeves, P. (2007, November 5). Pakistan's Musharraf declares State of Emergency. *NPR*. Retrieved October 20, 2018, from https://www.npr.org/templates/story/story.php?storyId=15994958

Ricchiardi, S. (2012). Challenges for independent news media in Pakistan: A report to the Center for International Media Assistance. Washington, DC, National Endowment for Democracy. Retrieved August 23, 2019, from http://www.centerforinternationalmediaassistance.org/wp-content/uploads/2015/01/Challenges-for-Independent-News-Media-in-Pakistan_Ricchiardi-updated.pdf

Rohlinger, D. & Brown, J. (2009). Democracy, action, and the Internet after 9/11. *American Behavioral Scientist, 53*(1), 133–150. doi: 10.1177/0002764209338791

In consideration: Saudi-style YouTube mulled. (2014, January 18). *The Express Tribune*. Retrieved October 23, 2019, from https://tribune.com.pk/story/660226/in-consideration-saudi-style-youtube-mulled/

Sethi, Ali (2013, August). Banistan: Why is YouTube still blocked in Pakistan? *The New Yorker*. Retrieved March 15, 2018, from https://www.newyorker.com/tech/annals-of-technology/banistan-why-is-youtube-still-blocked-in-pakistan

Shackle, S. (2018, July 27). Imran Khan has won over Pakistan. But real power still lies with the army. *The Guardian*. Retrieved October 03, 2019, from https://www.theguardian.com/commentisfree/2018/jul/27/imran-khan-won-pakistan-power-army-military-election

Shahid, J. (2010, May 21). PTA blocks access to YouTube. *Dawn*. Retrieved April 16, 2017, from https://www.dawn.com/news/536922

Siddiqui, T. (2018, July 26). Pakistan elections: How Imran Khan won with the army's help. *Bloomberg*. Retrieved October 22, 2019, from https://www.bloombergquint.com/quint/pakistan-elections-imran-khan-prime-minister#gs.8T4sRuZj

Wilkes, T. (2016, January 18). Pakistan lifts ban on YouTube after launch of local version. *Reuters*. Retrieved November 02, 2018, from https://www.reuters.com/article/us-pakistan-youtube/pakistan-lifts-ban-on-youtube-after-launch-of-local-version-idUSKCN0UW1ER

World Bank. (2018). Pakistan country profile. Retrieved December 04, 2019, from http://databank.worldbank.org/data/views/reports/reportwidget.aspx?Report_Name=CountryProfile&Id=b450fd57&tbar=y&dd=y&inf=n&zm=n&country=PAK

World Bank. (2019). Education statistics: Country at a glance- Pakistan. Retrieved October 20, 2019, from http://datatopics.worldbank.org/education/country/pakistan

X, A. (2016, November 10). The history of YouTube. *Engadget.com*. Retrieved June 22, 2019, from https://www.engadget.com/2016/11/10/the-history-of-youtube/

YouTube ban. (2013, June 10). *The Express Tribune*. Retrieved May 08, 2017, from https://tribune.com.pk/story/561386/youtube-ban-3/

You want an interactive map of where Facebook is used? Happy to help. (2010, July 22). *The Guardian Technology Blog*. Retrieved from https://www.theguardian.com/technology/blog/2010/jul/22/facebook-countries-population-use

Zephoria.com (2019, March). The top 20 valuable Facebook statistics—Updated March 2019. Retrieved May 29, 2019, from https://zephoria.com/top-15-valuable-facebook-statistics/

Part III

Egypt

With a population of 99 million people, Egypt is "slightly more than three times the size of New Mexico" (CIA, 2019, para.1). Located in Northern Africa, Egypt borders the "Mediterranean Sea, between Libya and the Gaza Strip, and the Red Sea north of Sudan, and includes the Asian Sinai Peninsula" (CIA, 2019, para. 3). The country's literacy rate is 80.8%, with 27.8% population living below the poverty line (CIA, 2019).

Tunisia's next-door neighbor, Egypt was the second-most important country to go through political uprisings after the Tunisian revolution. Also, in October 1993, Egypt was the first-ever country with Internet access in the Arab World, and all other countries in the region followed its lead (Abdulla, 2010). The existing scholarship on political activism argues that the success of the Tunisian social movement and revolution paved the way for the Egyptian revolution. That is why Tunisia and Egypt are seen as the icons of the Arab Spring of the 2010–11 uprisings. This part of the book provides a detailed analysis of social movements in Egypt and examines whether it was because of Tunisia that Egypt witnessed its Arab Spring, or if such political activism was already taking place on the political horizons of the country.

References

Abdulla, R. (2010). Arab media over the past twenty years: Opportunities and challenges. In B. Korany (Ed.) *The changing Middle East: A new look at regional dynamics* (pp. 59–84). Cairo, Egypt: The American University in Cairo Press.

Central Intelligence Agency (CIA). (2019). Egypt. In *The World Factbook*. Retrieved on May 21, 2019 from https://www.cia.gov/library/publications/the-world-factbook/geos/eg.html

7

"We Are All Khaled Said"

Who Was Khaled Said (January 27, 1982–June 6, 2010)

A computer programmer, music composer and entrepreneur from Alexandria, Egypt, Khaled Mohamed Said, was just 28 years old when he was brutally murdered (Chew, 2011; "Egypt Police Jailed," 2014; Meky, 2014). Growing up in a middle-class family in the Sidi Gaber neighborhood of Alexandria, Khaled "liked fishing, taking care of pets and composing music for his friends" (Meky, 2014, para. 3). It is pertinent to mention here that Khaled's last name has been widely cited and referred to with two different spellings "Saeed" and "Said." In the Arabic language, both of these spellings yield the same pronunciation of Khaled's last name. In this chapter, unless a direct quote that uses the "Saeed" spelling is being used, the "Said" spelling will be used as a reflection of the Facebook campaign, "We are all Khaled Said," which also uses "Said" as the preferred the spelling of his last name.

Said, whose father passed away when he was quite young, was raised by his mother along with his two siblings (Meky, 2014; Preston, 2011; "White House Honours," 2011). Growing up in an era of the Internet, Khaled, like hundreds and thousands of other educated youth around the world, had an obsession with computers, smartphones and the Internet. Khaled also had the opportunity to study computer programming in the United States (Chew, 2011). All of these factors—from getting an exposure to the freedom of speech and expression in a society such as the United States and having access to the Internet at his doorsteps—may have contributed to Khaled's Internet activism. Such activism was evident when Khaled decided to expose police corruption in his country by posting "a video on the Internet depicting officers sharing the profits of a drug bust" (Human Rights First, 2010, para. 3). This YouTube video went viral, which embarrassed and enraged the cops. It motivated them to find the person responsible for this act and punish him as a message to discourage further activism against their corruption. For this purpose, the local police officials started to target Internet cafes so as to find the person responsible for exposing their wrongdoings on social media outlets. Unaware of such a search operation by the security forces, Khaled kept his routine to keep on using the Internet cafes: "On the evening of June 7, 2010 … Khaled … was at an Internet café that he frequented in the Sidi Gaber district of Alexandria when two officers from the local police station entered the café and demanded to see everyone's ID cards, claiming that they were authorized to do this under the Emergency Law" (Human Rights First, 2010, paras. 3&5).

To provide context here, it is important to understand how Internet cafes function in countries like Egypt and Pakistan and why the police were demanding IDs from everyone while they were searching for Khaled. With the rise of the Internet on a global scale in the early 2000s, developing countries including Pakistan, Egypt and Tunisia witnessed an explosive growth of the Internet cafes. These cafes were designed purely as profit-making businesses, providing relatively cheap access to this new media. In these developing countries it was not cost-effective for an average citizen to buy a computer and pay for the extremely expensive monthly Internet access. Thus, Internet cafes offered a quick solution where one could pay an hourly fee and enjoy the access to a relatively fast-paced and reliable Internet service.

The incidents of the September 11, 2001 terrorist attacks on the United States, however, changed this scenario of much-easier access to the Internet in several developing nations, including the ones under study (Arif, 2010). After receiving reports of terrorists' and extremists' use of Internet cafes, governments in Pakistan, Egypt and other countries started to require users to bring their government-issued national identity cards, if they wished to use an Internet cafe. The Internet cafe operators were required to document the timestamp along with the ID card numbers of each user, so that they could be tracked down in case of any suspicious activity.

Ironically, none of these countries ever documented any report of catching a terrorist via this surveillance tactic. Governments did, however, start using this excuse to target political opponents who were using Internet blog posts and social media sites to complain against their rulers (Fackler, 2002). This was the case with Egypt, where Khaled Said was tracked down while he was sitting on the second floor of an Internet cafe (Chew, 2011). After arresting Khaled, the two police officers, Awad Suleiman and Mahmoud Salah ("Egypt police jailed," 2014):

> knelt over him beating his head against the marble floor tiles of the café. Khaled was then dragged outside the Internet café, covered in blood, and the beating continued in full view of many witnesses, some of whom pleaded with police to stop. Two doctors even tried to help … Eyewitnesses said his head was banged against an iron door, steps and walls of an adjacent building. He was thrown into a police vehicle, and fifteen minutes later, his gruesomely disfigured dead body was deposited in the street. (Human Rights First, 2010, para. 6)

It may be mentioned here that four years after Khaled Said's death, and as a result of countless protests and demands, both of the police officers involved in the torture and killing of Said were sentenced to only 10 years in jail by an Egyptian court ("Egypt Police Jailed," 2014).

Khaled Said Sets the Stage for Citizen Journalism in Egypt

While such a scenario of freedom of speech and expression—where average citizens play an active role in exposing corruption and social ills in their societies—may be praised in Western societies, it can easily put people's lives in danger in closed societies and dictatorial regimes, where information and communication are seen as the biggest threat to the sustainability of a particular regime. Thus, a strong case can be made that having an exposure to nations of the free world, such as the United States, and having access to latest means of digital communication, such as a smartphone equipped with a recording camera and access to the Internet, were among the main factors that got Khaled Said killed.

Egypt, like many other closed societies in the Muslim world, had absolute control over the flow of information and communication before the arrival of the Internet. Mass media was simply a mouthpiece of the Mubarak regime. In this scenario, a young Egyptian who grew up with access to social media started to realize that he could use this tool to expose law enforcement corruption without waiting for the traditional media outlets to perform their social role. This act speaks to an era of citizen journalism. Citizen journalism is not exclusive to the case of Egypt. In fact, a majority of the world has started to witness more and more citizens coming forward and performing their journalistic role to inform their respective societies whenever and wherever traditional media outlets fail them (de Oliveira & Cardoso-da-Silvia, 2018). Khaled was beaten and killed simply because of performing a citizen journalistic role in a society that was not ready for it (de Oliveira & Cardoso-da-Silvia, 2018; Tufekci & Wilson, 2012).

The so-called law enforcement in Egypt had a history of torturing its own people and was never questioned or challenged by the traditional media outlets. Therefore, it must have been equally shocking and embarrassing for the cops to get exposed and busted by an ordinary young man, Khaled, via an apparently ordinary social media platform, YouTube. Not only this, the cops, when they decided to torture and murder Khaled, must have underestimated the power of social media, as they were not expecting any organized and sophisticated online protests in response to their brutality.

Wael Ghonim: "We are all Khaled Said"

The same Internet that can be seen as a contributing factor to the circumstances for the death of Khaled Said, also became the tool used to protest and demand justice in the case of the most heinous crime committed by Egypt's law enforcement against one of its citizens. The shocking images of the torture-disfigured face of Khaled Said started floating on the Internet via blog posts and social media sites, and less than a week after his death, a Facebook page named "We Are All Khaled Said" was launched by an anonymous human rights activist. The page showed photos of Said's battered and bloodied face from the morgue, and YouTube videos offered up contrasting pictures of him happy and smiling next to the graphic images from the morgue. Within two weeks of Khaled Said's death, the Facebook page went viral, and by mid-June, more than 120,000 people had joined the page and were sharing updates about the case (Preston, 2011). The Facebook page created in memory of Khaled Said was perhaps the biggest nightmare of president Mubarak, whose decades-old regime was terribly exposed to the world with the speed of light.

Several aspects need to be discussed here regarding the creation and popularity of the Facebook page, which essentially became the most powerful voice of dissent against the Mubarak regime. These aspects include location, anonymity, use of language and the use of iconic images of Khaled Said as an icon of outrage. The following sections explore them individually.

Location. The Google marketing executive who created the "We Are All Khaled Said" Facebook page, Wael Ghonim, lived in Dubai, another Arabic country in the Middle East (Chew, 2011; "Egypt police jailed," 2014). Even though Ghonim was an Egyptian citizen, he launched his online activism outside of Egypt. In this way, Ghonim successfully avoided any chance of being caught and tortured by the Egyptian law enforcement. His decision to use a Facebook page while located in another country was also very practical because of the popularity of social media in Egypt. For example, out of 45 million Internet users in Egypt, "37 million Egyptians access Facebook every month with over 22 million or 59% of monthly active people returning every day" (Ahmad, 2017 para. 8), and the number of Facebook users continues to rise. Ghonim was extremely successful in spreading and sharing his pain for his fellow citizen, Khaled Said, via the Facebook page, "We Are All Khaled Said." Because Facebook had a direct reach in almost every household in Egypt, the country's laws at that time could not stop or control the spread of the campaign. Mubarak's control over mass media did not extend to the social media platforms, allowing uncensored information to spread quickly. Finally, it would have not been possible for Ghonim to launch any such campaign if there was no such a thing as the Internet or social media. Thus, we can say that the outreach of the Internet and modes of communication associated with it are making geographical limitations irrelevant in today's digital age.

Anonymity. The second important aspect in this case is the factor of being anonymous while still being politically active. Average citizens of Egypt had never witnessed such an opportunity before the era of the Internet. People knew if they ever tried to resist or raise their voice against the regime, they would be immediately exposed and would have to bear the cost of speaking out in a similar fashion to what happened to Khaled. That's why people's anger and unhappiness toward their rulers had not previously been shared with fellow citizens on a bigger scale.

This, however, changed with the ability of people to create fake profiles to express their grievances, views and ideologies with others on social media platforms and still be anonymous. Thus, anonymity became a resource that protesters and activists started to deploy for their political activism. Ghonim knew about this factor and the opportunity associated with being anonymous better than anyone else, because he was already working for Google. Also, he was cognizant of the fact that one day he would have to go back to his country, and if his identity were revealed, he would also get into trouble like his fellow Egyptians. That's why Ghonim kept running the page as an anonymous entity.

Language. Ghonim created the Facebook page in two languages: Arabic and English. Since Arabic is widely understood and spoken in the Middle East, including Egypt, the page had an excellent ability to target citizens of Egypt who were mostly residing in that country. The English version of the Facebook page, on the other hand, was a smart move to get the attention of the world so that global leaders, human rights organizations and others using social media could witness the human rights violations under Mubarak regime. This strategy also worked well. People from all across the planet were startled to see the torture-disfigured face of Khaled Said and started to demand justice for this poor soul.

Torture-Disfigure Face of Khaled Said: Egypt's Icon of Outrage

The Facebook page and the associated images of Khaled Said became icons of outrage not only for the residents of Egypt, but for many other people residing in different countries, including among those working with human rights organizations. People in Egypt started to like, share and follow this page, which soon became a powerful social movement online and in the streets, simultaneously. Even though this movement had a powerful narrative that had influenced the society, it was eventually successfully suppressed by the Mubarak regime.

It may be mentioned here that the online social movement, "We Are All Khaled Said" that was started in 2010 via a Facebook page was later joined by protesters from the Egyptian Arab Spring of 2011, who followed the Tunisian political uprisings of 2010. In order to further understand the connection of the "We Are All Khaled Said" movement with the political activism of 2011 against the Mubarak regime, this book looked at the most viewed videos of Egyptian political uprisings on YouTube. Two images of Khaled Said were found present among the 20 most viewed videos of protests related to Egyptian Arab Spring (Arif, 2014). One of these images showed Khaled Said as a charming young man with a smiling face. The second image of him was of his torture-disfigured face. In some of the videos, these two images were juxtaposed to each other to show the intensity of the brutality and torture of state agencies as they turned a bright smiling face into an example of horror. This strategy that was being deployed by digital activists on YouTube one year later against the Mubarak regime had stark similarities with that of the Facebook page that was created by Ghonim. Thus, social media activists, this time, had just decided to utilize YouTube as a medium of communication more frequently than that of the Facebook page. This could be because YouTube was offering more anonymity as compared to Facebook pages, or it might be because YouTube had an excellent ability to replace television as an alternate platform of media and thus spread the narrative of protests in the form of moving images. Hence, the online political activists learned to deploy their strategies from still to moving images to gain more support and attention of potential sympathizers.

Another angle to the iconic power of Khaled Said's image can be looked at this way. On the one hand, Egyptian police under the Mubarak regime tortured and killed Khaled Said to make him an iconic example of horror and spread a fear among others that if anyone else tried to mess with state agencies of Egypt, he or she would face the same consequences as Khaled Said. On the other hand, when people of Egypt came across this image on social media, they immediately felt connected to it. Among young Egyptians, the image was interpreted as "if this can happen to Khalid Said, it can happen to me." This association for most people with Khaled Saeed resulted in the social movement "We are all Khaled Said." To Egyptians, the message was clear that if we don't protest the regime, and if we don't come out into streets, the state agencies that are operating under President Mubarak would do the same to each one of us. In other words, they thought, "it could be me."

Perlmutter (1998) describes this phenomenon as the metonymic quality of an iconic image, which refers to an image's ability to represent a greater event because of its "summing up" quality. Thus, we can infer that the metonymic quality of this image summarized this feeling among Egyptians when they came out into streets during the 2011 Arab Spring to protest the Mubarak regime. People who produced and uploaded protest-related videos on YouTube were very well aware of the pain they would generate, and they were aware of the Egyptian people's association to Khalid Said. That's why this image was used in the videos as a symbol of resistance and to protest the regime. The image also reminded the protesters of why they were out there in streets and why they wanted to get rid of the regime.

Furthermore, the overall theme of the 20 most viewed videos was to sympathize with the protesters and gain support of an online community to sustain anti-Mubarak protests. In this context, the torture-disfigured face of Khaled Said was shown in several videos. This image was used as an iconic example to remind people about the cruelties of the Mubarak regime on Egyptian people, and what this political struggle means to the people of Egypt.

Conclusion

To set the record straight, it is important to understand that Khaled Saeed's death cannot be seen in either isolation to the Arab Spring revolution, nor should it be interpreted that the revolution started with the Tunisian man, Mohamed Bouazizi. In fact, Arabic speaking countries that have been ruled by dictators have a long history of similar stories. Law enforcement authorities in such states serve at the pleasure of their ruling elites. Their main task is to protect only the dictators and their fellow elites. Average citizens of the state do not enjoy even basic human rights such as the freedom of expression and speech, let alone the justice, healthcare, education and economic opportunities. In such a scenario, when some incidents such as the torturous killing of Khaled Said happen, they serve as a catalyst of pain, bringing back all the terrible memories and experiences of people who have been suffering for decades under their dictatorial regimes.

To summarize, the sad incident of Khaled Said's killing shines light on two important aspects of change in Egypt's society. First, the country is witnessing a new era of citizen journalism where an average person was introduced to an ability to perform the journalistic role because of the Internet and social media tools in their hands. Second, the movement spurred by the killing served as a wake-up call for the Egyptian regime. It could no longer continue to control the national narrative by merely controlling the entire mass media in the country. Now there was a much bigger, faster and effective mode of sharing information and communication in the form of the Internet and social media. This gave people a ray of hope to craft and share their own narratives and grievances not only among their fellow citizens, but with the rest of the world. Hence, this demonstrates an era of the emergence of social media and a new generation of netizens, such as Khaled Said (Arif, 2016; Dencik & Leistert, 2015).

References

Ahmad, Y. (2017, December). 2017 Trends report: The top online statistics in Egypt. Retrieved March 08, 2019, from http://consultyasser.com/egypt-digital-report-2017-top-online-statistics/

Arif, R. (2010). *How terrorism killed the news: Pakistani journalism after 9/11*. Saarbrucken, Germany: Lambert Academic Publishing.

Arif, R. (2014). *Social movements, YouTube and political activism in authoritarian countries: A comparative analysis of political change in Pakistan, Tunisia & Egypt* (Unpublished doctoral dissertation). University of Iowa, Iowa City, IA.

Arif, R. (2016). Internet as a hope or a hoax for emerging democracies: Revisiting the concept of citizenship in the digital age. *Procedia-Social and Behavioral Sciences, 236*, 4–8.

Chew, K. (2011, June 6). Khaled Mohamed Saeed (January 27, 1982—June 6, 2010) and the Arab Spring. *Care2.com*. Retrieved March 17, 2019, from https://www.care2.com/causes/khaled-mohamed-saeed-january-27-1982-june-6-2010-and-the-egyptian-revolution.html

Dencik, L., & Leistert, O. (2015). *Critical perspectives on social media and protest: Between control and emancipation.* Lanham, MD: Rowman & Littlefield International.

de Oliveira, L. G. & Cardoso-da-Silva, M. (2018). From Tahrir Square to Facebook and vice versa: The public sphere, cyber-space, and the reach of post-revolution in Egypt. In Julie Dee (Ed.), *From Tahrir Square to Gezi Park: Social networks as facilitators of social movements.* (pp. 23–38). New York, NY: Peter Lang Publishing.

Egypt police jailed over 2010 death of Khaled Said. (2014, March 3). *BBC News.* Retrieved March 19, 2019, from https://www.bbc.com/news/world-middle-east-26416964

Fackler, M. (2002, August 5). War on terrorism hits Pakistani web cafes. *Government Technology.* Retrieved February 08, 2017, from https://www.govtech.com/security/War-on-Terrorism-Hits-Pakistani-Web.html

Human Rights First. (2010, June 11). Beaten to death for using the Internet. Retrieved June 28, 2018, from https://www.humanrightsfirst.org/2010/06/11/beaten-to-death-for-using-the-internet

Meky, S. (2014, January 25). Remembering Khaled Saeed, whose death sparked Egypt's revolution. *Al Arabiya English.* Retrieved March 08, 2019, from http://english.alarabiya.net/en/perspective/features/2014/01/25/Khaled-Saeed-Egypt-s-Jan-25-icon-remembered-unlike-before.html

Perlmutter, D. D. (1998). *Photojournalism and foreign policy: Icons of outrage in international crises.* Westport, Conn.: Praeger.

Preston, J. (2011, February 5). Facebook and YouTube fuel the Egyptian protests. *The New York Times.* Retrieved May 27, 2019, from https://www.nytimes.com/2011/02/06/world/middleeast/06face.html

Tufekci, Z. & Wilson, C. (2012). Social Media and the decision to participate in political protest: Observations from Tahrir Square. Journal of Communication, *62.* 363–379. doi: 10.1111/j.1460-2466.2012.01629.x

8 Social Movements in Egypt

Egypt has witnessed the rise of several social movements that have used social media to promote revolution. These groups included: The Muslim Brotherhood, the Rebel Movement, the Egyptian Popular Current, the National Association for Change, the Revolutionary Youth Coalition, The April 6 Youth Movement, Kefaya, and "We are All Khaled Said" (Carnegie, 2010a, 2010b, 2013). The April 6 Youth Movement of 2008 was among the most prominent information movements to use Facebook to organize and protest poor economic conditions in the country (Korany & El-Mahdi, 2012). President Mubarak's regime was successful in crushing the movement by using force and strict censorship laws. The Egyptian Movement for Change (Kefaya), started in 2004, was also aimed at political change in the country. Kefaya, which means "Enough" in Arabic, was a "coalition of political forces united only by a shared call for an end to President Hosni Mubarak's rule" (Carnegie, 2010a). Although this book is primarily about the social movement commonly known as the "Arab Spring" of Egypt, it is important to revisit the history of political activism and social movements in the country. This will be helpful to understand whether the introduction of social media was the prime factor for the origination of multiple social movements in the country, or if such political activism existed well before the age of the Internet in Egypt.

History of Social Movements in Egypt

Egypt, which is located in the northeastern corner of the African continent, is a country with a deep-rooted ancient history of human civilization that lasted for over 3000 years (CIA, 2019; Hopwood, William, Holt, Goldschmidt, Smith, & Little, 2019). The country is among the oldest civilizations, and its archeological treasures continue to inspire and surprise the world. Examples of these treasures include thousand-year-old mummified bodies of kings and pharaohs, pyramids, proofs of centralized governments, religion, culture and urbanization, in addition to the ancient Egyptian's progress in science, agriculture and architecture (Hopwood, et al., 2019; "Ancient Egypt," 2019). All of these factors make this country among only a few remaining parts of the world that have a strong and well-developed sense of identity. The sense of identity is the prime factor among humans to engage in any collective action, whether religious, political, social or economic.

Despite its rich cultural and historical foundations, modern Egypt has witnessed multiple eras of monarchs both in the form of external colonizers (such as the British and Turkish Empires) and internal dictatorial rule wherein the military establishment has dominated the political landscape of the country (CIA, 2019). The country has a history of political activism both against the external rule of the British Empire and then later against its own military dictatorships. The following sections will discuss some of the iconic examples of social movements in Egypt to contextualize the Arab Spring of 2011 in a better way.

The 1952 Revolution

In order to break free from their colonial masters, the people of Egypt revolted in 1952, a movement which became known as the "July 23rd Revolution" ("Arab Unity," 2008; Yasmina, 2017). It is interesting to note that this revolution started within the ranks of the military, as we had discussed in the case of 1857 war for independence on the Indian subcontinent. However, this revolution, which was initiated by the "Free Officers Movement," unfolded in the form of a military coup (Hopwood, et al., 2019). Led by Lieutenant Colonel Gamel Abdel Nasser and General Muhammad Naguib, the "Free Officers Movement was a group that consisted of army officers who wanted to abolish the monarchy allied to the British Empire and end the Muhammad Ali dynasty of Egypt and Sudan" (Yasmina, 2017, para. 2). After the successful revolt against British imperialism, "Egypt was declared a republic on 18 June 1953 after the RCC [The Revolutionary Command

Council] was dissolved in January and Muhammad Naguib became Egypt's first president and commander in chief, a popular choice due to the respect he had gained in Egypt for his role in the 1948 war" (Yasmina, 2017, para. 6).

To put things in perspective, just like the war for independence of 1857 in the case of undivided Indian subcontinent, the revolution was aimed at getting rid of British colonialism in the region ("Arab Unity," 2008; CIA, 2019; Yasmina, 2017). However, unlike the 1857 war, this revolution was a successful one. In fact, the success of this bloodless coup was seen as a movement for Arab unity that encouraged other nations in the Arab and African region to launch their own social movements to end European and British colonialism in the region ("Arab Unity," 2008). Therefore, Egypt's revolution of July 23rd can also be seen as an informational cascade, not only for the people of Egypt, but also for the neighboring states who were inspired by the success of this military-led movement and were ready to launch their own collective actions. The signals of success coming from Egypt helped them understand the cost-benefit aspect of taking part in this kind of political collective action (Look at Lohmann's (1994) model of informational cascades for more details in Chapter 1 of this book). Another aspect that can be extracted from this case is the fact that the Arab Spring, which is celebrated as a unique case in history because of its spread across national borders, was, in fact, not a new phenomenon. Political activism in this region has had a history of inspiring neighboring states, which is evident in the case of the July 23, 1952 revolution of Egypt. Thus, this region's soil had always been fertile to welcome any political collective action, regardless of if it started inside of a particular country or came from across the borders, as long as it was connected with the national and ideological frames of the protesters and potential sympathizers. This historic lens, then, helps us understand why the Tunisian burning man, Mohamed Bouazizi, had a direct impact on Egypt's political landscape, even though these two countries are separate sovereign states in North Africa.

The Muslim Brotherhood Movement

The Muslim Brotherhood (MB) Movement has a long history of political activism in Egypt, dating back to 1928 when the movement was formally launched by an Islamic scholar and a teacher, Hassan Al-Banna ("What is the Muslim Brotherhood," 2017; Frampton, 2018). The MB, which is considered as the "oldest political Islamist group in the Arab world" ("What is the Muslim Brotherhood," 2017, para. 11), can be seen as an example of a highly centralized political organization that used religion to gain the support of potential sympathizers, sustain its ideology and organize its members to take part in collective actions, including violent ones. This movement also supported the 1952 military coup that resulted in the end of British colonial rule in Egypt ("What is the Muslim Brotherhood," 2017; Awad, 2017; Frampton, 2018). Even though the MB has no more than "900,000 full members … inside Egypt … with their families, low level members, and supporters, the Muslim Brotherhood represents an important minority in Egyptian society" (Awad, 2017, para. 4).

Because of its involvement in violence and violent tactics, the Muslim Brotherhood continues to remain controversial inside and outside of Egypt. Several countries including Egypt, Russia and the United Kingdom have labelled it a terrorist organization (Arraf, 2017). Interestingly enough, the Muslim Brotherhood was among one of the most significant participants in the Arab Spring of 2011 that resulted in the overthrow of President Mubarak, who had ruled the country for 30 years (1981 to 2011). President Morsi, who was the first ever democratically elected leader of the country after the fall of Mubarak, was subsequently overthrown and jailed because of his alleged involvement in the Muslim Brotherhood. This factor, in fact, once again paved the way for the Egyptian military to take back the reins of the country's politics as the then Army Chief General el-Sisi led a military coup on July 3rd, 2013 and removed Morsi from office (Kingsley, 2015). Later via a controversial election process, el-Sisi became president of the country ("Egypt's Sisi," 2018). This was a major blow to the Muslim Brotherhood, as several of its leaders were arrested, including the deposed president, Morsi (Kingsley, 2015). It may be mentioned here that the "[o]usted Egyptian President Mohamed Morsy collapsed and died in a Cairo court Monday [on June 17, 2019], soon after making a final statement in his trial on espionage charges" (Samaan & Fox, 2019, Para 1). This shocking development at the country fragile political stage resulted in another wave of demonstrations and protests. According to media reports, "[d]ozens of supporters of former Egyptian President Mohamed Morsi demonstrated […] in his hometown of Al Edwa in the eastern province of the Nile Delta" (Rezeg, 2019, Para 1). Only time will tell if such a political scenario will result in another wave of protests and collective action in the country.

Kifaya & the April 6 Youth Movements

In order to better understand the political uprisings of 2011 in Egypt and the contribution of social media in organizing and sustaining subsequent social movements in the country, one must look at the two most important social movements in the recent history of Egypt when the Internet had already taken its place as a new medium of communication. One of these movements is known as "Kifaya" began in 2004; the other movement, recalled as the "April 6 Youth Movement," was launched by the activists four years later in 2008.

Kifaya. Kiyafa, an Arabic term, which means "enough" was the most powerful voice of dissent against President Mubarak's regime prior to the Arab Spring (Oweidat et al., 2008; Shorbagy, 2007). The movement, which was "founded in November 2004 by 300 Egyptian intellectuals from various ideological backgrounds at a meeting in the home of al-Wasat party leader Abu al-'Ila Madi" (Carnegie, 2010a, para. 3), is regarded as a mother movement that paved the way for future social movements, including the Arab Spring of 2011 (El-Gundy, 2011). The movement demanded an end to President Mubarak's rule and the transformation of the country into a genuine democratic state, where everyone would have equal opportunities to thrive politically, economically and socially (Carnegie, 2010a; Oweidat et al., 2008; Shorbagy, 2007).

Even though President Mubarak's regime was successful in suppressing this social movement by utilizing violent tactics, including using the state media's propaganda against the movement organizers, the movement set the stage for the "formation of other groups, including the March 9 movement for university independence, Workers for Change, Youth for Change, Doctors for Change, Writers and Artists for Change, the Egyptian judges movement" (Carnegie, 2010a, para. 6). Not only this, Kifaya is also regarded as the "first political initiative in Egypt to truly explore and capitalize on new social media and digital technology as its main means of communication and mobilization" (Carnegie, 2010a, para. 6).

The April 6 Youth Movement. After Kifaya had set the stage for modern political activism in Egypt, there was no looking back. Regardless of President Mubarak's attempted suppression of his opponents, voices of dissent continued to erupt. These dissenting voices were not only using the streets as a form of protest, but they had now found alternative platforms for communicating and organizing themselves against their powerful opponent. One of such voice was the "April 6 Youth Movement," which was "originally formed in the spring of 2008 with a small event on Facebook (relatively new to Egypt at the time) that called for a general strike in Egypt on 6 April in solidarity with workers in Mahalla .... The Mahalla uprising has now come to be considered one of the primary precursors to the January 25 revolution" (El-Gundy, 2011, para. 17).

It is worth noting that the movement was launched "in support of a planned textile workers' strike in the city of Mahalla al-Kobra to protest low wages and high food prices" ("April 6 Youth Movement," 2011, para. 1) as an entirely online political movement. The organizers of the youth group launched a Facebook page in support of the textile workers. To everyone's surprise, the Facebook page had 3,000 members "and within a few weeks, 70,000 had joined the call for strikes across Egypt in support of Mahalla's workers" ("April 6 Youth Movement," 2011, para. 2).

This online social movement that was launched on Facebook was followed by street protests as thousands of people joined the protest call on April 6, 2008 ("April 6 Youth Movement," 2011). Just like the Kifaya movement, President Mubarak was able to contain this social movement as the "Egyptian security police struck back, killing four and arresting 400" ("April 6 Youth Movement," 2011, para. 3). However, despite being defeated, the April 6 Youth movement changed the political landscape of Egypt forever for two reasons: First, people of Egypt for the very first time in the history of the country realized the true power of social media in the form of Facebook. With this new tool in their hands, they did not need the traditional media outlets to come forward and amplify their demands. This could easily and most effectively be done by the activists themselves via social media platforms. Second, in addition to the communicative power of social media, the citizens of Egypt learned how to bring online political activism to the streets. The discovery of this powerful connection between the online activism and street protests was not forgotten in the hearts and minds of the people who later launched an online campaign via the Facebook page, "We are All Khalid Said," in 2010, "The National Association for Change" in 2010, and then eventually the most-talked about social movement, the "Arab Spring Revolution" of Egypt in 2011, which resulted in an end to the 30 year rule of President Mubarak.

The National Association for Change

Sometimes a political action or a social movement becomes notable, not because of how many people participated in that collective action, but because of the critical moment when a collective action takes off. In dictatorial regimes, when a dictator is all-powerful and there are no visible signs of division among the ruling elite, challenging a regime requires so much courage because of the level of cost associated with political activism. In this context, the "National Association for Change" stands out on its own. This movement

> was formed by former International Atomic Energy Association head Mohammed ElBaradei and a close group of supporters in February 2010, at a time when opposition activity was at a low point, and became the most visible movement challenging the regime until the January 2011 uprising. (Carnegie, 2010b, para. 2)

It is pertinent to mention here that the so-called Arab Spring of Egypt and Tunisia was not yet visible in the political arena of the region when this movement began. The Tunisian political uprisings started in December 2010 and the Egyptian political mass protests followed in late January 2011 ("The Arab Spring," 2014). Thus, in this context, Mohammed ElBaradei's decision to launch a political movement was at that time the most significant step forward in challenging the powerful President Mubarak, who was enjoying the full support of the civil and military establishments.

The movement was supported by prominent politicians, activists, and intellectuals and had a very clear agenda and set of demands. Some of these demands included:

> Ending the state of emergency; ensuring judicial oversight over the election process; allowing local and international civil society groups to monitor elections; allowing equal access to media for all candidates, particularly during presidential elections; giving Egyptians living abroad the right to vote at Egyptian embassies and consulates; ensuring the right to run for president without arbitrary restrictions in accordance with Egypt's obligations under the International Covenant on Civil and Political Rights as well as limit the president's service to two terms; voting by using the national identification card rather than a special voters' registration card. (Carnegie, 2010b, para. 7)

One of the factors contributing to this social movement's ability to withstand the pressures of the dictatorship was the international stature and popularity of Mohammed ElBaradei ("ElBaradei," 2010) who was known to the world for his efforts "to prevent nuclear energy from being used for military purposes and to ensure that nuclear energy for peaceful purposes [was being] used in the safest possible way" (The Nobel Prize, 2005, para. 6). For this work, ElBaradei "and the IAEA were jointly awarded the Nobel Peace Prize" (The Nobel Prize, 2005, para. 6) in 2005. Despite being the most powerful person in Egypt, President Mubarak was well aware of the popularity of his political opponent ElBaradei, and that is why there was no evidence of direct clashes between the supporters of the National Association for Change and the ruling elite. Even though the *National Association for Change* did not take off the way the Arab Spring and later movements did, the social movement should be seen as the foundational step that set the stage for mass political uprisings in the region in the following year.

Revolutionary Youth Coalition (February 2011–July 2012)

The "Revolutionary Youth Coalition" was perhaps the first ever offshoot of the Egyptian Arab Spring of 2011. This movement was formed at Tahrir Square, Egypt on February 1, 2011 but was dissolved on July 08, 2012 after the country transitioned to a democracy by electing its first-ever civilian president, Morsi, in June 2012 (Amrani, 2012). The movement referred to itself as an umbrella social movement that supported the social movement of ElBaradei, "the April 6 Movement, the Youth Movement for Justice and Freedom, the Youth of the Democratic Front Party, the Muslim Brotherhood Youth, in addition to the following independent individuals: Nasser Abdel Hameed, Sally Toma, and Abdel Rahman Fares" (El Amrani, 2012, para. 5). The coalition movement also had a Facebook page to promote its agenda of activism. The page was also deactivated after the successful presidential elections in Egypt (Taha, 2012). Even though this coalition movement was disbanded, it kept the momentum of political activism going. In other words, as the coalition itself stated, "the disbanding would not be the end of revolutionary youth, but instead the beginning of a new story" (Taha, 2012, para. 8).

The *Tamarud*-Rebel Movement (2013)

The Rebel Movement, which is also known as the "*Tamarud*-Rebel" movement should, in fact, be looked at as a movement to counter the Islamic Brotherhood. This movement started as an effort to remove president Morsi from his office and hold early elections in the country. The movement launched by Mahmoud Badr, a 28-year-old activist, is another example of youth activism in Egypt after the Arab Spring. The movement is known for its association with the political power of Egyptian youth as "[a] bunch of kids in T-shirts had changed the course of the Arab world's most populous nation by mobilizing mass protests against the ruling Muslim Brotherhood, then threatening to turn on anyone who resists their demands" (Saleh & Taylor, 2013, para. 8).

Unlike the Arab Spring of 2011, where protesters had started coming out on the streets in a relatively less organized way and did not have a clearly defined leadership, the Tamarud movement took a different path. The movement, which had an organized network, well-defined demands (remove Morsi and hold early elections) and leadership (Mahmoud Badr), opted for "collecting signatures on a red-printed petition demanding the recall of Morsi" (Saleh & Taylor, 2013, para. 21). The youth leadership and its supporters launched campaigns to collect signatures of supporters and sympathizers instead of instigating them to come out on the streets. The movement claimed that "they got 22 million signatures with names, signatures and national identity numbers, nine million more than the electors who voted to elect the president" (Saleh & Taylor, 2013, para. 21). The number of signatories on the petition, however, was never verified by independent sources (Ateyya, 2013; Childress, 2013). There are a lot of controversial statements about the credibility of this social movement, as it is believed that the movement was already infiltrated by the secret police and former president Mubarak supporters and had a strong backing of the Egyptian military (Ateyya, 2013; Childress, 2013; Saleh & Taylor, 2013).

In any case, one conclusion from the launch and success of this movement can be drawn: for the very first time in Egypt, the civil and military establishment had realized the power of the common man on the streets. That's why they did not opt to take the matters of the state in hand directly. Rather, they supported and infiltrated an already existing social movement, Tamarud, that was launched by an average, middle-class youth group. This helped the military establishment achieve its end goal—to regain the power that it had lost during the Arab Spring of 2011. The then military chief, Abdel Fattah Said Hussein Khalil el-Sisi, eventually succeeded in becoming the president of the country on June 8, 2014 ("Egypt's Sisi," 2018).

Thus, forthcoming social movements in the region may witness this kind of strategy and tactic, where the ruling elites might secretly mobilize and/or infiltrate already existing grassroot social movements in order to benefit from the outcome of the movement. This new strategy enacted by Egypt's military invites a re-examination of Olson's (1965) free-rider problem. As discussed earlier, the free-rider problem states that to avoid the challenges of participating in a movement, sometimes people instead rely on others to participate. These "free riders" then benefit from the outcome of a particular social movement, since group benefits are shared by default with everyone (Olson, 1965). Researchers and scholars in political science and communications disciplines should look at and study this new emerging phenomenon, where the ruling elites have started to act as potential free-riders in grassroots social movements, particularly in the era of digital communication. For example, el-Sisi's strategy to reap the fruit of the Rebel Movement can be seen and interpreted in this context. Because of the fast-paced communication technologies and social media tools, we will witness more and more political and social activism online and in the streets, and these social movements may be easily hijacked by the political elites and civil and military establishments (such as in Pakistan and the Middle East) or simply by strong lobbying firms (such as in the United States).

The Egyptian Popular Current (EPC)

Hamdeen Sabahi, a leftist politician and a former presidential candidate, launched the "Egyptian Popular Current" (EPC) in September of 2012, less than a year after the beginning of the Arab Spring. This movement was geared toward promoting liberal ideals not only in the country's political sphere, but in all walks of life including the economy, culture, foreign policy, trade and education (Carnegie, 2013; "Egyptian Popular Current," 2013). Also, it was because of its liberal ideology, "[t]he EPC became a key player in the secular opposition to former Egyptian president Mohamed Morsi, participating in the National Salvation Front and supporting the protests that resulted in military intervention to remove Morsi on July 3" (Carnegie, 2013, para. 1). The movement, which was relying heavily on youth participation, promoted a widespread agenda to incorporate urban, rural, educated, labor class and pro-democratic people to gain more support and participation across the country (Abdalla, 2013; Carnegie, 2013). This liberal agenda contributed to the popularity of this collective action, and "[a]s a populist movement with roots in Nasserist, socialist, and nationalist strains of Egyptian politics, the EPC's goals emphasized freedom, social justice, and dignity" (Carnegie., 2013, para. 3). The movement also tried to capitalize on people's anger toward the International Monetary Fund (IMF) by rejecting the government's negotiations with the IMF, which the movement blamed for what they saw as promoting economic suicide for the country (Abdalla, 2013).

It is interesting to note that the Tamarud-Rebel movement of Egypt and the EPC shared a common interest in ousting president Morsi from his office. In this regard, "Sabahi and the EPC also supported Egypt's Rebel Movement in its attempt to bring down Morsi's government through popular protest and demands for early presidential elections" (Carnegie, 2013, para. 9). However, unlike the Tamarud-Rebel movement, the EPC appealed "to a range of liberal, left-wing and secular-minded Egyptians who reject[ed] both military and Islamist rule" ("Left-wing outsider," 2014, para. 13). In the later years, particularly after el-Sisi took office as the president of Egypt, the movement could not sustain itself and died down because of lack of resources and leadership (Abdalla, 2013).

Conclusion

This chapter provides an overview of the long-standing history of political activism in Egypt and describes how such activism gained new soul and spirit because of the introduction and popularity of social media in the society. This country, which was politically and socially stagnant for over 30 years until the Arab Spring of 2011, immediately started to witness a new era of political activism with the arrival of social media. The citizens of Egypt, for the very first time in their recent history, realized the power of social media and collective action, which could topple a powerful 30-years-long rule of Mubarak in less than 30 days. The success of this one social movement (the Arab Spring) led to the launch of several social movements in the country. Hence, the political climate of this country has changed forever. Soon after 2011, the country witnessed at least three mass political uprisings including the Revolutionary Youth Coalition, the EPC and the *Tamarud*-Rebel Movement within a short span of two years (2012–13). This is unprecedented for a country like Egypt. This speaks to Tarrow's (1998) claim that once a social movement is triggered in a society, it challenges the status quo and subsequently changes the political landscape of that particular region forever. At the same time, the ruling forces are also becoming smarter in dealing with the rise of this new era of social movements and political activism. Their tactics to contain such social movements are also evolving and changing according to the demands and challenges of this information age. We might see the political elite utilizing tools of misinformation, such as fake news and artificial intelligence (AI), in order to create confusion among protesters and activists. These infiltrators would then benefit from the chaos without even using a direct force against the protesters.

References

Abdalla, N. (2013). Egypt's revolutionary youth: From street politics to party politics. *German Institute for International and Security Affairs*, 1–8. Retrieved March 11, 2019, from https://www.swp-berlin.org/fileadmin/contents/products/comments/2013C11_abn.pdf

Ancient Egypt. (2019, March 13). *History.com*. Retrieved June 08, 2019, from https://www.history.com/topics/ancient-history/ancient-egypt

April 6 Youth Movement: How it started. (2011, February 22). *PBS: Frontline*. Retrieved March 16, 2019, from https://www.pbs.org/wgbh/pages/frontline/revolution-in-cairo/inside-april6-movement/

Arab unity: Nasser's revolution. (2008, June 20). *Al Jazeera.com*. Retrieved June 26, 2018, from https://www.aljazeera.com/focus/arabunity/2008/02/200852517252821627.html

Arraf, J. (2017, February 22). Muslim Brotherhood, mainstream in many countries, may be listed as terrorist group. *NPR Morning Edition*. Retrieved May 25, 2019, from https://www.npr.org/sections/parallels/2017/02/22/516437938/muslim-brotherhood-mainstream-in-many-countries-may-be-listed-as-terror-group

Ateyya, A. (2013, May 17). 'Rebel' Egyptian movement defies Morsi through petitions. *Al-Monitor*. Retrieved April 11, 2019, from https://www.al-monitor.com/pulse/fr/originals/2013/05/rebel-movement-egypt-early-elections.html

Awad, M. (2017, November 6). The Rise of the violent Muslim Brotherhood. *Hudson Institute*. Retrieved May 18, 2019, from https://www.hudson.org/research/13787-the-rise-of-the-violent-muslim-brotherhood

Carnegie Endowment for International Peace. (2010a). Kifaya: A backgrounder on Kifaya. Retrieved May 29, 2019, from https://carnegieendowment.org/2010/09/22/kifaya-pub-54922

Carnegie Endowment for International Peace. (2010b). National Association for Change. A backgrounder on the National Association for Change. Retrieved May 29, 2019, from https://carnegieendowment.org/2010/09/22/national-association-for-change-pub-54923

Carnegie Endowment for International Peace. (2013). Egyptian Popular Current: A backgrounder on the Egyptian Popular Current. Retrieved May 30, 2019, from https://carnegieendowment.org/2013/09/03/egyptian-popular-current-pub-54824

Childress, S. (2013, September 17). Timeline: What's happened since Egypt's revolution? *PBS: Frontline*. Retrieved May 26, 2019, from https://www.pbs.org/wgbh/frontline/article/timeline-whats-happened-since-egypts-revolution/

CIA Factbook (2019, March 25). Africa: Egypt. The World Factbook. Retrieved May 15, 2019, from https://www.cia.gov/library/publications/the-world-factbook/geos/eg.html

Egyptian Popular Current will boycott parliamentary elections. (2013, February 20). *Ahram Online*. Retrieved May 15, 2019, from http://english.ahram.org.eg/NewsAFCON/2017/65180.aspx

Egypt's Sisi: From coup leader to authoritarian strongman. (2018, March 27). *France24.com*. Retrieved June 02, 2019, from https://www.france24.com/en/20180327-egypt-president-abdel-fattah-sisi-coup-leader-strongman-portrait

El Amrani, I. (2012, July 18). In translation: The Revolutionary Youth Coalition's final report. *The Arabist*. Retrieved May 30, 2019, from https://arabist.net/blog/2012/7/18/in-translation-the-revolutionary-youth-coalitions-final-repo.html

ElBaradei to form 'National Association for Change'. (2010, February 24). *BBC News*. Retrieved May 20, 2019, from http://news.bbc.co.uk/2/hi/middle_east/8534365.stm

El-Gundy, Z. (2011, July 30). Kefaya and April 6 Youth Movement: Post-revolution allegations in Egypt. *Ahram Online*. Retrieved July 10, 2019, from http://english.ahram.org.eg/NewsContent/1/64/17559/Egypt/Politics-/AboutUs.aspx)

Frampton, M. (2018). *The Muslim Brotherhood and the west: A history of enmity and engagement.* Cambridge, MA: Harvard University Press.

Hopwood, D., William, R. B., Holt, M. P., Goldschmidt, A. E., Smith, C. G., & Little, D. P. (2019, March 6). Egypt. *Encyclopedia Britannica.* Retrieved May 24, 2019, from https://www.britannica.com/place/Egypt

Kingsley, P. (2015, June 1). How Mohamed Morsi, Egypt's first elected president, ended up on death row. *The Guardian.* Retrieved August 29, 2019, from https://www.theguardian.com/world/2015/jun/01/mohamed-morsi-execution-death-sentence-egypt

Korany, B. & El-Mahdi, R. (Eds.) (2012). *Arab Spring in Egypt: Revolution and beyond.* Cairo, Egypt: The American University in Cairo Press.

Left-wing outsider to run for Egypt president. (2014, February 8). *Al Jazeera.* Retrieved September 4, 2019, from https://www.aljazeera.com/news/middleeast/2014/02/leftist-politician-run-egypt-president-20142914424645634.html

Lohmann, S. (1994). The dynamics of informational cascades: The Monday demonstrations in Leipzig, East Germany, 1989–91. *World Politics, 47*(1), 42–101.

Olson, M. (1965). *Logic of collective action.* Cambridge, MA: Harvard University Press.

Oweidat, N., Benard, C., Stahl, D., Kildani, W., O'Connell, E., & Grant, A. (2008). *The Kefaya Movement: A case study of a grassroots reform initiative.* Santa Monica, CA: RAND Corporation. Retrieved May 14, 2019, from http://www.jstor.org/stable/10.7249/mg778osd

Rezeg, A.A. (2019, June 18). Protests in Egypt after absentia funeral for Morsi. Retrieved June 27, 2019, from https://www.aa.com.tr/en/middle-east/protests-in-egypt-after-absentia-funeral-for-morsi/1508059

Saleh, Y. & Taylor, P. (2013, July 8). Mahmoud Badr, Tamarod protest leader, 'owns the streets' in Egypt. *Huffington Post.* Retrieved May 05, 2019, from https://www.huffingtonpost.com/2013/07/08/mahmoud-badr-tamarod-protest-leader-egypt_n_3559487.html

Samaan, M. and Fox, K. (2019, June 18). Mohamed Morsy, ousted Egyptian president, dies in court. *CNN.* Retrieved June 20, 2019, from https://www.cnn.com/2019/06/17/middleeast/mohamed-morsy-dies-egypt-intl/index.html

Shorbagy, M. (2007). Understanding *Kefaya*: The new politics in Egypt. *Arab Studies Quarterly, 29*(1), 39–60. Retrieved January 10, 2018, from http://www.jstor.org/stable/41859016

Taha, R. M. (2012, July 8). Revolutionary youth coalition disbands. *Daily News Egypt.* Retrieved January 12, 2018, from https://dailynewsegypt.com/2012/07/08/revolutionary-youth-coalition-disbands/

Tarrow, S. G. (1998). *Power in movement: Social movements and contentious politics.* Cambridge, Mass: Cambridge University Press.

The Arab Spring: Made in Tunisia, broken in Egypt. (2014, January 16). *The Guardian: Editorial.* Retrieved May 20, 2019, from https://www.theguardian.com/commentisfree/2014/jan/16/leader-2-arab-spring-tunisia-egypt

The Nobel Prize (2005). Mohamed ElBaradei: Biographical. Retrieved May 15, 2019, from https://www.nobelprize.org/prizes/peace/2005/elbaradei/biographical/

What is the Muslim Brotherhood?. (2017, June 18). *Al Jazeera*. Retrieved from https://www.aljazeera.com/indepth/features/2017/06/muslim-brotherhood-explained-170608091709865.html

White House honours Khaled Said's sister. (2011, June 23). *AhramOnline*. Retrieved May 12, 2019, from http://english.ahram.org.eg/News/14874.aspx

Yasmina, A. (2017, July 23). Remembering the 1952 Egyptian Revolution. *Middle East Monitor*. Retrieved June 03, 2019, from https://www.middleeastmonitor.com/20170723-remembering-the-1952-egyptian-revolution/

9 Politico-Cultural Context of Egypt

Egypt, a transcontinental Arabic speaking country, has a population of over 99 million people with a population growth rate of 2.38% (CIA, 2019; Cook, 2012). Greeks, Romans, Byzantines, Persian, Arabs and the British ruled Egypt, whose history dates back to 3200 BCE (CIA, 2019). The country gained its full freedom from the British-backed monarchy in 1952, although its freedom came with the challenges of a poor economy, debt, a rapidly growing population and limited resources (CIA, 2019). The legal system of the country is a complex one. It practices a "mixed legal system [,which is] based on Napoleonic civil and penal law, Islamic religious law, and vestiges of colonial-era laws" (CIA, 2019, para. 8). With a steady unemployment rate of 12.2%, more than 27.8% of the population of Egypt is currently living below the poverty line (CIA, 2019). In terms of ethnicity, nearly 90% of Egyptians are Muslims, and the rest of the population represents different sects of Christian minorities in the country (CIA, 2019).

Just like several other countries in the Muslim world, Egypt continues to share similar challenges on its social and political fronts that include, but are not limited to: a long history of dictatorship, lack of freedom of expression and speech, government-controlled mass media, corruption, nepotism and unequal distribution of economic opportunities among the citizens. Among these challenges, the most significant one that needs to be discussed and understood is the constitutional framework of free speech in the country and how the ruling elite have manipulated this basic human right of Egyptians by introducing controversial amendments. This discussion will also help us better understand why the Internet and social media were seen as a ray of hope in the country when the status quo was being maintained by absolute control over the traditional media outlets.

Constitutional Framework of Free Speech in Egypt

In order to discuss the media situation in Egypt before and after the Arab Spring, let's revisit the Egyptian Constitution of 1971. Articles 47 and 48 of the Egyptian Constitution of 1971 (amended) are about the freedom of expression and the freedom of media, respectively. According to the Article 47:

> Freedom of opinion is guaranteed. Every individual has the right to express his opinion and to disseminate it verbally, in writing, illustration or by other means within the limits of the law. Self-criticism and constructive criticism is a guarantee for the safety of the national structure. ("Comparing Egypt's," 2012; "Egypt's Constitution," 2018)

Article 48, on the other hand, provides extremely limited media freedom particularly during the times of emergency rule in the country. The Article states:

> Freedom of the press, printing, publication and mass media shall be guaranteed. Censorship on newspapers is forbidden. Warning, suspension or abolition of newspapers by administrative means are prohibited. However, in case of declared state of emergency or in time of war, limited censorship may be imposed on newspapers, publications and mass media in matters related to public safety or for purposes of national security in accordance with the law. ("Comparing Egypt's," 2012; "Egypt's Constitution," 2018)

It may be mentioned here that after the Arab Spring, Egypt proposed a new Constitution in 2012. The proposed Constitution had to wait another two years for a referendum to be adopted by the state ("Voters overwhelmingly back," 2014). The constitutional referendum that was held on 14–15 January 2014 overwhelmingly voted for the adoption of the revised Constitution (CIA, 2019; Sayah & Tawfeeq, 2014). While it was in its proposal stage, this revised Constitution draft of 2012 was supposed to provide a little more freedom to the media and freedom of speech to its citizens. In this regard, the revised constitutional draft had two new articles (Article 48 & Article 49) dedicated to media freedom, with wording slightly different from the previous versions. These Articles state:

> **Article 48:** Freedom of the press, printing, publication and mass media shall be guaranteed. The media shall be free and independent to serve the community and to express the different trends in public opinion, and contribute to shaping and directing in accordance with the basic principles of the State and society, and to maintain rights, freedoms and public duties, respecting the sanctity of the private lives of citizens and the requirements of national security. The closure or confiscation of media outlets is prohibited except with a court order. Control over the media is prohibited, with the exception of specific censorship that may be imposed in times of war or public mobilization.
>
> **Article 49:** Freedom to publish and own newspapers of all kinds is a guaranteed subject of notification for every natural or juridical Egyptian person. The establishing of radio stations, television broadcasting and digital media is regulated by law. ("Comparing Egypt's," 2012)

The final version of the constitutional draft that was approved and adopted via a constitutional referendum, however, had its Chapter 3 dedicated to "Public Rights, Freedoms and Duties … and Information Security Space" (de Oliveira & Cardoso-da-Silva, 2018, p. 25), with Articles 31, 65, 70, 71, 72, 73, 92 and 93 defining these issues. These articles have been somewhat revised in a way that leverage more power to the government, which deals with the information as an integral part of national economy and security. Article 31, for example, addresses issues of freedom of thought and freedom of press by stating, "The security of information is an integral part of the system of national economy and security. The government is committed to taking the necessary measures to preserve it in the manner organized by law" (De Oliveira & Cardoso-da-Silva, 2018, p. 25). Article 31, if looked at carefully, leaves large grey areas related to the power of government in controlling information. The government can determine any scenario of information sharing as a potential breach or threat to the security of the state and damaging for the economy of the country. Thus, leaving little room for free flow of information in the society.

Another article regarding the freedom of expression, however, provides a much more encouraging scenario for individual freedoms: "Article 65: Freedom of thought and opinion is guaranteed. All individuals have the right to express their opinions through speech, writing, imagery, or any other means of expression and publication" ("Egypt's Constitution," 2018, p.23). Likewise, Article 70 deals with the protection of the freedom of the press in a more elaborate way:

> Freedom of press and printing, along with paper, visual, audio and digital distribution is guaranteed. Egyptians … have the right to own and issue newspapers and establish visual, audio and digital medium outlets. Newspapers may be issued once notification is given. The law shall regulate the ownership and the establishment of procedures for visual and radio broadcast stations in addition to online newspapers. (de Oliveira & Cardoso-da-Silva, 2018, p. 25)

Even though, this article is relatively more comprehensive in nature, it leaves enough room for the ruling elite to exercise their influence over the issuance of licenses for newspapers. They may then regulate the press based on the procedures that the government decides to establish. Since Egypt has gone back in the hands of a former military chief, el-Sisi, who enjoys full support of the military establishment, the regulating procedures that have been mentioned in the Constitution can once again be new tactics and tools that the government will continue to apply to control the freedom of the press. As some scholars have already noted:

> Despite the ostensible clarity of definitions that protect the individual liberties of Egyptian citizens in its Constitution, rewritten in 2014 by the Joint Military Command led by current President Abdel Fattah el-Sisi, in reality, freedom of expression and freedom to join political organizations are governed by a tangle of confusing and imprecise laws. (de Oliveira & Cardoso-da-Silva, 2018, p. 26)

Not only this, the political uprisings of 2011 and its aftermath have taught the military and civil establishment of the country the undeniable power of social media, particularly when it is being utilized by educated youth. And that's why, under el-Sisi's leadership, the "censorship of the Internet hit mostly young university activists who had already established social networking as a platform for organization of protests" (de Oliveira & Cardoso-da-Silva, 2018, p. 27).

This brief overview of the proposed (2012) version of the constitutional draft, which was later altered, and the existing Constitution of Egypt (adopted in 2014), help us understand that Egypt still has a long way to go in order to achieve the goal of true media and individual freedoms, particularly with regard to the articles related to the media freedom in the country. The following discussion on the media situation of Egypt will further elaborate on this point.

A Brief History of the Media Situation in Egypt

Since 1960, when President Gamal Abdel Nasser nationalized the mass media, Egyptians have not had a private press. Despite the change of leadership in Egypt, there was no change in the media situation as "Nasser's successors, Anwar Sadat and Hosni Mubarak, both military officers, continued the direct government control of the mass media" (Eko, 2012, p. 135). Even after the Arab Spring when the world witnessed Egypt's first-ever democratic presidential elections, media freedom was still facing repeated bans and threats to journalists were common. This did not end with the end of Morsi's short stay in power. The former military chief, el-Sisi, soon after becoming the president of Egypt and started tracing the same line of curbing individual and media freedoms that the country had been witnessing for the past seven decades. To some scholars and independent observers, el-Sisi's control over the media and individual freedoms is even stricter and organized than his predecessors (ElHaies, 2019).

To revisit a quick history of controversial media laws in Egypt, let's look at how President Mubarak dealt with media freedom during his three decades-long stay in power. Vagueness is an old tactic, which every single ruler of Egypt applied when it came to devise media strategies and laws. President Mubarak's 31 years of emergency rule introduced several controversial media laws, and most of these laws were intentionally kept vague in nature. The Audiovisual Broadcast Law of 2008 is among one of several such examples where uncertainty was kept in the law to maintain control over journalists by keeping them in a vulnerable position (Arab Media and Society, 2008). There are no laws that guarantee an individual right to information or access to information in Egypt (Cook, 2012; Eko 2012; Mendel, 2011). According to a 2018 Freedom House report, in advance of the March 2018 presidential elections, "[n]umerous bloggers, activists, and journalists were arrested for nonviolent political, social, or religious posts on social media, while others languish[ed] in arbitrary detention" (Egypt, 2018, para. 4).

It is interesting to note that on the one hand, Mubarak's government opened up broadband Internet in Egypt for economic reasons, yet the regime was concerned with how Egyptians would use the Internet. Before and during the Arab Spring uprisings, the government required national identification cards from those using Internet cafes so that no one could benefit from the anonymity factor of the digital media (OpenNet Initiative, 2009). In order to keep absolute control over the Internet, cell phones and satellite media, the Mubarak regime made the regulatory agency *Telecom Egypt*, which was granted

> the exclusive right to establish, operate and exploit international transmission networks between Egypt and any other country through international gateways via submarine and terrestrial cables, microwave links and satellites for fixed services and provide Telephone, Fax, Telex, and Telegraph Services over such networks. (Eko, 2012, p. 135)

During the revolution of 2011, when Al Jazeera provided live coverage of Tahrir Square protests, the Mubarak government vandalized Al Jazeera offices, canceled its license, arrested its journalists, and confiscated all their equipment.

It may be noted that the challenges to mass media and individual freedoms in Egypt were not a new phenomenon, rather it was a consistent practice that spanned over decades, going all the way back to the British colonizers. Somehow people around the world simply did not notice it or maybe had turned a deaf ear to the media situation in Egypt. However, the political uprisings of 2011 led international media scholars to become more interested in the Egyptian media. Although plenty of information exists about the state of media freedom in Egypt, the report, "Political and Media Transition in Egypt" by Mendel (2011) covers almost every aspect of Egypt's traditional and online media, including controversial legislation that still exists despite the political and constitutional changes in the country. The following paragraphs introduce key findings of this report in order to better understand the history of the media situation in Egypt and whether mass media played any role in the political activism of 2011.

According to the report that appeared six months into Egypt's revolution, Mendel (2011) maintains that during 31 years of emergency rule by the Mubarak regime, the government introduced controversial legislation to control journalists, which led to high levels of self- censorship that has become deeply rooted in the culture at many media outlets. The Egyptian Penal Code includes several provisions on defamation. These include Article 179, making it a crime to insult the president; Article 184, protecting the Majlis al-Shaab (People's Assembly), the army, the courts and other public authorities; and Article 186, protecting the judiciary (Mendel, 2011). Furthermore, saying or publishing anything against the president, army, and ruling elite was considered a crime according to Egypt's media laws. Also, any defamation case was dealt with via the criminal defamation law rather than civil defamation law. This tendency to deal with defamation as a criminal offense violates international information protection laws.

It is pertinent to mention here that under the Emergency Law of President Mubarak (and then later by el-Sisi for a short while), cases against the media could be pursued in military courts, a procedure that is highly problematic from the perspective of media freedom, as well as other basic due process human rights (OpenNet Initiative, 2009). Content restrictions on media freedom pertaining to religious speech, hate speech, and racial comments, continue to remain a problem in today's Egypt. Furthermore, in his report, Mendel (2011) observed that the "Egyptian revolution has directly impacted Egyptian Radio & Television Union (ERTU)'s governance systems, most significantly with the removal (at least temporarily) of the Minister of Information. Following Mubarak's departure, the Chair of the ERTU Board of Trustees was replaced by Dr. Samy Sherif, formerly a media and communications professor" (Mendel, 2011, p. 9). The appointment of Dr. Sherif was a step forward in right direction. This appointment of an intellectual, however, did not suit the military establishment, and:

> In early June … Dr. Sherif was replaced by Tarek El-Mahdy, a military general, and the organization has reportedly been put under the direction of a council appointed by the Supreme Council of the Armed Forces. As a result, it appears that ERTU is presently largely under the control of the governing military authorities. (Mendel, 2011, p. 9)

The report further adds that before the revolution, applications for newspaper licenses reportedly had to be approved by the security forces; shortly after the Arab Spring, the interim government announced that this practice would be stopped. Currently, no laws restrict media ownership monopolies. Also, in post-revolution Egypt, there are no specific rules on concentration of media ownership or cross-ownership.

In order to control and regulate the Internet, the Mubarak regime introduced the Telecommunications Law (NTRL) in 2003. This law makes the use of Skype illegal in Egypt (Egypt Telecommunication Regulation Law, 2003), and "renders the operation of a local Wi-Fi operation illegal, although these are extremely common in homes and businesses in the country" (Mendel, 2011). The National Telecommunication Regulatory Authority (NTRA) was also established under this law. According to the Article 13 of the law, the NTRA, which was financially an independent authority with a privately-owned bank, was given powers including:

> Setting up the rules and conditions for granting special licenses for the establishment of Telecommunication Networks Infrastructure without prejudice to the provisions of the laws governing construction, urban planning, environmental and local administration, as well as the licenses for the operation and management of such networks, and the licenses for providing Telecommunication Services. Also issuing such licenses and monitoring their execution in accordance

> with the provisions of this Law in a manner that guarantees the rights of the Users, especially their privacy rights in accordance with the Law, and without disturbing the National Security, the State top interests, urban planning and health and environmental standards that are specified by the relevant Ministries and Heads of concerned entities. (Egypt Telecommunication Regulation Law, 2003, p. 9)

By 2009, the country had 20 million Internet users and 83 million Egyptians (out of 85 million in total) had mobile cellular/ telephone service available to them. By 2019, this number rose to over 50 million Internet users and 28 million people (out of 100 million total population) have access to smartphone services (CIA, 2019; "Internet user penetration," 2019). According to the data provided by the Dubai Press Club's annual Arab Media Outlook report (2013), by 2013, Egypt had 19 daily newspapers with a total circulation of 4 million. In the post-revolution Egypt, there was not much growth in the total number of newspapers, as by 2018 there were around 20 daily newspapers (state-run and privately owned). Their readership continues to decline (Allam, 2019; "Egypt Profile," 2018). As for TV media, the total television penetration rate in the country is 93% (satellite TV penetration: 43%; cable TV penetration: 0.2%) and "[n]early all Egyptians (98.8%) have television sets in their home. Television is by far the most common source of news as nearly all Egyptians (94.1%) use the TV to get news at least once a week, and 84.2% use it daily or most days a week" (Allam, 2019, p. 7).

The broadband penetration in the country is 7.4%, whereas mobile phone penetration is 72% (Dubai Press Club, 2013). By 2017, over 100 million people in Egypt were using mobile cell phones, which makes the country number 16 among the list of the top 20 cellphone using countries in the world (CIA, 2019). Traditional media sources including broadcast media are mostly under state control ("Egypt Profile," 2018) with "2 national and 6 regional terrestrial networks as well as a few satellite channels." Similarly, state-run radio "operates about 30 stations belonging to 8 networks" (CIA, 2019).

Nature of Pre-revolutionary Regime

Several studies on the Egyptian revolution agree on four major factors that have contributed to the political uprising of 2011 in the country. These factors include: unemployment among educated youth, rising food prices, emergency rule since 1981 and the lack of freedom of expression because of the state-controlled mass media (CIA, 2019; Cook, 2012; Eko, 2012; Ghannam, 2011; Harb, 2011; Lynch, 2013; Mendel, 2011; OpenNet Initiative, 2009). This chapter argues that it was because of the history of the state's absolute control over traditional media outlets that people in Egypt started to look at alternative media platforms to express themselves. With the dawn of the information age, when digital communication started to shrink the globe in the 21st century, the Internet and the associated social media emerged as rays of hope in many closed societies such as Egypt (Gerbaudo, 2018). That's why, with its debut in the Middle East, digital communications technologies including cell phones, text messages, the Internet, blogs, and other alternative forms of digital communication started to become more and more popular among Egyptians. This kept adding to the regime's frustration with digital media. During the time of the 2011 revolution in Egypt, a scholar, Ghannam (2011) observed the popularity of this new medium this way:

> Although Egypt's interior ministry maintains a department of 45 people to monitor Facebook, nearly 5 million Egyptians use the social networking site among 17 million people in the region, including journalists, political leaders, political opposition figures, human rights activists, social activists, entertainers, and royalty who are engaging online in Arabic, English, and French. (p. 5)

It is worth noting that these numbers represent the scenario in Egypt in 2011. These numbers have now dramatically changed as people are increasingly joining social media platforms and use their smartphones to benefit from alternative platforms of communication when traditional media has a history of failing its people.

In an effort to control the mushroom growth of these new modes of communication such as mobile smartphones, social media and the Internet, and satellite channels, the Mubarak regime introduced the Audio-Visual Media Bill in 2008, which required media professionals to "avoid damaging 'social peace,' 'national unity,' 'public order,' and 'public values" (Arab Media and Society, 2008; "Egypt Faces," 2008). Furthermore, according to the bill:

> Violators of the rules face imprisonment, cancellation of broadcasting licenses, the confiscation of equipment, and fines. The bill will create a National Agency for Regulation of Audio and Visual Broadcast, which will comprise national security and military intelligence representatives, to enforce the implementation of the proposed rules. The bill coincided with an increase in government's closure of TV channels. (OpenNet Initiative, 2009)

Another important aspect that we need to discuss here in order to keep the record straight is the history of online political activism in Egypt that finds its roots way before the Arab Spring of 2011. In contrast to claims that Egyptian political activism started after the Tunisian revolution of 2010, a report by the OpenNet Initiative (2009) provides evidence that online political activism was already happening in the country in 2007, when a majority of Egyptian youth started using cellphones, blogs, YouTube and Facebook to express their unhappiness toward the Mubarak regime. For example, at the time of the Arab Spring, out of 17 million Facebook users in the Arab world, 5 million users were in Egypt alone (Ghannam, 2011). Similarly, as compared to the 34% offline news seekers in Egypt, the number of online newspaper readers was already about 50% in the country by the year 2009 (Arab Advisors Group, 2009).

Furthermore, it was because of the growing popularity and influence of online media that more than three years before the Egyptian revolution, a blogger, Abdel Kareem Nabil Suleiman Amer was "sentenced in February 2007 to four years in prison … and was charged with offending the state institutions, destabilizing public security, and inciting others to demonstrate and strike via the Internet" (Open Net Initiative, 2009, pg. 3). Also, on April 6, 2008 (long before the Arab Spring), a group of Egyptian activists "managed to recruit supporters using Facebook for a general strike … protesting against rising food prices and President Hosni Mubarak's government" (Open Net Initiative, 2009, pg. 4). The report highlights that, beginning around 2004, the Internet had started becoming more popular among Egyptians, adding:

> The number of blogs in Egypt has risen from just 40 in 2004 to an estimated 160,000 in July 2008 …. More than three fourths of Egyptian bloggers write in Arabic only, 20 percent write in both Arabic and English, and nearly 10 percent write in English only. More than 30 percent of Arabic-language blogs are Egyptian. Most Egyptian bloggers are young men in their 20s, while just over one fourth are female. More than half of Egyptian bloggers are between the ages of 20 and 30. (Open Net Initiative, 2009, p. 2)

This data and the numbers of Internet users, both in terms of social media and people accessing networking sites via their smartphones, have multiplied since the Arab Spring of 2011. For example, by 2017, Egypt had 49.2 million Internet users, which is around 49.5% of the population of Egypt (BBC.COM, 2018). On the one hand, el-Sisi's government is utilizing the same old tools and strategies to curb media and individual freedoms by revising existing controversial laws along with introducing the new ones. An example of this can be found in "[a] 2018 cybercrime law [, which] allows the authorities to block any website deemed to threaten national security or the economy" ("Egypt Profile," 2018, para. 11). On the other hand, youth in and outside of Egypt continue to find new and alternate means and modes of information and communication to continue their struggle against the powerful ruling elite, so as to ensure that their government does not take away their basic constitutional rights of freedom of speech and thought.

Conclusion

Even though the Arab Spring of Egypt 2011 brought down a regime through the collective action of political activists both online and on the streets, it could not ensure freedom of speech for the media and individuals who continue to bear the cost of speaking up. Journalists and bloggers continue to face life threats and are put behind bars after the government has labelled them as terrorists or terrorist supporters. Controversial laws continue to be passed by the legislative branches to control and contain the Internet and social media activities among the Egyptian youth. The revised Constitution of 2014 has already failed to protect the rights of freedom of individual speech and media. In the near future, there seems to be little hope for the betterment of freedom of thought and press freedom. The country, in fact, might experience tougher laws and regulations against media freedoms before it experiences any easing of these regulations in the future. In this politically complex scenario, where the Telecommunication Regulation Law of Egypt is designed to give el-Sisi absolute power to curb constitutional rights of freedom of speech and expression of citizens and mass media, "[i]t will be up to the Egyptians inside and out of Egypt, especially the younger ones, to continue their fight for the revolutionary values of the 2011 Arab Spring" (de Oliveira & Cardoso-da-Silva, 2018, p. 36).

So far, the discussion on Pakistani and Egyptian media laws and telecommunication regulations show clear similarities between the two countries. Both countries keep national security, military institutions, religion and heads of states as supreme and untouchable. Also, both countries established telecommunication regulatory authorities during dictatorial regimes, not through their parliaments or elected representatives. In part III of this book, we look at the legal situation of media in Tunisia and see whether that country, much smaller in size as compared to Pakistan and Egypt, pursued similarly aggressive and controversial media laws both for traditional media and the Internet.

References

Allam, R. (2019). Egypt: Media Landscape. *European Journalism Centre: Media Landscapes.* Retrieved May 30, 2019, from https://medialandscapes.org/country/pdf/egypt

Arab Advisors Group. (2009, August 31). *A survey of Internet use and online advertising consumption and effectiveness in Egypt.* Retrieved February 06, 2018, from http://www.arabadvisors.com/survey-internet-use-and-online-advertising-consumption-and-effectiveness-egypt-0

Arab Media and Society. (2008, July 29) Draft Egyptian broadcast law. Retrieved April 02, 2019, from https://www.arabmediasociety.com/full-text-draft-egyptian-broadcast-law/

Central Intelligence Agency (CIA). (2019). Africa: Egypt. *In The World Factbook.* Retrieved May 22, 2019, from https://www.cia.gov/library/publications/the-world-factbook/geos/eg.html

Comparing Egypt's 1971 Constitution to today. (2012, December 9). *Al Jazeera English.* Retrieved May 25, 2019, from https://www.aljazeera.com/indepth/spotlight/egypt/2012/12/2012129173710651270.html

Cook, S. A. (2012). *The struggle for Egypt: From Nasser to Tahrir Square.* Oxford, England: Oxford University Press.

de Oliveira, L. G. & Cardoso-da-Silva, M. (2018). From Tahrir Square to Facebook and vice versa: The public sphere, cyber-space, and the reach of post-revolution in Egypt. In J. Dee (Ed.) *From Tahrir Square to Gezi Park: Social networks as facilitators of social movements.* (pp. 23–38). New York, NY: Peter Lang Publishing.

Dubai Press Club. (2013). *Arab media outlook 2009–2013: Inspiring local content* (3rd. ed.). Retrieved June 09, 2019, from https://fas.org/irp/eprint/arabmedia.pdf

Egypt (2018). Freedom on the net 2018. Freedom House.org. Retrieved from https://freedomhouse.org/report/freedom-net/2018/egypt

Egypt's Constitution of 2014. (2018). The Constitute Project. Retrieved from https://www.constituteproject.org/constitution/Egypt_2014.pdf

Egypt faces new media censorship. (2008, August 7). *Al Jazeera English.* Retrieved May 25, 2019, from https://www.aljazeera.com/focus/2008/08/20088791952617974.html

Egypt Profile: Media. (2018, October 23). *BBC News.* Retrieved May 25, 2019, from https://www.bbc.com/news/world-africa-13313373

Egypt telecommunication regulation law (2003). University of Minnesota Human Rights Library. Retrieved May 25, 2019, from http://hrlibrary.umn.edu/research/Egypt/Egypt%20Telecommunication%20Regulation%20Law.pdf

Eko, L. (2012). *New media, old regimes: Case studies in comparative communication law and policy.* Lanham, MD: Lexington Books.

ElHaies, M. (2019, May 7). Egypt tests new censorship law with handling of al-Mashhad website block. CPJ. Retrieved July 11, 2019, from https://cpj.org/blog/2019/05/egypt-tests-new-censorship-law-with-handling-of-al.php

Gerbaudo, P. (2018). *Tweets and the streets: Social media and contemporary activism.* London, U.K.: Pluto Press.

Ghannam, J. (2011). Social media in the Arab world: Leading up to the uprisings of 2011. *Center for International Media Assistance, 3*(1), 1–44. Retrieved May 29, 2019, from http://

www.cima.ned.org/wp-content/uploads/2011/02/Ghannam-Jeffrey-Arab_Social_Media-Report-10-25-11.pdf

Harb, Z. (2011). Arab revolutions and the social media effect. *M/C Journal, 14*(2). Retrieved July 20, 2019, from http://journal.media-culture.org.au/index.php/mcjournal/article/view/364Two

Internet user penetration in Egypt from 2013 to 2019. (2019). Statista. Retrieved June 01, 2019, from https://www.statista.com/statistics/484939/internet-user-reach-egypt/

Lynch, M. (2013). *The Arab uprising: The unfinished revolutions of the new Middle East.* New York, NY: Public Affairs.

Mendel, T. (2011). *Political and media transitions in Egypt. A snapshot of media policy and regulatory environment.* Commissioned by Internews. Retrieved August 01, 2018, from http://hrlibrary.umn.edu/research/Egypt/Internews_Egypt_MediaLawReview_Aug11.pdf

OpenNet Initiative. (2009, August). *Egypt.* Retrieved March 17, 2018, from https://opennet.net/sites/opennet.net/files/ONI_Egypt_2009.pdf

Sayah, R. & Tawfeeq, M. (2014, January 2018). Egypt passes a new Constitution. *CNN.* Retrieved May 14, 2019, from https://www.cnn.com/2014/01/18/world/africa/egypt-constitution/index.html

Voters overwhelmingly back new Egypt Constitution. (2014, January 17). *Associated Press.* Retrieved May 22, 2019, from https://www.aikenstandard.com/news/voters-overwhelmingly-back-new-egypt-constitution/article_55e1f63a-62db-5979-bd4f-c29e3642e143.html

Part IV

Tunisia

With a population of 11.52 million people, Tunisia is slightly larger than Georgia (CIA, 2019). Located in Northern Africa, Tunisia borders the "Mediterranean Sea, between Algeria and Libya" (CIA, 2019, para. 3). The country's literacy rate is 81.8%, with 15.5% of the population living below the poverty line (CIA, 2019).

It is widely believed that the political uprisings in the Muslim world started in Tunisia when a Tunisian street vendor, Mohamed Bouazizi, doused himself with gasoline and self-immolated protesting against poor economic conditions and police brutality in the country. Bouazizi's protest suicide got national and global attention when Ali Bouazizi posted the cellphone-recorded video of the "Tunisian burning man" on Facebook. The Arabic channel, Al Jazeera, "picked up Ali Bouazizi's footage from the man's Facebook page, and transmitted it to its transnational Arabic satellite audience that same evening" (Eko, 2012, p. 130). This part of the book looks at Tunisian political uprising as the iconic social movement that acted as a catalyst for change in several other Muslim majority countries.

References

Central Intelligence Agency (CIA). (2019). Tunisia. In *The World Factbook*. Retrieved July 03, 2019, from https://www.cia.gov/library/publications/the-world-factbook/geos/ts.html

Eko, L. (2012). *New media, old regimes: Case studies in comparative communication law and policy*. Lanham, MD: Lexington Books.

10

Catching Fire

Let's revisit the incident of the Tunisian burning man that is believed to have been the spark of the political uprisings in Tunisia, commonly referred to as the Jasmine Revolution, which triggered political unrest in different parts of the Muslim world. Since age 10, Mohamed Bouazizi was the sole breadwinner for his family, selling fruits and vegetables from his wooden cart in the local market of Sidi Bouzid (Ryan, 2011a). Because of his poor economic conditions, he did not graduate from high school, but made sure that his five younger siblings had a chance to continue their education (de Soto, 2011). In other words, Bouazizi was no more than an average Tunisian who had no political interests nor a powerful background. There was nothing charming about his everyday struggles to get up in the morning and leave his home to push his cart through the streets selling vegetables and fruits. Neither was he known for spending a crazy amount of time on the Internet as a social media star. He probably did not even own a smartphone. One might wonder how, then, did such an average young Tunisian became the reason for revolutions that not only shook the Muslim world, but in fact brought the political hierarchy of several Middle Eastern countries down in a matter of weeks.

This chapter explores the events and circumstances associated with Bouazizi's radical step to take his own life by setting himself alight. The still and moving images of this suicide reached every nook and cranny of the world, and were seen as "a man on fire," rather than as just someone taking his own life. Put this way, the incident was interpreted as an act of courage and valor to stand up against the most powerful and corrupt regime of its time and challenge its authority over the lives of Tunisian citizens. It may be mentioned here that suicide is forbidden in Islam, and such an act is usually treated as a sin in Muslim-majority countries. However, Bouazizi's attempted suicide was revered as an act of a martyr who died to highlight the plight of his fellow citizens:

> Within days of Mohamed Bouazizi's attempted suicide in front of the local government office, students, teachers, lawyers, journalists, human rights activists, trade unionists, and opposition politicians took to the streets in several cities, including Tunis, to condemn the government's economic policies, its repression of all critics, and a mafia-style corruption that enriches members of the president's family. (Alexander, 2011, para.1)

This leads us to build an important connection between Bouazizi and the citizens of Tunisia, to understand what that connection was as well as why the people of Tunisia (and later Egypt) sympathized so much with this isolated incident that they decided to come out on the streets to challenge a powerful regime knowing that they might have to pay a heavy price for such activism.

In this context, it is imperative to mention here that the case of Bouazizi should not be looked at as an isolated incident, but in fact his life shares the story of an overwhelming majority of Tunisian people. Nor was he the first Tunisian to take his own life as a protest against government abuse. A similar incident, in fact, took place during the same year when "street vendor Abdesselem Trimech had set himself on fire in the coastal city of Monastir in March 2010" (Fraleigh, 2018, p. 4). Even though the incident did not gain iconic status, it served as a precursor to Bouazizi's attempted suicide and what came after his death. The circumstances that led to Bouazizi's self-immolation are a history of abuse, harassment, heavy monetary fines and humiliation by the local authorities. In one of its investigative reports on Bouazizi, Al Jazeera describes the circumstances this way:

> Six months before [Bouazizi's] attempted suicide, police sent a fine for 400 dinars ($280) to his house—the equivalent of two months of earnings. The harassment finally became too much for the young man on December 17. That morning, it became physical. A policewoman confronted him on the way to market. She returned to take his scales from him, but Bouazizi refused to hand them over. They swore at each other, the policewoman slapped him and, with the help of her colleagues, forced him to the ground. The officers took away his

> produce and his scale. Publicly humiliated, Bouazizi tried to seek recourse. He went to the local municipality building and demanded to a meeting with an official. He was told it would not be possible and that the official was in a meeting. (Ryan, 2011a, paras. 15–20)

Disappointment, helplessness and humiliation led Bouazizi to take the extreme step: On December 17, 2010 Mohamed Bouazizi doused himself with gasoline and set himself on fire in Sidi Bouzid in front of a government building as a mark of protest against his poor economic conditions and police brutality (Brown, 2012). The only difference between Abdesselem Trimech's burning himself alive and the Bouazizi's attempted suicide was the use of social media and in the latter case: "Ali Bouazizi, a relative of Mohamed Bouazizi, used his cellphone to record the self-immolation and the protest which followed" (Fraleigh, 2018, p. 4). This cellphone recording of the horrific incident did not stay within a close circle of those who witnessed the incident live, but, in fact, that same evening, Ali Bouazizi "posted the recording and several photographs" (Fraleigh, 2018, p. 4) of the Tunisian burning man on social media, including on Facebook (Lim, 2013).

Bouazizi, who was hospitalized after his attempted suicide, died of his burns on January 4, 2011 (de Soto, 2011). This story does not begin or end with Bouazizi. In fact, this practice of abuse and injustice was a prevailing one in the society, and most of the victims were middle-class youth. People of Tunisia had been grieving and protesting in their closed circles about their unhappiness towards the dictatorial regime of Tunisian President Ben Ali. They had maintained their grievances within their private spheres because they were afraid of the consequences for going public against the tyrant regime of Ben Ali. Besides, there was no independent traditional media to raise and highlight the plights of average Tunisians. In 2010, the poverty rate of the country was 20.5% with an unemployment rate of 23% (World Bank, 2018). An overwhelmingly large proportion of these unemployed youth were university graduates with higher degrees (World Bank, 2018). Such a youth who was well-educated and was relatively aware about the world around him had much higher levels of frustrations about his poor economic conditions even before these political protests erupted in the country. It may be mentioned here that in the wake of the Tunisian Arab Spring of 2010, even though the official poverty rate has declined to 15.2% from 20.5%, the unemployment rate had jumped to 31% by the end of 2017 (World Bank, 2018), which is an indication of an uncertain future for the country when it comes to long term political and economic stability.

Tunisian youth were having a difficult time expressing their frustration, as they lacked the support of any traditional mass media outlet in the country. In other words, since all the traditional media outlets were state-controlled and/or state-run, Tunisians did not have independent mass media to amplify their voices and share their grievances to their fellow citizens. For decades, their voices, grievances and frustrations were gagged by the same media that was supposed to give voice to the voiceless. Instead, the mass media was busy praising Ben Ali and his regime 24/7. Subsequently, for Tunisians there was no point in coming out in public and protesting the powerful elite, because there was no one to hear them out, all the way up until late 2010.

So, what changed this time? Why did Bouazizi become a symbol of resistance so quickly and why and how did the average vegetable seller bring down the most powerful man in Tunisia, Ben Ali, in a matter of weeks, not months? The simplest and most concise answer to these questions could be associated to just one phrase: alternative media. For the very first time in the history of this country, Tunisians found a way to tell their *own* stories via their *own* platforms of communication. They could also disseminate these stories to the rest of the world on their *own* terms. This new sense of ownership in terms of media was an important paradigm shift that the country had started to witness in the middle of the 2000s. In other words, the dawn of the Internet and digital communication in the form of social media on global horizons including Tunisia was, in fact, a game changer. By 2010, Tunisians—like people in many other developing countries in the world—had access to the Internet and smartphones. They could connect to the globe, record audio-visual stories via their smartphone cameras and share, store and re-share the information to their fellow citizens around the world. In such a scenario—where digital communication was already redefining the world—Bouazizi's voice of dissent was heard across the globe right at a time when he screamed, so to speak. On the one hand, unlike the past, this time the whole online world was watching and listening to the Tunisian man who burned himself as a mark of protest against the regime. On the other hand, the Ben Ali regime, consistent with its past practices, was still giving a deaf ear to Bouazizi and his supporters' screams.

Since President Ben Ali and his administration were used to suppressing the voices of dissent so easily and successfully because of their absolute control over the traditional media, the government miscalculated the power of social media this time. Ben Ali and his administration did not pay heed to the self-immolation of a street vendor, who apparently was neither important nor a political threat to the stability of the regime. By the time the government realized the powerful role that social media had played in spreading the images of the burning man to the world, it was already too late for Ben Ali. It took President Ben Ali two weeks to visit the hospital where Bouazizi was admitted (Ryan, 2011a). And by that time, the genie of people's anger and resentment against his regime was already out of the bottle.

Meanwhile, something unique was happening in terms of narrative sharing between the social media and traditional media. Bouazizi's protest suicide got national and global attention when the cellphone-recorded video of the "Tunisian burning man" was posted on Facebook. The Arabic channel, Al Jazeera, "picked up Bouazizi's footage from the man's Facebook page, and transmitted it to its transnational Arabic satellite audience that same evening" (Eko, 2012, p. 130). Thus, this unique and informal collaboration between Al Jazeera and social media was in fact the beginning of a new era that set the stage for social media to begin telling stories of political dissent while traditional media outlets were trying to readjust by engaging with these alternative media platforms.

This new intermedia collaboration between Al Jazeera and Facebook had also baffled the Ben Ali regime, not to mention researchers and scholars in the field of media and communication. Youth who had direct access to and knowledge of the Internet and social media started mobilizing their fellow citizens on social media platforms such as Facebook, YouTube and Twitter. At the same time, the older generations in Tunisia, who lacked the basic access or knowledge to operate these social media tools, were relying on the traditional televised media platform, including Al Jazeera. Put this way, both factions of the society were being informed and educated about people's grievances against the Ben Ali regime and how a young man ended up burning himself alive as a result of the system's failure to provide him justice.

Also, it is interesting to note that even though many Tunisians were already online before the Jasmine Revolution, Tunisia witnessed real online activism when President Ben Ali tried to suppress protesters by shutting down the entire country's mass media outlets. The absence of the mass media in the country created an informational vacuum, which was later filled by the alternative media, as "[i]n the face of the national media blackout, blogs, Facebook, Twitter, and other social media became virtual bulletin boards where videos of governmental violence were posted, shared and discussed" (Eko, 2012, p. 130). Consequently, the emergence of the Internet took away the ruling elite's exclusive control over the information flow in the country. Now citizens had an alternate platform to express their opinions and unhappiness toward the regime via online activism.

Bouazizi:Tunisia's Icon of Outrage

After laying the foundation of how social media bridged the communication gap in Tunisian society at the time of the political unrest of 2010 against the Ben Ali regime, let us explore the iconic status of Bouazizi in light of Perlmutter's "icons of outrage" concept (1998). According to Perlmutter (1998), celebrity, prominence, frequency, profit, instantaneousness, transposability, fame of subjects, importance of events, metonymy, primordiality and/or cultural resonance and striking composition, are all the conditions that contribute to make an image iconic. An iconic image has the power to get public and elite attention simultaneously and thus can create social upheaval if turned into action. Also, the scholar "divides photojournalistic icons into two broad categories: generic and discrete" (Smith Dahmen, Mielczarek & Perlmutter, 2018, p. 273). Where generic iconic images contain a recurring situation or theme, discrete iconic images, on the other hand, "[are] connected to a specific event that usually becomes a defining single image of that occasion or that historical time" (Smith Dahmen et al., 2018, p. 273). In light of this differentiation among types of iconic images, this chapter treats Bouazizi's image as a discrete iconic image.

Let us apply each single element of Perlmutter's characteristics of icons of outrage to the images of Bouazizi to understand its iconic power, which figuratively shook the world and even today continues to inspire and trigger more political uprisings in several other countries, such as Sudan and Algeria (El Wardany, 2019). (For more discussion on the Sudanese and Algerian Springs, refer to Chapter 14 of this book)

Celebrity

According to Perlmutter (1998), a "famous image is one which people can identify when prompted, or are vaguely familiar with even if little is known about the context of events" (p. 11). Additionally, he writes, "the celebrity status of a picture is often signaled by the fact people assume others must know of it" (p. 12). In the context of this definition of the celebrity element of an iconic image, we can say that when the image of Bouazizi surfaced in 2010, it did not enjoy celebrity status right away, even though the image shocked the world. However, almost nine years after the Tunisian Spring, the image fulfils the property of being a celebrity one. Therefore, whenever this image is brought up in the news media or academic discussions, people can now not only identify it, they also assume that others must know of it.

Prominence

Terming it as the least ambiguous quality of an icon, Perlmutter describes an icon as a "much more visible [image] than any other. Its greater likelihood to achieve a higher rank in our collective memory is influenced by its place order in the agenda of media" (p. 13). In the case of the image of the burning man, it is evident that the image was placed as the central theme to express people's anger against the Ben Ali regime. However, such an agenda setting was not done by the traditional media of Tunisia, but by the social media activists who had started sharing this image on online platforms to a wider audience. At the same time, the image kept achieving higher status in the collective memories of not only Tunisians, but also to the people of the globe, because anyone who saw this image online became a part of this collective memory process. After all, the Internet phenomenon is not country-specific, rather its boundaries are determined by the aspect of connectivity. Therefore, Perlmutter's (1998) element of prominence is also evident in the case of this iconic image, even though the circumstances in terms of media role and collective memory were dramatically shifted in this case.

Frequency & Transposability

Perlmutter (1998) defines the phenomenon of repeated use of famous images in mass media as "frequency." According to him, "A flood of repetitious, similar images may have more of an influence than a single, non-recurring one" (p. 13). On the other hand, "transposability" refers to the replication of icons across media, facilitating retention of that icon in people's collective memories. Bouazizi's image of self-immolation in the middle of a street is often thought of as *the image* that triggered revolutions in the Arab region. The image was repeatedly used and replicated on social media platforms during the Tunisian revolution of 2011. It was also carried as a protest theme on the streets of Tunisia while protesters gathered against the Ben Ali regime.

Profit

Perlmutter (1998) believes that "icons sell" (p. 13) and have the tendency to keep appearing and reappearing in different venues for years and decades. In this cycle of reappearances, "[e]ach appearance earns the copyright holder a fee, especially for the celebrity images repeated in thousands of publications" (p. 13). He adds, "[t]he more sensational, specific icons adopt the uniqueness of *objects d' art;* they are commensurably more valuable" (p. 13). In this case, however, there were no copyrights, neither was there any artistic aspect associated with the image. Rather, the profit aspect of the image can be revisited and seen in terms of Tarrow's (1998) "repertoire of collective action," where people with limited resources deploy anger in addition to cultural and ideological themes to sustain a social movement. (For more details, refer to Chapter 1 of this book). Hence, it can be argued that because of the sensational power of the Bouazizi's image, the protesters profited from deploying it as a resource to sustain their movement (both online and on the streets) against the Ben Ali regime.

Fame of Subjects

Sometimes recognizability or notoriety of subjects in an image can contribute to its iconic status. Therefore, "Icons often draw their fame from the presence of a well-known person" (Perlmutter, 1998, p. 15). In the case of Tunisia, however, Bouazizi was not a well-known person, but the President Ben Ali was. Perlmutter (1998) justifies the unknown aspect of an iconic image this way: "[I]n many icons the subjects are unknown, ordinary people caught up in some important moment or some striking composition that eventually is lifted to iconic status" (p. 15). Keeping this explanation in perspective, recall how Bouazizi's image was lifted to an iconic status: When social media activists, particularly YouTubers, started juxtaposing the image of a burning man next to Ben Ali's image, the result amassed fame to Bouazizi and notoriety to Ben Ali. An icon of outrage was being put next to an "icon of arrogance" (Perlmutter, 1998, p.120), as a strategic resource so as to motivate potential sympathizers to join the collective action against the regime. Thus, it can be stated that in the age of the Internet, when icons of outrage collide with icons of arrogance, revolutions may occur, as it was witnessed in the case of Tunisia in 2011.

Importance of Events

Perlmutter (1998) adds, "Another criterion for iconic status is that the event pictured has significance in itself. Quite often, icons are tied to important social events or historical occurrences" (p. 16). This element is most relevant in the case of Bouazizi's image. It was not the person or even the act that earned Bouazizi's image an iconic status, but rather the poor economic conditions of people. In addition, injustices and a history of exploitation by an authoritarian regime were among the circumstances that made Bouazizi's suicide an immortal act.

Metonymy

Among all the previously discussed elements of an iconic image, metonymy stands out the most because of its "said it all" (Perlmutter, 1998, p. 17) quality. Perlmutter writes, "The use of one image to illustrate a news story implies, without need of a caption, that the picture represents the greater event. This 'summing up' quality is a special value of the news picture" (Perlmutter, 1998, p. 17). The "summing up" quality of the Tunisian burning man's image is so powerful that despite the passing of several years since the Tunisian Spring, the image is still being referred to as a metonymic representation of the Arab Spring. The image, "a man on fire," is, in itself, a whole story and needs little to no interpretation whenever it is looked back upon through the window of recent history and political activism in the Middle East and beyond.

Primordiality and/or Cultural Resonance

For an image to reach an iconic status, it must resonate with a person's common cultural and/or historical belief system. Such a primordial characteristic and/or cultural resonance ignites an emotional response every time its viewers see it. For example, during the 1989 Tiananmen Square protests in China, the iconic image of a "man facing the tanks at Tiananmen recalls—to some observers—David's confrontation with Goliath" (Perlmutter, 1998, p. 18). In other words, "[o]nce we make a picture an icon, it too becomes a frame to which newer images will be compared. Every icon, therefore, creates a new standard for new icons" (Perlmutter, 1998, p. 18). The definition of primordiality connects us to the previous discussion about metonymy; because Bouazizi's image of burning himself alive is not just an image that gained fame, but a frame or lens through which future social movements and political activism in the Muslim world will be compared. The image itself resonates with the deep-rooted cultural realities from the Arab region, where average citizens share a collective memory of the denial of basic human rights such as freedom of speech and expression by their rulers, not to mention other issues including injustice, poor economic conditions and unemployment.

Outrage

Outrage can be defined as a quality of the icon that is set to engender strong negative reactions. Perlmutter (1998) further describes outrage as an emotional reaction. So far, the discussion of Perlmutter's elements of icons has focused on understanding what makes an ordinary image an iconic one, but this last part is, in fact, about the outcome: what happens when an image acquires an iconic status, and that is the most important aspect of this chapter. Bouazizi's image of dousing himself with gasoline and setting himself alight in broad daylight did not end at just being referred to as an iconic picture because of its shocking and sensational qualities, but, in fact, the image is directly associated with the outrage and emotional reaction of Tunisians, and they have been carrying it in their hearts and minds for nearly a decade. Bouazizi's suicide was not the sole action that resulted in the Arab Spring, but it represents a critical moment in time when the volcano of people's outrage erupted, which later engulfed a decades-old authoritarian regime within matter of days. Such volcanic activity in the form of collective actions and social movements continue to spread even several years after this incident (For example, look at the recent protests in Sudan and Algeria in 2019). Therefore, Bouazizi was not only an icon in history, and neither can he be summarized as simply an example of outrage. He is "a man on fire" and the Muslim world is catching fire from this burning man.

Conclusion

From the discussion provided in this chapter, we can draw two important conclusions: first, the Tunisian political uprisings commonly referred to as the Arab Spring of 2010 did not start with this one random incident when a young vegetable and fruit seller decided to burn himself alive. In fact, Tunisia had a history of injustice and corruption, and when one man came forward to protest these discriminations by burning himself, his pain and grievances were felt, shared and connected with the rest of the population of the country and beyond. Once the revolution was over, "[t]he new Tunisian government estimated that the previous regime's forces killed more than 300 protesters in December 2010 and January 2011" (Fraleigh, 2018, p.15). Their sacrifices were not the result of a random protest rally but tell us the sad tale of a history of injustice and discriminations in the Tunisian society at large. Thus, we should look at Bouazizi's burning image as Tunisians on fire, rather than just a one man's story. Bouazizi's self-immolation just served as a trigger for social change and social movements that followed at a very precise moment in time.

Second, the success of the Tunisian social movement that made this movement itself an iconic one and was termed as the Arab Spring, is associated with the fact that people of Tunisia had an alternative platform of communication in their hands known as social media. Therefore, "[t]he growth of Facebook, Twitter, and a Tunisian blogosphere—much of it based outside the country—made it increasingly easy for Tunisians to learn about the latest arrest, beating, or illicit business deal involving the president's family" (Alexander, 2011, para 4). In addition to the popularity of social media among Tunisians, the successful and intelligent collaboration of social media and traditional media (Al Jazeera) in order to mobilize and organize potential sympathizers and protesters, resulted in mass protests on the streets that toppled Ben Ali regime in less than a month. Therefore, social media had a direct contribution to social change of Tunisian society. Once this revolution was over, it spread to other societies and triggered more social movements and collective actions in the days to come. The collective memory of social media and the Internet, which can now be referred to as digital memory, also played a powerful role in the spread of social movements and revolutions to other societies. This aspect will be discussed in detail in a separate chapter (#13) to discuss how the Internet is becoming a platform of record to store political activism of the 21st century in digital form and how these collective memory themes are contributing to create more social movements because of their fluidity.

References

Alexander, C. (2011, January 3). Tunisia's protest wave: Where it comes from and what it means. *Foreign Policy*. Retrieved July 02, 2019, from https://foreignpolicy.com/2011/01/03/tunisias-protest-wave-where-it-comes-from-and-what-it-means/

Brown, B. (2012, February 14). The Jasmine Revolution: A timeline. *Tunisia Weekly* [blog post]. Retrieved July 02, 2019, from https://tunisiaweekly.wordpress.com/2012/02/14/the-jasmine-revolution-a-timeline/

de Soto, H. (2011, December 16). The real Mohamed Bouazizi. *Foreign Policy*. Retrieved July 07, 2019, from https://foreignpolicy.com/2011/12/16/the-real-mohamed-bouazizi/

Eko, L. (2012). *New media, rld Regimes: Case studies in comparative communication law and policy*. Lanham, MD: Lexington Books.

El Wardany, S. (2019, March 8). Is Algeria finally having its Arab Spring moment? *The Washington Post*. Retrieved July 10, 2019, from https://www.washingtonpost.com/business/is-algeria-finally-having-its-arab-spring-moment/2019/03/07/1061218c-4141-11e9-85ad-779ef05fd9d8_story.html?utm_term=.7ce32b599e3f

Fraleigh, D. (2018). The Tunisian Revolution: A social movement of courage assisted by social media. In J. Dee (Ed.), *From Tahrir Square to Gezi Park: Social networks as facilitators of social movements* (pp. 3–18). New York, NY: Peter Lang Publishing.

Lim, M. (2013). Framing Bouazizi: 'White lies', hybrid network, and collective/connective action in the 2010–11 Tunisian uprising. *Journalism, 14*(7), 921–941. doi: 10.1177/1464884913478359

Perlmutter, D. D. (1998). *Photojournalism and foreign policy: Icons of outrage in international crises.* Westport, Conn.: Praeger.

Ryan, Y. (2011a, January 20). The tragic life of a street vendor. *Al Jazeera.* Retrieved June 28, 2019, from https://www.aljazeera.com/indepth/features/2011/01/201111684242518839.html

Ryan, Y. (2011b, January 26). How Tunisia's revolution began. *Al Jazeera.* Retrieved June 28, 2019, from https://www.aljazeera.com/indepth/features/2011/01/ 2011126121815985483.html

Smith Dahmen, N., Mielczarek, N., & Perlmutter, D. D. (2018). The influence-network model of the photojournalistic icon. *Journalism & Communication Monographs, 20*(4), 264–313. doi: 10.1177/1522637918803351

Tarrow, S. G. (1998). *Power in movement: Social movements and contentious politics.* Cambridge, England: Cambridge University Press.

World Bank (2018, April 16). Tunisia's economic outlook. Retrieved June 23, 2019, from: https://www.worldbank.org/en/country/tunisia/publication/economic-outlook-april-2018

11 Social Movements in Tunisia

The so-called Jasmine Revolution of Tunisia was started with the self-immolation of a Tunisian street vendor and was aimed at changing the regime of President Ben Ali. The term Jasmine—after the country's national flower symbol—was used by the mainstream media to refer the Tunisian uprisings of 2010 (Fraleigh, 2018). However, because of its significant presence and the role that social media played during these uprisings, the Tunisian protests are also referred to as the Twitter Revolution by some media researchers and scholars (Breuer, Landman & Farquhar, 2015; Esseghaier, 2012; Fraleigh, 2018). This chapter makes a case that the Jasmine Revolution was not an overnight phenomenon, but the outcome of a decades-old history of political, economic and social unrest in the country that goes all the way back to the Tunisian Bread Riots of 1984, even before Ben Ali assumed the office of president. Put this way, "Tunisia's history has been dotted with such mini-uprisings, each one breathing new life into a continuous struggle to address socio-economic inequality" (Aboueldahab, 2018, para. 3). This struggle is far from over, even after the highly celebrated Jasmine Revolution of 2010. This chapter highlights some of the recent political unrests in the country and argues that the term "Tunisian Arab Spring" should be seen as a terminology of the past. Moreover, this chapter argues that a coalition of social movements made up of the Tunisian General Labor Union (UGTT), the Lawyers' Union, and the

Student Movement were involved in information activism and street protests and had "roots in workers' movements, starting with a strike in 1978 under [Tunisia's] first post-independence president, Habib Bourguiba" (Aboueldahab, 2018, para. 3). The workers' movement demands were no different from several other follow-up movements, though it was specifically asking for "better contract terms, higher salaries, working conditions, and a solution to rampant unemployment" (Aboueldahab, 2018, para. 3). Even though the Workers' Movement of 1978 and many other subsequent movements were mostly suppressed by the ruling elites, these protests served as the foundation for the Tunisian Arab Spring of 2010. The following paragraphs in this chapter will discuss some of the significant social movements in the country's history that led to the Jasmine Revolution of 2010.

Labor Activism in Tunisia

Tunisian labor activism has a long history of struggle both on social and political fronts. Its roots are in an era when Tunisia was still colonized by France, and begins with "the establishment of General Confederation of Tunisian Workers by Mohamed Ali El Hammi in 1924 and the foundation of the Tunisian General Labor Union in 1946 under the leadership of Farhat Hached" (Zayani, 2015, p. 54). The main goal of these organizations was to protect the rights of the working class under French colonial rule. Hence, the labor union has played an active role in politics and social issues of Tunisia, even after the independence of the country in 1956 (Zayani, 2015). The popularity of the labor union as a political force on national forefronts, however, was seen as a threat by the post-independence president, Bourguiba. When the labor union started organizing protests against the government's poor economic policies, "[r]ising tensions [between the government and protesters] culminated in the bloody riots of January 26, 1978" (Zayani, 2015, p. 54). Afterward, President Bourguiba made sure to replace the union's democratically elected leadership with a leadership more favorable to the government to keep the union under its control from then onwards. In the later years of Ben Ali's presidency, the movement was never a big impediment to the government, but still played an active role in organizing and supporting small scale protests, mostly in southern parts of Tunisia where laborers and miners were feeling economically marginalized, despite having been blessed with oil, gas and phosphate as natural resources. In its later stages, the UGTT was joined by lawyers, students and other members of civil society, who continued to play an active role in political, social, economic and nation building fronts.

Tunisian Bread Riots of 1984

Soon after getting independence from France, Habib Ben Ali Bourguiba, became the first-ever president of Tunisia in 1957 and continued to rule the country for around 30 years, until 1987 (Alexander, 2011; Zayani, 2015). Bourguiba, who was once considered a hero for his role in gaining independence from France, was seen as a dictator who continued to rule the country against the people's will and who kept on suppressing any resistance effort against him by force until 1987, when Zine El Abidine Ben Ali ousted him from the office in a bloodless coup (Zayani, 2015).

One of the most significant resistance movement that contributed to the overthrow of Bourguiba erupted three years prior to the coup against Bourguiba in 1983, is known as the Tunisian Bread Riots or *intifadat al khubz* (Aboueldahab, 2018). It is interesting to note that just like the Jasmine Revolution of 2010, the Bread Riots also started in December (of 1983) and ended in January of 1984 (Aboueldahab, 2018; Mullenbach, n.d.; Pérez-Altable & Blanco, 2016; Zayani, 2015). In other words, "January traditionally has been Tunisia's month for political drama—a general strike in January 1978; a Libyan-supported insurrection in January 1980; bread riots in January 1984" (Alexander, 2011, para. 1). This coincidence of the same months for several Tunisian political uprisings including the Jasmine Revolution may not be planned, but still speaks to the relevance of the Tunisian past to its future. The Bread Riots erupted after the government decided to stop subsidizing wheat and other grains, resulting in soaring prices of bread in the country (Alexander, 2011; Gana, 2013; Zayani, 2015). Simultaneously, the country's economy was not doing great, and the southern part of Tunisia was already witnessing a drought. All these conditions added to the economic woes of the citizens of Tunisia. When Bourguiba's government announced an end to all subsidies on wheat in order to secure an International Monetary Fund (IMF) loan, it served as a catalyst for protesters to come out in the streets against the regime and demand the overthrow of Bourguiba (Gana, 2013; Walton & Seddon, 2008). Even though Bourguiba successfully suppressed the protestors through violence—after he declared a state of emergency in the country and over 100 protesters died and over 1000 people were injured as a result (Aboueldahab, 2018)—his iron grip on the government was finally challenged. In the aftermath of these riots, Bourguiba could never regain the same level of control over his country and ended up losing the office in a matter of three years, when Ben Ali ousted him from power. These incidents and the outcome point us to two important implications: one is related to the theoretical underpinning of Tarrow (1998) and the other is about the role of media and communication.

As I have discussed in the first chapter of this book, Tarrow (1998) believes that even if a social movement against a regime fails to achieve its goals, it challenges the status quo and changes the political scene of a society forever. In such a situation, an authoritarian regime has no choice but to readjust to the new realities. It will either have to get tougher on its people so that such political activism does not take place again or will have to accommodate the demands of the protesters and loosen its control to avoid future conflicts. In the case of Tunisia, the aftermath of the Bread Riots was of significant impact, as this was the first ever time for this relatively young country to experience more suppression and limits on individual freedoms since the country got its independence from France. Bourguiba did not only declare a state of emergency, he used violence and force to overcome the riots and banned any political activity that involved protests, gatherings and processions. All these tactics deployed by the government apparently worked. Tunisians had no choice but to accept the new realities of limited freedoms in terms of expression and participation in the country's mainstream politics.

The second implication is about the importance of communication among the masses. Despite the fact that the participants in the 1984 Bread Riots were representatives of the poor, youth, students, farmers and middle-class communities, they could not sustain their social movement for long. These protesters lacked access to mass media, which was directly under state control. That's why they could not spread their narrative of grievances against the regime so that potential sympathizers could join them on the streets. The protesters' narrative was further lost and compromised when violence erupted among the ranks of protesters. This was seen as the rioters destroying the national infrastructure and people's properties on the streets of the capital city. Had there been a mass media supportive of these protesters, or had there been a medium like the Internet, where protesters could organize and spread their narrative of protests, there might have been a different outcome to the Bread Riots of 1984. Also, even though several lives were lost and so much anger against the Tunisian president was there, it took another three years for the Tunisians to get rid of Bourguiba because they lacked their own network of communication and could not judge or gauge how other Tunisians were thinking or feeling about the Bourguiba regime.

Unemployed Demonstrators in Redeyef 2008

A number of political uprisings in Tunisia find their roots in economic instability and unemployment among the Tunisian youth. This connection that goes all the way back to the Bread Riots of 1984, was also found as a dominant factor during the protests against unemployment at "Redeyef in the country's southwestern Gafsa region" ("Tunisian Police," 2008, para. 2) in 2008. These protests of 2008 are considered the beginning of the Jasmine Revolution and began as a protest of "corrupt hiring practices at the mines of Gafsa" (Gall, 2014, para. 1). Often referred to as the "Revolt of the People of Mines" (Gantin & Seddik, 2008), the Redeyef protests, which lasted for six-months, were seen as "a mass revolt against unemployment and economic inequality in the town of Gafsa." These protests "resulted in several deaths and many injuries" (Aboueldahab, 2018, para. 7).

Ironically, President Ben Ali, who had toppled the Bourguiba regime for the very same reasons, did not refrain from using his predecessor's fear tactics when it came to handle the protesters. Ben Ali imposed a curfew, and the security forces did not refrain from shooting bullets at the demonstrators, resulting in one casualty and several others injured ("Tunisian Police," 2008). Interesting enough, just like Bourguiba, Ben Ali also was successful in putting down the protests. yet despite his apparent success, the Tunisian president was ousted from his office within two years of the Redeyef demonstrations, as a result of the iconic Tunisian social movement of 2010. Looking more closely at these demonstrations, one can easily observe the government's efforts to use the same old-fashioned fear tactics to suppress the protesters (Aboueldahab, 2018). At the same time, the protesters were finding themselves less and less afraid of the government's tactics and kept on challenging the regime against all odds. This chapter argues that this shift in being less afraid of the government's tyranny should be seen in the context of social media. For the very first time in the history of this country, Tunisians had access to smartphones and the Internet, and were able to connect with each other to gain the support of their fellow citizens, thus, defusing any fear of government suppression in their hearts and minds. For the very first time, Tunisians could express themselves and their grievances freely to a wider audience and could realize that their fellow citizens felt the same way. Hence, a new era of collective thinking was dawning at the forefronts of decades-old dark practices of the regime. The world and Tunisian citizens could see it and were ready to embrace this new era of informational activism. Meanwhile, Ben Ali and his team were still living under the mistaken belief that merely controlling the traditional media outlets would be enough to contain the narrative of protesters as it had in the past. By the time Ben Ali realized the true power and potential that the informational activism on social media had brought as a challenge to his regime, it was already too late for him.

Anti-censorship Protests of 2010

When Ben Ali realized the true potential and power of social media activism, he started going after cyber activists by imposing tougher censorship measures against social media including "Twitter, Facebook, blogs, and even popular multimedia-sharing websites, as YouTube or Flickr" (Pérez-Altable & Blanco, 2016, p. 10–11). Tunisian youth—who were already falling in love with these new modes of digital communication—could not stand the government's decision to take away the Internet from them. As a reaction, Tunisian activists launched an online anti-censorship movement in April 2010 (Pérez-Altable & Blanco, 2016), only eight months in advance of the Jasmine Revolution. Utilizing Twitter to organize and disseminate their narrative of protest, the activists deployed symbolic means to protest, so as to avoid direct confrontation with the regime. On May 22, 2010, these "Tunisian activists took the main street in Tunis, Habib Bourguiba Avenue, and wore their white t-shirts in order to protest against the censorship" (Pérez-Altable & Blanco, 2016, p.15). This activism was a turning point in modern Tunisia's history because, for the very first time, Tunisian "bloggers [and] cyber activist[s] decided to leave their screens and online campaigns and to come on the ground, protest on the ground against censorship and for freedom of speech" (Pérez-Altable & Blanco, 2016, p.15). While the movement was still gaining traction, Ben Ali met with a powerful blow to his presidency when Mohamed Bouazizi's incident of self-immolation unfolded. As a result, the tsunami of the so-called Jasmine Revolution had already begun to sweep the presidency, and now could not be reversed.

It is pertinent to mention here that after the Jasmine Revolution was over, and Ben Ali had fled the country, Tunisian political activism did not stop. Rather, we continue to witness more political, social and economic uprisings on the country's horizon. For example, within 10 days of the Jasmine Revolution, "[o]n January 23, thousands of young protesters and activists occupied Al Kasbah Square in front of the seat of [transitional] government to demand the expulsion of cabinet members associated with the Ben Ali regime" (Zayani, 2015, p. 190). The protesters were worried that the acting government was still inclusive of Ben Ali's former allies, including the Ben Ali regime's Prime Minister Mohamed

Ghannouchi, who was playing an active role to "constitute a transitional government" (Zayani, 2015, p. 190). The protests of January 23 were followed by a second wave of sit-ins on February 25th, "demanding the departure of Ghannouchi and his government, the suspension of legislative assembly, the banning of the ruling party, the dismantling of Ben Ali's security apparatus, and the electing of a new legislature to write a new constitution" (Zayani, 2015, p. 190).

These new cycles of political activism kept on moving forward in post-revolutionary Tunisia. Some such examples of social movements range from "'Protests Against Thirst' (Summer 2012) to '*Manich Mymeh*' ('I do not forgive'), against the so-called 'National Reconciliation' law 2015–17) and '*Fach Nestannaow*' ('What are we waiting for?'), …[and] ('Association for the Protection of the Palm Grove of the Oasis of Jemna') 2011–2017" (Saidani, 2018). Even though these movements could never become as significant as the Jasmine Revolution of 2010, they still continue to keep the post-revolution government in check and ensure that the country moves forward in achieving better human rights, civil liberties and equal economic opportunities for all citizens. Among these many post-revolution movements, some of the most significant are discussed below.

The Kamour Movement and Civic Protests of April 2017

Unlike the past examples of failures to the social movements and political uprisings of Tunisia, the Jasmine Revolution set the stage for the beginning of a new era of protest politics. People have started to realize the power of a collective action. In the aftermath of the Arab Spring, political activists and protesters in Tunisia participate in collective actions believing that the outcome will be in their favor. A Tunisian political analyst, Youssef Cherif describes this new trend this way: "Since the fall of former president Zine el-Abidine Ben Ali in 2011, such events have become more frequent, due to expanded civic freedoms and a relatively greater respect for human rights, coupled with a weaker state apparatus and economic turmoil" (Cherif, 2017, para, 4). One such example is of the Kamour Movement and Civic Protests of April 2017, which started within six years of the Tunisian Arab Spring (Cherif, 2017; Souissi, 2017).

The Kamour Movement was essentially another example of a social movement that was triggered because of the poor economic conditions and unemployment among Tunisian people. The southern region of Tunisia is an oil and gas rich area of the country, but it has been historically marginalized by Tunisian governments. The same is the case with "Tataouine, an area of high poverty and unemployment" (Saussi, 2017, para. 2). When the people of southern Tunisia realized that the promises that were made to them during the transition of Tunisia following the Jasmine Revolution were not delivered to this part of the country, they decided to launch their own social revolution by blocking access of the government and multinational companies to oil and gas sites, and "in April 2017, hundreds of protesters occupied an oil and gas facility at Kamour in southern Tunisia." (Cherif, 2017, para. 1). The protesters had a list of demands, and almost all of the demands were focused on their economic conditions. As Cherif (2017) puts it:

> They asked for a fair share of the region's oil and gas revenues, requesting that 20 percent of these revenues be invested in Tataouine. They also demanded that private companies operating in the country (including in the oil and gas sector) be obliged to create at least 4,500 jobs for local residents, while also insisting that the state invest $40 million in infrastructure and development funds for Tataouine. (para. 6)

Just as a reminder for the readers of this chapter, such a blockage of natural energy resources as a mark of protest was not a new tactic in Tunisian history of political activism. As has been discussed earlier in this chapter, Tunisians had utilized the same strategy during the Redeyef demonstrations of 2008. However, unlike the unfortunate outcome of Redeyef demonstrations, the Kamour Movement witnessed a relatively happy ending. The protesters ended their sit-ins on June 16, 2017, when "[t]he government and the private oil and gas companies ... accepted most of the protesters' initial demands" (Cherif, 2017, para. 18). The fulfillment of all the promises that were made to end the protests remain uncertain, however. Only the future will tell us whether Tunisians will go through more episodes of political activism if the government fails to execute its promises to the citizens in a timely fashion.

As for the role of media during these protests, one would hope that the Tunisian mainstream media might have changed its course by starting to give more coverage to the people's demands. In fact, this was not the case. The Tunisian mainstream media continued to ignore the Kamour Movement and the demands of the participating protesters. Just like the Jasmine Revolution, social media, once again, served the role of an alternative media outlet for the protesters, both in terms of organizing the protesters and amplifying their demands to the rest of the country. Hence, for example, "it was through Facebook that most Tunisians heard about the sit-in. A Facebook page and a logo were created in the early weeks of the movement" (Cherif, 2017, para. 12). This Facebook page was seen as the lifeline of communication throughout the duration of the sit-ins. The motto of the Facebook page was "*ar-rakh la,*" which translates to "no surrender" (Cherif, 2017, para. 13).

Manich Msemah Anti-corruption Campaign

While the Tunisian government was still recovering from the difficult negotiations and outcomes of the Kamour Movement, it was met by another wave of political activism with the turn of the new year in 2018. The Tunisian government passed a controversial reconciliation law in 2017, "which grant[ed] certain civil servants immunity from prosecution for corruption and economic crimes" (Aboueldahab, 2018, para. 10). The law, which was adopted on September 13, 2017 by the Tunisian parliament, "grant[ed] complete impunity to civil servants who were implicated in corruption under former dictator Zine El Abidine Ben Ali and allow[ed] them to return to positions of power" (Guellali, 2017, para. 1). Furthermore, the law also "obstruct[ed] any investigation into the systematic corruption that prevailed in Tunisia for decades and prevent[ed] courts from ruling on human-rights violations" (Guellali, 2017, para. 1). This protection goes completely against the narrative and demands of the Jasmine Revolution of 2010, which had taken a tougher stance against corruption and nepotism. However, the reconciliation law seems to be doing otherwise because of its protections to some of the corrupt elements in the society. Tunisians who are now used to of using political activism as a tool to get their demands accepted, once again launched the "*Manich Msemah* anti-corruption campaign to call for a reversal of this unjust law" (Aboueldahab, 2018, para. 10). The activists created a Facebook page with the logo of *Manich Msemah* (which means "I Will Not Forgive"), and at time of writing this chapter (in April 2019), the Facebook page had over 83,000 followers. The language of communication on the page was Arabic and it was mostly dedicated toward fellow Tunisians rather than with connecting to the outside world.

Conclusion

This chapter provides an overview of social movements and political activism in Tunisia that started long before the Jasmine Revolution. It helps average reader to understand that the Jasmine Revolution was not an overnight or abrupt phenomenon, rather it represents a turning point in Tunisian history, which is full of injustices, economic and political dilemmas, and denial of basic human rights by the country's rulers for decades. Thus, the Jasmine Revolution of 2010 is in fact sitting on the shoulders of many other past political and social movements in the country's history that led to the uprisings of the Tunisian Arab Spring. Bouazizi's suicide was not an isolated incident, but a powerful and courageous refusal to keep bearing the atrocities being committed by the powerful elite on its people. That is why Bouazizi's act of defiance was well received and well heard by his fellow citizens, who were quick to come out and join online and street protests and made history by ousting the most powerful man in the nation from his office in a matter of days.

Looking at the two presidents and their respective overthrows from their offices and the chronology of events and timeframes associated with these developments, we can clearly see how the communication factor made a difference in these two cases. With little to no media freedom during the 1984 riots, President Bourguiba continued to rule for another three years because he had absolute control over the national narrative. However, the 2008 example of Redeyef, which saw relatively more presence in media—particularly the social media and Al Jazeera—sped up the process of ending Ben Ali's regime, as the monarch was ousted by another political uprising within two years.

Therefore, while highlighting the significant political activism in Tunisia, this chapter contextualizes the developments that were taking place in the field of media and communication, and which might have contributed to the pace of making future social movements successful ones.

References

Aboueldahab, N. (2018, January 29). Unrest in Tunisia: Another turning point in a legacy of economic injustice. *Brookings Institute*. Retrieved May 08, 2019, from https://www.brookings.edu/blog/order-from-chaos/2018/01/29/unrest-in-tunisia-another-turning-point-in-a-legacy-of-economic-injustice/

Alexander, C. (2011, January 3). Tunisia's protest wave: Where it comes from and what it means. *Foreign Policy*. Retrieved June 06, 2019, from https://foreignpolicy.com/2011/01/03/tunisias-protest-wave-where-it-comes-from-and-what-it-means/

Breuer, A., Landman, T., & Farquhar, D. (2015). Social media and protest mobilization: Evidence from the Tunisian revolution. Democratization, 22(4), 764–792.

Cherif, Y. (2017, August 8). The Kamour Movement and civic protests in Tunisia. *Carnegie Endowment for International Peace*. Retrieved June 12, 2019, from https://carnegieendowment.org/2017/08/08/kamour-movement-and-civic-protests-in-tunisia-pub-72774

Esseghaier, M. (2012). "Tweeting out a tyrant:" Social media and the Tunisian revolution. *Journal of Mobile Media, 6*(3). Retrieved June 14, 2019, from http://wi.mobilities.ca/tweeting-out-a-tyrant-social-media-and-the-tunisian-revolution/

Fraleigh, D. (2018). The Tunisian revolution: A social movement of courage assisted by social media. In Julie Dee (Ed.), *From Tahrir Square to Gezi Park: Social networks as facilitators of social movements* (pp. 3–18). New York, NY: Peter Lang Publishing.

Gall, C. (2014, May 13). Tunisian discontent reflected in protests that have idled mines. *The New York Times*. Retrieved July 28, 2019, from https://www.nytimes.com/2014/05/14/world/africa/tunisian-discontent-reflected-in-protests-that-have-idled-mines.html

Gana, N. (Ed.) (2013). *The making of the Tunisian revolution: Contexts, architects, prospects*. Edinburgh, England: Edinburgh University Press.

Gantin, K. & Seddik, O. (2008, July). Revolt of the "people of mines" in Tunisia. *Le Monde Diplomatique*. Retrieved August 04, 2019, from https://www.monde-diplomatique.fr/2008/07/GANTIN/16061

Guellali, A. (2017, October 2). New reconciliation law threatens Tunisia's democracy. *Human Rights Watch*. Retrieved August 04, 2019, from https://www.hrw.org/news/2017/10/02/new-reconciliation-law-threatens-tunisias-democracy

Mullenbach, M. J. (n.d.). French Tunisia (1881–1956). *University of Central Arkansas, Dynamic Analysis of Dispute Management (DADM) Project*. Retrieved May 7, 2019, from https://uca.edu/politicalscience/dadm-project/middle-eastnorth-africapersian- gulf-region/french-tunisia-1881-1956/

Pérez-Altable, L. & Blanco, S. (2016). Social movements and network analysis in Tunisia before the Arab Spring. *Hipertext.net, 14*, 1–21. doi: 10.2436/20.8050.01.30

Saidani, M. (2018, October 25). A decade of social movements in Tunisia: Review and prospectus. Report presented at Conference of the Research Initiative: Social Movements in the Global Age, Paris, France. Retrieved May 14, 2019, from http://www.fmsh.fr/en/college-etudesmondiales/29614

Souissi, Z. (2017, May 15). In marginalized south Tunisia, unrest over gas tests government. *Reuters*. Retrieved August 05, 2019, from https://www.reuters.com/article/us-tunisia-protests/in-marginalized-south-tunisia-unrest-over-gas-tests-government-idUSKCN18B0VA

Tarrow, S. G. (1998). *Power in movement: Social movements and contentious politics*. Cambridge, England: Cambridge University Press.

Tunisian police shoot at demonstrators. (2008, June 7). *France24*. Retrieved August 04, 2019, from https://www.france24.com/en/20080607-tunisia-police-shoot-demonstrators-protests-unemployment

Walton, J. K., & Seddon, D. (2008). *Free markets and food riots: The politics of global adjustment*. Hoboken, NJ: John Wiley & Sons.

Zayani, M. (2015). *Networked publics and digital connection: The politics of everyday life in Tunisia*. Oxford, England: Oxford University Press.

12 Politico-Cultural Context of Tunisia

Tunisia, a country with a population of 11.516 million (98% Muslim) is seen and celebrated as the birthplace of the Arab Spring revolutions that have sparked political activism across the Muslim world since 2010 (CIA, 2019b; Ghannam, 2011; Harb, 2011; Lynch, 2013; Mir, 2011; World Bank, 2018). Known for its liberal policies toward women in contrast to other Arab states, Tunisia gained its independence from France in 1956 (Charrad & Zarrugh, 2014; CIA, 2019b). From its independence until December 2010, two dictators ruled the country and dominated the country's politics. Habib Bourguiba ruled for 31 years, until he was overthrown by Zine el Abidine Ben Ali. Ben Ali ruled Tunisia for 24 years and dominated the country's politics up until the Jasmine Revolution of 2010 (CIA, 2019b; Fraleigh, 2018; Zayani, 2015).

Located in Northern Africa, Tunisia borders the Mediterranean Sea, between Algeria and Libya. According to the CIA Factbook (2019b) country profile, in terms of ethnic representation, 98% of Tunisians are Arab. The country's official language is Arabic, but French is another widely spoken and understood language in Tunisia. Since Tunisia was colonized by France from 1881 to 1956, the French influence on the country's language, food and culture remains dominant (Mullenbach, n.d.; Zayani, 2015). Unlike other North African and Arab countries, Tunisia has a high literacy rate and a strong middle-class. Neither Islamist groups nor political Islam played a significant role in the country's recent revolution for change (Mir, 2011). It may be mentioned here that high numbers of educated, unemployed youth was among one of the primary reasons that Tunisia, as compared to other Arab nations, witnessed relatively stronger and more organized political activism. These middle-class, young university degree holders were well-versed about the world around them and were quick to adopt new modes of information sharing and communication when the Internet was debuted in the country in 1996 (Freedom House, 2018).

Ben Ali's Business Empire & WikiLeaks Contribution to the Jasmine Revolution

Despite Tunisia's success in bringing in foreign investment and developing a flourishing tourism industry, the country failed to transfer economic prosperity to educated but unemployed youth because of corruption and nepotism (Ghannam, 2011). Since Ben Ali and his "extended family of about 140 people" (Fraleigh, 2018, p. 6) had direct interests in business and investments, the president kept introducing and implementing controversial laws and regulations that benefitted his family and close allies (Dreisbach & Joyce, 2014). Once the revolution was over and independent investigations about Ben Ali and his family's empire began, Tunisia and the world started to learn more of the alarming details about the former president's convoluted business interests:

Looking at 220 companies owned by family members [of Ben Ali] that were seized by Tunisian authorities after the regime fell, the World Bank determined that while the firms accounted for only three percent of economic output, they controlled 21% of net private sector profits (Dreisbach & Joyce, 2014, para. 4).

Ben Ali's direct and indirect business empire included interests and holdings ranging from luxury brand cars to mining industry kickbacks, shares in media industry, assets in the private education sector, investments in the sports world, cell phones and the mobile banking industry, to name a few (Dreisbach & Joyce, 2014; Fraleigh, 2018; Zayani, 2015).

It is believed that the WikiLeaks revelations of Ben Ali's corruption played a huge role in fueling the revolution of 2010 because many Tunisians were able to easily access the information regarding their ruling elites online (Mir, 2011). To provide context, WikiLeaks, a whistleblower website, released a set of 10 diplomatic cables in November of 2010, just a month before Mohamed Bouazizi's attempted suicide (Azzam, 2011; Sanina, 2011; Sullivan & Pérez-Peña, 2019;

Zayani 2015). These confidential cables—compiled by the U.S. Embassy in Tunis between January 2006 and June 2009—labeled Ben Ali and his family a "quasi-mafia" family involved in mega corruption projects (Sanina, 2011). One of the leaked cables from 2008 said, "Whether it's cash, services, land, property, or yes, even your yacht, President [Zine el Abidine] Ben Ali's family is rumored to covet it and reportedly gets what it wants" (Azzam, 2018, para. 3). The stories about Ben Ali and his family's involvement in nepotism and corrupt practices had already been circulated in smaller circles of Tunisian society well before the WikiLeaks revelations. But because of his absolute control over the mass media of the country, Ben Ali had managed to control the narrative in his favor. None of the traditional media platforms in Tunisia had ever challenged Ben Ali's misuse of power and shady involvement in taking kickbacks from foreign companies for awarding contracts in the mining districts of Southern Tunisia, a place where poverty and unemployment were at its peak. The WikiLeaks revelations immediately broke open this private sphere in Tunisian society. The people of Tunisia who were already on the Internet and were obsessed with using this platform for entertainment and communication purposes found this news about their leader's direct and indirect involvements in corruption. The details provided by WikiLeaks supported their doubts, which they already had in mind about Ben Ali and his family. Soon after the WikiLeaks revelations about Ben Ali started to flood social media, Tunisians broke their decades-old silence and started to comment, share, like/dislike these pieces of information on the social media platforms, without even bothering with what their traditional media outlets had to say.

In other words, Tunisians were already realizing the power of social media and the Internet in their hands. They could not only react to an issue important to them, but also be a part of online activism, which was far more efficient than the private sphere of information sharing that Tunisians had been maintaining for so long. Therefore, the WikiLeaks revelations to Tunisians not only informed the society about the corrupt practices of their president but set the tone for a revolution that was about to follow. In addition to several other shocking revelations pertaining to the U.S. and global affairs, these documents also released details about a "secret 2009 cable by U.S. Ambassador Robert Godec … which classified Tunisia as 'a police state, with little freedom of expression or association, and serious human rights problems' " (Fraleigh, 2018, p. 5).

It may be noted that when WikiLeaks broke the news about Ben Ali's corruption, Tunisia was going through major economic challenges. The government's promises to provide jobs to educated youth were not being fulfilled, and the middle class had already started to get frustrated with the regime and its false commitments. Even the post-revolution Tunisia continues to portray a bleak picture of the country's economic sector. According to some statistics, the national unemployment rate in the country rose from 13% (pre-Jasmine Revolution) to 15.5% (after the Jasmine Revolution), and more than 15.5% of the population was still living under the poverty line, even when the revolution was over (Barnell, 2017; CIA, 2019b). Discriminatory economic policies and unemployment among educated youth were among two of the most important factors that contributed to the political unrests and uprisings in Tunisia in 2010–11. However, as I have mentioned earlier, almost nine years after the Jasmine Revolution, the situation has yet to improve in the country. Contrary to the expectations of the Tunisian protesters who risked their lives for a better tomorrow, the country has yet to enjoy a better economic, political and social environment. For example, in the post-revolutionary era, the youth employment rate of Tunisia rose to 36%, which is more than double the national average of 15.5% (Reguly, 2019; The World Bank, 2018), but the "laws that rigged the system, however, remain" (Dreisbach & Joyce, 2014, para. 22).

Ben Ali's Control over the Judiciary

The Ben Ali regime had a system of control in place that not only kept the mass media under its absolute control, but the judiciary as well. In any country, a free and independent judiciary is the biggest threat to monarchs and dictators. Ben Ali knew it well and that is why he made sure that throughout his tenure, the judicial branch was among least of his problems. Under his presidency, "[t]he judicial system was used as a tool for prosecuting members of opposition parties, along with labor leaders, reporters, students, and human rights advocates" (Fraleigh, 2018, p. 6). The regime established a system of rewards and punishments for the judges: "Judges who failed to follow orders could be denied promotions and find themselves transferred to jurisdictions away from their homes" (Fraleigh, 2018, p. 6). Others were rewarded with promotions, and in some cases, kickbacks (Aleya-Sghaier, 2012; Angrist, 2013; Fraleigh, 2018). It is interesting to note that a similar phenomenon of judicial control was observed in the cases of Pakistan and Egypt. These dictatorial regimes adopted similar tactics to make sure that the judicial branch could never be autonomous enough to start questioning the ruling elite. Therefore, based on the analysis of the politico-cultural contexts of the three countries under investigation, we can argue that dictatorial and tyrannical regimes flourish on the shoulders of three branches: judiciary, journalism, and generals. If any of these three tries to deviate from the path of maintaining the status quo or gains autonomy, the regime is destined to be threatened and may be overturned. In Ben Ali's case, the judiciary and generals (military and security forces) were not a problem, but journalism slipped away from his clutches, thanks to the power of social media and citizen journalism that bridged the void during the political uprisings of 2010–11.

Controlled Privatization of Media under Ben Ali

The country's entire broadcasting system was directly owned and operated by the government until 2003 (Fraleigh, 2018). Tunisians were very clear about mass media's disappointing role whenever it came to highlight the issues of common people. They knew that the broadcasting network of Tunisia was just a mouthpiece of Ben Ali and his machinery. The level of distrust in their own media forced Tunisian audiences to look for alternative sources of information. Tunisians began using the Internet to access Al Jazeera online and French news organizations. They quickly started embracing these outside sources more than their own media. Such a shift in audience behavior and the availability of choice forced Ben Ali to allow "some space for private sector broadcasting" (Fraleigh, 2018, p. 7) in the country. This controlled privatization of media, however, was another attempt to control the narrative of the government on broadcast media platforms. Ben Ali's extended family was given exclusive opportunities to invest and own some of the popular media outlets. For example, Ben Ali's "son-in-law Mohamed Sakhr al-Materi owned *Radio Zitouna* and Belhassen Trabelsi, his brother-in-law, owned the holding company which controlled *Radio Mosaique*. Ben Ali's daughter and his private doctor's son directed two other FM stations" (Fraleigh, 2018, p. 8). Such a manipulation of the private media sector left little-to-no room for independent voices to flourish even on private platforms.

Ben Ali and his family used their control of the country's mass media sector to promote their business interests. These vested and financial interests in the media sector started to become more damaging to the society when:

> The Ben Ali family's financial interests intersected with restrictions on public expression. Tunis-based radio and TV stations, in addition to newspapers and magazines, were at least part-owned by a member of the family. El-Materi, the car dealership-owning son-in-law, also owned Radio Zitouna. (Dreisbach & Joyce, 2014, para. 18)

After the revolution was over and the newly appointed government started to confiscate and liquidate Ben Ali and his family's properties and investments, one of the most "[p]opular radio station Mosaique FM was also confiscated as a Ben Ali family asset" (Dreisbach & Joyce, 2014, para. 18).

Tunisians Distrust over the Country's Traditional Media

Since the entire Tunisian media was connected to the regime of Ben Ali, Tunisians did not trust their country's media. International sources of information, such as France 24 and Al Jazeera, carried far more weight in the forming of public opinion than local news sources (Mir 2011). The country banned Al Jazeera several times before and during the revolution. In 2009, when the Arab TV network decided to host opposition leaders during Tunisian presidential elections, Tunisia suspended its diplomatic relations with Qatar as a mark of protest. During the Arab Spring revolution, the Ben Ali government canceled Al Jazeera's license and arrested its staff.

Likewise, when the Tunisian street vendor attempted to commit suicide by burning himself in front of a government building, Tunisian state media completely ignored the incident "until four days after the event [, when] the national media reported on the protests, and then it was only to condemn them" (Zayani, 2015, p. 184). Just like in the past, Tunisians did not trust the narrative of their state media and turned to foreign news networks to get a better picture about what was happening on the streets of Sidi Bouzid, the Tunisian city where Bouazizi was from. This time, Al Jazeera did not disappoint them: "Relying extensively on user-generated information circulated on the social web, Al Jazeera latched onto the events in Tunisia, positioning itself as a leading source of news" (Zayani, 2015, p. 185). Such a scenario helps us understand two things. First, Tunisians did not get hooked to the storytelling power of social media because they were in love with it, but, in fact, their history of distrust towards their own traditional media outlets left Tunisians with no choice but to find alternatives. Second, any traditional media, including television, radio and print, that was not directly or indirectly connected to the Ben Ali regime, carried more respect and trust in the hearts of Tunisians. Further, for the very first time in the history of the region, not only in Tunisia, Al Jazeera was there to tell the story of their grievances in their own language, Arabic. Moving forward in the post-revolutionary era, it remains to be seen whether Tunisian mass media will ever be able to earn back the trust it lost decades ago among Tunisians. In other words, Tunisian mass media has a long walk to walk in order to gain the support and viewership/readership of its people. The newly adopted Tunisian Constitution, which reveals a judiciary role in interpreting the provisions of free speech and assembly in the Constitution and the level of support for the opening of independent private media outlets, are among some of the factors that will determine whether Tunisians will trust their own media.

Constitutional Framework of Free Speech in Tunisia

In order to better understand the politico-cultural context of Tunisia, it is important to revisit the country's constitutional framework of free speech, freedom of media and basic human rights. This will help us contextualize the events that unfolded in the overthrow of two of the post-revolutionary dictators, Bourguiba and Ben Ali.

The 1988 Constitution of Tunisia (amended) provides the country with "no freedom of information law and citizens have little access to the government's financial information" (Freedom House, 2011, para. 53). Only the Article 8 of the Constitution refers to terms such as freedom of opinion, expression and the press. However, Article 8 spends more time and space on discussing the roles and expectations of political parties in the country, rather than providing a comprehensive definition of the terms related to individual and press freedom. According to Article 8:

> Freedom of opinion, expression, the press, publication, assembly and association are guaranteed and exercised according to the terms defined by the law. The right to organize in trade unions is guaranteed. Political parties contribute to supervising citizens, in order to organize their participation in political life, and they should be established on democratic foundations. Political parties must respect the sovereignty of the people, the values of the republic, human rights, and the principles pertaining to personal status. Political parties pledge to prohibit all forms of violence, fanaticism, racism and discrimination. No political party may take religion, language, race, sex or region as the foundation for its principles, objectives, activity or programs. It is prohibited for any party to be dependent upon foreign parties or interests. The law sets the rules governing the establishment and organization of parties. (WIPO, n.d.)

Since the 1988 Constitution was not enough to guarantee basic freedoms of speech, expression and freedom of media for the society, participants in the

Jasmine Revolution of 2010–11 demanded to amend or introduce a new Constitution to the country. Freedom House and the Committee to Protect Journalists are among two of the most prestigious thinktanks that gauge country-specific civil liberties and the state of media freedom and the freedom of expression every year. According to the Freedom House reports issued during and after 1994, Tunisia was consistently rated between #11 and #12 "on a scale from 2 (most free) to 14 (least free)" (Fraleigh, 2018, p. 5), under the Ben Ali regime. Likewise, the Committee to Protect Journalists included Ben Ali's name as among " 'Top Ten Enemies of the Press' list" (Fraleigh, 2018, p. 5), in addition to describing the country as the worst place to be a blogger in 2009, just a year before the Tunisian revolution unfolded.

Once the revolution was over and Ben Ali had already fled the country to seek refuge in Saudi Arabia, the new interim government of Tunisia, led by the Islamist Ennahda party, proposed a new Constitution (Fraleigh, 2018). In January 2014, almost three years after the Tunisian revolution, the new Constitution was adopted by the legislative assembly (Fraleigh, 2018). At that time, it was believed that, if adopted, the new Constitution would have better provisions for the freedom of the media and individual freedoms in the country (Freedom House, 2012; Gall, 2014). Despite the fact that the newly proposed Constitution was passed and adopted by the Tunisian government on January 26, 2014, its promises of freedom of media and individual freedoms are still debatable (DIHR, 2018; Guellali, 2017; Hofmann, 2014).

The newly adopted Constitution of 2014 dedicates Articles 31 and 32 specifically to freedom of expression and free access to information as basic rights of Tunisian citizens. According to the Article 31 of the Constitution, "Freedom of opinion, thought, expression, information and publication shall be guaranteed. These freedoms shall not be subject to prior censorship" ("Tunisia's Constitution," 2019, p. 7). Taking these freedoms further, Article 32 states, "The state guarantees the right to information and the right of access to information and communication networks" ("Tunisia's Constitution," p. 8). In addition to these, Articles 19, 24, 33, 35 and 37 are also about the individual's freedoms, their privacy rights, political participation rights including the rights to assemble, and peaceful demonstrations.

Despite the fact that these constitutional freedoms are guaranteed in the newly adopted Tunisian Constitution, the reality on the ground tells us a different story in post-Ben Ali Tunisia. According to a report issued by the Freedom House in 2017, journalists continue to face threats and interference by the country's security forces. Some journalists are being punished by military courts, while others are losing their jobs as a result of low or no salaries (Freedom House, 2017). The report adds:

> In a January 2016 speech, President Beji Caid Essebsi blamed journalists and media outlets for amplifying social turmoil in the country as demonstrators protested persistent unemployment. Such hostile rhetoric from senior officials during the year indirectly encouraged arrests and other mistreatment of reporters. Between September and November, journalists Jamel Arfaoui, Mohamed Naem Haj Mansour, and Rached Khiari were arrested and charged by military prosecutors with insulting the armed forces. (Freedom House, 2017, para. 6)

This trend in post-revolutionary Tunisia does not send an encouraging message to the rest of the world, let alone to other countries in the Middle East where the Tunisian example is seen and celebrated as the most successful one. Furthermore, even though the new Tunisian Constitution is perhaps the only Constitution in the Muslim world that guarantees the rights and freedoms of future generations of Tunisians, the country has yet to introduce and implement such laws and regulations to carry out the Constitutional philosophy. For example, although the new Constitution "includes guarantees of freedom of speech, assembly, and association" (Fraleigh, 2018, p. 17), it leaves several grey areas where these freedoms can be curbed "based on 'national defense,' 'public health or public morals,' and 'public order' " (Fraleigh, 2018, p. 17). These exceptions to freedom of speech, expression and collective action contain enough room for the current and future governments to curb people's basic rights in the name of "national defense" and/or "public order." Tunisia has witnessed such cloak-and-dagger tactics by the regimes of the past. Only time will tell us whether the country goes through more eras of censorship and hurdles in the pursuit of free expression. In order to achieve a genuine openness and a positive change in the society, stakeholders from all walks of life should be brought on the table. A Tunisian law scholar explains it this way:

> Such a task demands a reconsideration of the broader group of inequitable legislative texts addressing various segments of society (children, youth, women)—texts that do not reflect the desired development model. According to the Constitution, this should be based upon participatory democracy, "good governance", "balance between regions", and "the proper exploitation of national resources." (Ferchichi, 2017)

In addition to the lack of Constitutional guarantees for free speech, Tunisia's penal and press codes "contain broadly-worded articles that provide prison terms of up to five years and fines for various types of peaceful speech, notably speech deemed defamatory toward individuals but also toward state institutions and speech deemed liable to disturb the public order or harm Tunisia's image" (Goldstein, 2011, para. 29). Several international organizations working on human rights and media freedom are skeptical of the post-revolutionary government's level of sincerity to ensure media freedom in the country, particularly when the Tunisian Press Code continues to be used against its citizens:

> Outdated press and penal codes continue to restrict expression in the media sector. For example, on March 28, 2012, Ghazi Mohamed Beji and Jaber Ben Abdallah Majri were sentenced to seven-year prison terms and heavy fines for "mocking Islam" on Facebook and other social media websites. Alarmingly, the government has remained silent on violent encounters between Salafists and the police, as well as Salafist attacks on secular activists and academics. (Freedom House, 2012, p. 6)

This Freedom House report that came out only within two years of the revolution, highlights two important issues: First, the freedom of media and individual expression were not welcomed in the post-revolution Tunisia. Second, just like its predecessors, the newly founded government also retained the same old tactic of using religion, national interests and the country's security as tools to silence social media activists in the country.

Tunisian Media before & after the Revolution

In light of this discussion on Tunisian Constitutional provisions on media freedom and the functioning of Tunisian press and penal codes, we will take an in-depth look at the media situation in Tunisia before and after the revolution, particularly what has changed after the country got its new Constitution, which, as compared to past Constitutions, provides more freedoms and protections for expression and free speech.

During the earlier phase of post-revolutionary Tunisia, when the country was still going through multiple transitions of political leadership and the new Constitution was still being debated, no significant change was observed in the traditional media landscape. According to data provided by the Dubai Press Club's (2013) annual *Arab Media Outlook* report, Tunisia had 10 daily newspapers with a total daily circulation of 399,000. As for electronic media, the total television penetration rate in the country was 92.5%, all from satellite. The broadband penetration in the country was 24%, which, at that time, was much higher than Egypt's broadband penetration rate (only 7.4%). More than 18% of the Tunisian population had a Facebook account, in addition to having easy access to smartphones and computers (Mir, 2011). Also, the mobile phone penetration rate for Tunisia was 87%, higher than its next-door neighbor Egypt's 72% (Dubai Press Club, 2013; MBRF & UNDP/RBAS, 2009).

According to the most recent statistics provided by *Internet World Stats* in 2019, a little over 67% of the Tunisian population is using the Internet, and the Facebook penetration rate was recorded as 54.9%, which is many times higher than what it was during the Tunisian uprisings of 2010–11. Just like the Internet, Tunisian mobile phone usage in the post-revolutionary era also went up. By November 2017, the mobile phone penetration rate was recorded as 93% ("Major African," n.d.). Despite the fact that Tunisia dominated in cellphone and Internet penetration rates among the Arab states before and after the Tunisian uprisings, the country's mass media were predominantly controlled by the government even after the revolution was over. As for the broadcast media situation in post-revolutionary Tunisia, the most updated page of CIA World Factbook (retrieved in April 2019) does not provide a different picture from what was observed in pre-revolutionary Tunisia. According to the CIA Factbook report:

> [B]roadcast media is mainly government-controlled; the state-run Tunisian Radio and Television Establishment (ERTT) operates 2 national TV networks, several national radio networks, and a number of regional radio stations; 1 TV and 3 radio stations are privately owned and report domestic news stories directly from the official Tunisian news agency; the state retains control of broadcast facilities and transmitters through L'Office National de la Telediffusion; Tunisians also have access to Egyptian, pan-Arab, and European satellite TV channels. (CIA, 2019a)

As discussed earlier in this chapter, when Tunisia adopted its new Constitution in January 2014 with promises of freedoms of speech, expression and assembly, it was anticipated that the country's mass media would also witness a new era of freedom and objectivity where the traditional media outlets would serve as the Fourth Pillar of the state, rather than just serving the interests of the ruling elites. This was not the case, however. Within the few years of passing the new Constitution, the country's traditional media started to face hurdles and challenges, both from the government and pressure groups. Journalists who were covering security operations or were being critical of the government's controversial legislations were threatened, incarcerated, and, in some cases, were tried and sentenced in military courts ("Tunisia: Attack," 2018; "Tunisia tightens," 2017; Zayani, 2015). The ironhandedness of the Tunisian government was not only limited to the journalists working in traditional media outlets, but also it expanded its grip to the people involved in citizen journalism. One of such recent examples is of a Tunisian blogger, Yassine Ayari. In January of 2018, the "blogger and parliamentarian Yassine Ayari was tried in a military court for 'undermining the morale of the army' after a Facebook post in which he mocked the appointment of a senior military commander" ("Tunisia: Attack," 2018, para. 12). Not only this, singers and creative artists who had played an integral role in the overthrow of the Ben Ali regime, are also not safe in the post-revolutionary Tunisia. One such incident that was reported by Amnesty International describes:

> In July, singer Ahmed Ben Ahmed was assaulted by a group of police officers who had been assigned to protect him. The officers had been offended by Ben Ahmed's music, claiming that his songs insulted the police. A police union later filed a complaint before the Court of First Instance in the city of Mahdia against the artist, under the Penal Code crime of "insulting state officials." ("Tunisia: Attack," 2018, para. 13)

In order to raise their voice against the challenges to media freedom posed both by the government and the security agencies of the country, the National Syndicate of Tunisian Journalists organized a journalists' demonstration, which the Syndicate named a "Day of Anger" ("Tunisia: Attack," 2018). Despite these protests organized by journalists and human rights activists, Tunisia is seen to be headed toward adopting the same old practices that the previous two regimes invented. For example, in order to further limit the freedom of media, the Tunisian government proposed another controversial bill in July 2017. The proposed legislation known as "Repression of Attacks against Armed Forces" bill ("Tunisia: Proposed," 2017, para. 2) would not only provide impunity for security forces in the event they decide to use unnecessary lethal force, it also "includes provisions that could criminalize criticism of the security forces, including for human rights abuses" ("Tunisia: Attack," 2018, para. 14). It is believed that this proposed law would specifically target media professionals and whistleblowers on social media platforms.

Tunisian Internet Agency (ATI)

Even though dictatorships and authoritarian regimes are least flexible to change or adaptation when it comes to maintaining their hegemony over the masses, almost all tyrants are quick to adopt new means and tactics when dealing with information and communication networks. Ben Ali's regime was no different in this regard. Soon after the Internet made its debut in Tunisia in 1996, Ben Ali directed his focus to devise new laws and regulations to control this new medium. In order to instrumentalize the telecommunication infrastructure in the country, the Ben Ali regime established the Tunisian Internet Agency (ATI) in March 1996 (Eko, 2012). The ATI, which was the principal Internet Service Provider (ISP) in Tunisia, operated under the Ministry of Information and Communication Technologies, and had an absolute monopoly over the functioning of the Internet (Eko, 2012).

In the beginning, the government perceived the Internet and social media platforms as mere tools of entertainment and probably a nice way out for unemployed educated youth to kill their time on digital platforms, rather than complaining about the government's policies. In other words, the Internet and social media in societies like Tunisia, Egypt and Pakistan were seen as tools for entertainment and distraction, rather than a political threat to the system. That is why, during the introductory phase of the Internet in such countries as Tunisia, legislations to regulate these alternate forms of media were relaxed in nature, when compared to the traditional media. This relatively softer treatment on the part of the government, however, did not last long. Soon after social media started to criticize and highlight Ben Ali and his family's unethical practices, the Internet became the prime target to ban free speech (Howard et al., 2011). One particular incident that served as a catalyst for the government's anger against the Internet and social media is described below:

> The president [Ben Ali] was particularly angered after a video surfaced in 2007 showing his wife, Leila Trabelsi, making personal use of the presidential plane to visit prestigious shopping locations in Europe. From that point in time forward, YouTube, Facebook, and other sites were blocked for extended periods of time. (Fraleigh, 2018, p. 9)

Such activism over the Internet, causing embarrassment to the ruling family, paved the way for a new era of censorship and control primarily on the common citizens' use of the alternate media, so as to ward off any such incident in the future. In order to speed up the process of gaining control over the Internet and social media, the government did not bother to write new laws exclusively for the Internet, rather the "same laws that constrained the print media were extended to the Internet" (Fraleigh, 2018, p. 8).

The practice of control and censorship over the Internet and associated social media was multiplied manifold during the Tunisian Spring, commonly referred to as the Jasmine Revolution. The Ben Ali regime started blocking YouTube, The Daily Motion, blog sites, Facebook, and other digital communications networks to control the rapidly spreading anger and animosity of Tunisians toward the regime. For example, "[s]ecurity officials at Facebook discovered that Tunisian Internet Service Providers were using malware codes to steal passwords and other login information when Tunisians attempted to access that site" (Fraleigh, 2018, p. 10). Not only this, since the Tunisian government was the sole Internet Service Provider (ISP) in the country, it banned a number of sites including "some free electronic mail services like Hotmail as well as human rights organizations like Amnesty International, the Committee to Protect Journalists, the International Human Rights Federation, and Reporters Without Borders" (Eko 2012, p. 134), well before the political uprisings of Tunisia.

Conclusion

In post-revolution Tunisia, even though the Ministry of Information that used to control media has been abolished, controversial media laws such as the Press Code and the Penal Code continue to exist (Fraleigh, 2018; Mir 2011; Zayani, 2015). Similarly, *Agence Tunisienne d'Internet* (ATI) (Tunisian Internet Agency) established during Ben Ali's regime in 1996, continues to monopolize and control Internet traffic in the country even after the revolution, and new, stricter laws are being proposed by the post-revolution government to curb most of the freedoms that the country had just started to enjoy after it adopted a new Constitution in 2014.

Furthermore, it is interesting to note that just like Pakistan and Egypt, Tunisia also witnessed similar cloak-and-dagger policies by its authoritarian rulers. The country's security forces (about 130,000) were trained and deployed to maintain the regime's control over its citizens, not to protect their fundamental rights. Likewise, the Tunisian judiciary was not more than a rubber stamp authority to serve and protect the interests of the ruling elites, rather than upholding the constitutional rights of its citizens. Also, freedom of expression and freedom of media in Tunisia were among the worst in world rankings. Although, all of the tactics of control prolonged the stay of Ben Ali and his cronies in power, they could not stop the tsunami of the people's collective action, which was brought forward by the power of social media in the hands of young educated Tunisians, who were determined to see a better tomorrow for themselves and their future generations. Despite the growing pains of an emerging democracy, the people of Tunisia are now aware of the power they hold to keep their government accountable. Even if authoritarian rule comes to the country again, things will never be the same because the people have realized the power of their collective action.

References

Aleya-Sghaier, A. (2012). The Tunisian revolution: The revolution of dignity. *Journal of Middle East & Africa*, *3*(1), 18–45. Doi: https://doi.org/10.1080/21520844.2012.675545

Angrist, M. P. (2013). Understanding the success of mass civic protest in Tunisia. *Middle East Journal*, *67*(4), 547–564. doi: https://doi.org/10.3751/67.4.13

Azzam, M. (2011, January 18). Opinion: How WikiLeaks helped fuel Tunisian revolution. *CNN*. Retrieved June 09, 2019, from http://www.cnn.com/2011/OPINION/01/18/tunisia.wikileaks/index.html

Barnell, O. (2017, December 17). Seven years after Arab Spring revolt, Tunisia's future remains uncertain. *France 24*. Retrieved August 14, 2019, from https://www.france24.com/en/20171217-tunisia-seven-years-after-arab-spring-revolution-protests-economic-uncertainty

Central Intelligence Agency (CIA). (2019a, April 7). Tunisia: Broadcast media. In *The World Factbook*. Retrieved August 14, 2019, from https://www.cia.gov/library/publications/the-world-factbook/geos/ts.html

Central Intelligence Agency (CIA). (2019b, May 15). Tunisia: The World Factbook. Retrieved May 17, 2019, from https://www.cia.gov/library/publications/the-world-factbook/geos/ts.html

Charrad, M. M., & Zarrugh, A. (2014). Equal or complementary? Women in the new Tunisian Constitution after the Arab Spring. The Journal of North African Studies, 19(2), 230–243. Retrieved May 26, 2019, from https://www.tandfonline.com/doi/abs/10.1080/13629387.2013.857276

Danish Institute for Human Rights (DIHR). (2018). *Study of state actors in the Tunisian human rights system*. Retrieved July 15, 2019, from https://www.humanrights.dk/sites/humanrights.dk/files/media/researchpublications/downloads/tunis-rapport-version_english.pdf

Dreisbach, T. & Joyce, R. (2014, March 27). Revealing Tunisia's corruption under Ben Ali. *Al Jazeera*. Retrieved June 09, 2019, from https://www.aljazeera.com/indepth/features/2014/03/revealing-tunisia-corruption-under-ben-ali-201432785825560542.html

Dubai Press Club. (2013). *Arab media outlook 2009–2013: Inspiring local content*. (3rd. Ed). Retrieved August 18, 2019, from https://fas.org/irp/eprint/arabmedia.pdf

Eko, L. (2012). *New media, old regimes: Case studies in comparative communication law and policy*. Lanham, MD: Lexington Books.

Ferchichi, W. (2017, July 27). The new Tunisian Constitution: A reading into the rights of future generations. *Heinrich Böll Stiftung*. Retrieved August 04, 2019, from https://tn.boell.org/en/2017/07/27/new-tunisian-constitution-reading-rights-future-generations

Fraleigh, D. (2018). The Tunisian revolution: A social movement of courage assisted by social media. In Julie Dee (Ed.), *From Tahrir Square to Gezi Park: Social networks as facilitators of social movements* (pp. 3–18). New York, NY: Peter Lang Publishing.

Freedom House. (2011). Tunisia: Countries at the Crossroads, 2011. Retrieved March 24, 2019, from https://freedomhouse.org/report/countries-crossroads/2011/tunisia

Freedom House. (2012). Tunisia: Countries at the Crossroads, 2012. Retrieved March 24, 2019, from https://freedomhouse.org/sites/default/files/Tunisia%20-%20FINAL_1.pdf

Freedom House. (2017). Freedom of the Press 2017: Tunisia Profile. Retrieved July 18, 2019, from https://freedomhouse.org/report/freedom-press/2017/tunisia

Freedom House (2018). Tunisia: Country Profile. Retrieved July 18, 2019, from https://freedomhouse.org/report/freedom-net/2018/tunisia

Gall, C. (2014, January 14). Tunisian Constitution, praised for balance, nears passage. *The New York Times*. Retrieved May 14, 2019, from https://www.nytimes.com/2014/01/15/world/africa/tunisian-constitution-praised-for-balance-nears-passage.html

Ghannam, J. (2011). Social media in the Arab world: Leading up to the uprisings of 2011. *Center for international media assistance, 3*(1), 1–44. Retrieved February 10, 2019, from http://www.cima.ned.org/wp-content/uploads/2011/02/Ghannam-Jeffrey-Arab_Social_Media-Report-10-25-11.pdf

Goldstein, E. (2011, December 16). Tunisia's repressive laws: The reform agenda. *Human Rights Watch*. Retrieved April 29, 2018, from https://www.hrw.org/report/2011/12/16/tunisias-repressive-laws/reform-agenda#page

Guellali, A. (2017, October 2). New reconciliation law threatens Tunisia's democracy. *Human Rights Watch*. Retrieved August 01, 2019, from https://www.hrw.org/news/2017/10/02/new-reconciliation-law-threatens-tunisias-democracy

Harb, Z. (2011). Arab revolutions and the social media effect. *M/C Journal, 14*(2). Retrieved October 23, 2019, from http://journal.media-culture.org.au/index.php/mcjournal/article/view/364Two

Hofmann, K. (2014, May 2). Assessing Tunisia's new Constitution. *Democracy International*. Retrieved August 19, 2019, from https://www.democracy-international.org/assessing-tunisias-new-constitution

Howard, P. N., Duffy, A., Freelon, D., Hussain, M., Mari, W., & Mazaid, M. (2011). Opening closed regimes: What was the role of social media during the Arab Spring? *Project on Information Technology & Political Islam* [working paper]. Retrieved May 06, 2019, from https://deepblue.lib.umich.edu/bitstream/handle/2027.42/117568/2011_Howard-Duffy-Freelon-Hussain-Mari-Mazaid_PITPI.pdf?sequence=1&isAllowed=y

Internet World Stats (2019, April 8). Africa. Retrieved May 16, 2019, from https://internetworldstats.com/africa.htm#tn

Julian Assange: Wikileaks co-founder arrested in London. (2019, April 11). *BBC News*. Retrieved April 20, 2019, from https://www.bbc.com/news/uk-47891737

Lynch, M. (2013). *The Arab uprising: The unfinished revolutions of the new Middle East*. New York, NY: Public Affairs.

Major African Mobile Markets: Tunisia. (n.d.) *African Telecoms News*. Retrieved May 17, 2019, from https://www.africantelecomsnews.com/resources/AfricaOpp_Tunisia.html

Mir, J. (2011). Political and media transitions in Tunisia: A snapshot of media policy and regulatory environment. *Internews Report.*
Mohammed bin Rashid Al Maktoum Foundation (MBRF) & United Nations Development Programme/Regional Bureau for Arab States (UNDP/RBAS). (2009). *Arab Knowledge Report 2009.* Retrieved May 17, 2019, from https://www.undp.org/content/dam/rbas/report/ahdr/AKR2009-Eng-Full-Report.pdf
Mullenbach, M. J. (n.d.). French Tunisia (1881–1956). *University of Central Arkansas, Dynamic Analysis of Dispute Management (DADM) Project.* Retrieved May 7, 2019, from https://uca.edu/politicalscience/dadm-project/middle-eastnorth-africapersian-gulf-region/french-tunisia-1881-1956/
Reguly, E. (2019, March 19). In Tunisia, a youth crisis threatens the Arab Spring's only successful revolution. *The Globe And Mail.* Retrieved May 7, 2019, from https://www.theglobeandmail.com/world/article-in-tunisia-a-youth-crisis-threatens-the-arab-springs-only-successful/
Sanina, M. (2011, January 25). WikiLeaks cables help uncover what made Tunisians revolt. *PBS Newshour.* Retrieved June 01, 2019, from https://www.pbs.org/newshour/world/wikileaks-reveal-what-made-tunisians-revolt
Savage, C., Goldman, A., & Sullivan, E. (2019, April 11). Julian Assange arrested in London as U.S. unseals hacking conspiracy indictment. *The New York Times.* Retrieved April 13, 2019, from https://www.nytimes.com/2019/04/11/world/europe/julian-assange-wikileaks-ecuador-embassy.html?emc=edit_na_20190411&nl=breaking-news&nlid=69209290ing-news&ref=cta
Sullivan, E. & Pérez-Peña, R. (2019, April 11). Julian Assange charged by U.S. with conspiracy to hack a government computer. *The New York Times.* Retrieved April 13, 2019 from https://rivernetcomputers.com/julian-assange-charged-by-u-s-with-conspiracy-to-hack-a-government-computer/
Tunisia: Attack on freedom of expression must end. (2018, February 2). *Amnesty International.* Retrieved May 08, 2019, from https://www.amnesty.org/en/latest/news/2018/02/tunisia-attack-on-freedom-of-expression-must-end/
Tunisia: Proposed bill could give security forces carte blanche to use unnecessary lethal force. (2017, July 13). *Amnesty International.* Retrieved May 08, 2019, from https://www.amnesty.org/en/latest/news/2017/07/tunisia-proposed-bill-could-give-security-forces-carte-blanche-to-use-unnecessary-lethal-force/
Tunisia tightens restrictions on journalists, press freedom at risk—union. (2017, April 11). *Reuters.* Retrieved May 08, 2019, from https://www.reuters.com/article/us-tunisia-politics-censorship-idUSKBN17D1RQ
Tunisia's Constitution of 2014. (2019) *Constitute Project.* Retrieved May 08, 2019, from https://www.constituteproject.org/constitution/Tunisia_2014.pdf
World Bank (2018, April 16). Tunisia's economic outlook—April 2018. Retrieved May 24, 2019, from https://www.worldbank.org/en/country/tunisia/publication/economic-outlook-april-2018
World Intellectual Property Organization (WIPO). (n.d). *1955 Constitution of Tunisia.* Retrieved May 25, 2019, from https://www.wipo.int/edocs/lexdocs/laws/en/tn/tn028en.pdf
Zayani, M. (2015). *Networked publics and digital connection: The politics of everyday life in Tunisia.* Oxford, England: Oxford University Press.

Part V

What Happens Now?

The final part of this book is based on two chapters. Chapter 13, *Collective Memory: The Rise of Global Memories,* revisits the idea of collective memory in the field of media and communication and makes a case that the collective memory paradigm, which used to be a community, country or a culture specific approach, is now shifting. It is because of the Internet and associated social media tools of human communication that we are witnessing a new era of global memory themes, which are not static, but continue to be reshaped on digital media platforms. This phenomenon is resulting in the rise of global social movements where the idea of a *Collective We* is no more about the experiences of people located in a region or a country, but about the experiences of digitally connected global citizens.

Chapter 14, *Aftermath of Online Activism in Pakistan, Egypt & Tunisia,* is the concluding chapter of this book. After summarizing some of the common themes that were witnessed during the political unrests of the three countries, Pakistan, Egypt and Tunisia, the chapter looks at the most recent political uprisings of Sudan, Algeria and Morocco, and how these are connected to the previous movements of Pakistan, Egypt and Tunisia. The chapter puts forward an idea of *flash* social movements to better understand and study the changing dynamics of collective action on social media platforms. The chapter then concludes by providing a new model of collective action where the role of communication is provided as central, not peripheral, to social movements in the digital age.

13

Collective Memory: The Rise of Global Memories

This chapter explores the theoretical paradigm of collective memory in the field of media and communication and considers how the whole concept of collective memory is challenged when looking at the Arab uprisings. It discusses some of the Western cultural and ideological frames that were adopted and used by non-Western social protesters during the Arab Spring uprisings. The chapter makes a case that it was because of the emergence of social media that we have started to witness the formation and sustainability of global collective memories, rather than national and local ones. In this context, the chapter discusses the rise of the Internet and social media-based anonymous movements and the use of wider cultural icons to engage global audiences. The chapter also provides evidence of similar global memory themes that were utilized by later social movements such as: the Occupy Wall Street movement in the United States (2011), Gezi Park Protests in Turkey (2013) and protests in Brazil against the country's government corruption and spending before the world cup (2013). This chapter asserts that the information age continues to redefine existing media, communication and cultural approaches such as the concept of collective memory. I further argue that any current or future protests will utilize collective memory themes that are more global than local in nature because of social media and its outreach to global audiences. In other words, the social movements of the digital age utilize "glocal" memory themes that represent a combination of global and local collective memory themes, so as to attract and inspire potential sympathizers both at local and global fronts.

Revisiting the Concept of Collective Memory in Global Context

In order to understand the ideological underpinnings of collective memory and how it has contributed to political uprisings in the digital age—particularly during the Arab Spring—let's revisit some of the phenomenal works of social media and social movement scholars. The term, "collective memory" was first used by the European scholar Maurice Halbwachs (1992), and has since become associated with the field of psychology. The concept of collective memory was initially defined as the shared pool of information held in the memories of two or more members of a group (Coman, Brown, Koppel & Hirst, 2009; Olick & Robbins, 1998; Russell, 2006), but has now morphed into a complex phenomenon far broader than a fixed memory shared among only a few. Media and communication scholars now largely agree that collective memory can be shared, passed on and constructed both by small groups and large groups (Berkowitz, 2010; Birkner & Donk, 2018; Hoskin, 2011; Liu, 2018; Reading, 2011; Savage, 2007). In other words, collective memory refers to the common past that members of a community can associate with (Hoskin, 2011). Therefore, media and communication scholars have been obsessed with the idea of common pasts whenever looking at media practices from a collective memory approach. In journalistic terms, collective memory is a cultural tool that helps storytellers to predetermine how the story is supposed to go (Berkowitz 2010; Neiger, Meyers, & Zandber, 2011). This chapter, however, emphasizes the role of citizens as storytellers on social media platforms, thus making the cultural tool of collective memory a more complex phenomenon.

Historically, nation states, imagined communities and collective identities are also referred to in the idea of collective memory. Countries and nations also reassert the idea of collective memory through building monuments and memorials to a common past (Anderson, 1991; Berkowitz, 2010; Smith, 1991). While some of these theorizations of collective memory suggest rigidity and fixedness, French scholar Pierre Nora (1989; Nora & Kritzman, 1996), takes a different approach to the concept of collective memory. Nora looked at collective memory as a tool and an object of power that can be manipulated. He believed that memory is more than a fixed representation of the past. Rather, it is flexible and keeps morphing. Nora's definition of collective memory as being flexible provides an opportunity for scholars to revisit the concept—not as a fixed and unshakable common past, but as something that keeps on taking new shapes. Nora (1989) argues, "We speak so much of memory because there is so little of it left (p. 7)." He adds, modern societies invest so heavily in 'lieux de memoire' (memory sites, such as monuments, museums, archives, and historic places) because these have replaced real environments of memory (Nora, 1989).

According to some of the recent media scholarship, there are two kinds of processes involved in collective memory making: memory construction and memory selection. Memory selection refers to the process of pulling images and ideas from the a-historical past and is mostly used by advertisers to construct non-existent memories to sell their products. Memory construction, however, refers to the process of selecting some parts of the past while leaving the others (Neiger, Meyers, & Zandber, 2011). Furthermore, scholars interested in studying digital modes of communication argue that in the online media world audiences are equally involved in creating and reshaping of collective memory (Hoskin, 2011; Reading, 2011; Robinson, 2011). These scholars believe that in this "globital" world (a combination of global and digital), collective memory has become a porous, fluid phenomenon that keeps changing its significance. Hoskin (2011) argues that collective memory of digital media is different than that of the past, so we should call it "*connective* memory," instead. Hoskin's (2011) idea of connective memory also resonates with that of political science scholars studying social movements in the digital age, such as Bennett and Segerberg (2011), who present the logic of "connective action" in contentious political collective actions, including the Pakistani uprisings of 2007 and the wider Muslim uprisings of 2010–11. Highlighting the role of the Internet in storing and spreading collective memory themes during the Arab Spring uprisings, the scholars argue that the Internet has become "an often imperfect but easily accessible archive of action repertoires and software, presenting a dynamic memory of action for future perusal, inspiration and use" (p. 45). In other words, collective memory in this digital age is no more a concept that is determined by the common past of people in physical spaces, but by what gets archived on the Internet, social media and other digital spaces.

Another connection that the concept of collective memory seems to make is with Tarrow's (1998) theory of cultural and ideological frames, which protesters deploy to sustain their social movements against powerful elites. These cultural and ideological frames in Tarrow's theory about social movements, resonate with the mass media approach of collective memory. Recalling Tarrow's theory—which was discussed in Chapter 1 of this book—protesters in a social movement deploy their cultural and ideological themes to attract potential sympathizers to join the movement. These cultural and ideological frames, in fact, are representations of the collective past of a society where a social movement is taking place. In the light of this definition, if we agree that what gets archived on the Internet can also be considered as the collective memory of online users, then just like the idea of collective memory, Tarrow's cultural and ideological frames are also not stagnant or fixed, but are continuously morphing and taking new shapes on the digital platforms of human communication.

Looking at an incident involving the killing of an Iranian woman, Neda Agha-Soltan, by the Iranian state security forces, another scholar, Reading (2011), argues that the creation and dissemination of collective memories in the digital world is much different than the memories of the past. Neda Soltan was shot by Iranian security forces while she was protesting against then President Mahmoud Ahmadinejad. The whole incident was caught on someone's smartphone camera and was later uploaded on YouTube. The video of Neda's death went viral within minutes of its posting. The scholar compares this incident and how it got propagated on social media platforms with an incident of collective memory from the past. In this regard, after comparing the case of Neda Soltan (that took place in Iran on June 22, 2008) with the battle of Waterloo on the same date in 1865, Reading (2011) argues that because of digital (and social) media, the death of Neda Soltan was seen around the world almost instantly, and thus became a part of a global collective memory even though perhaps only a small number of people *actually* saw the incident. On the other hand, the Battle of Waterloo, even though it directly impacted many more people, took a much longer to become part of collective memory, and indeed may not even be part of a collective memory except for the countries and people who were directly involved. Today, social media platforms are not only involved in speeding up the process of collective memory creation, they are also expanding the reach of iconic memories to a much wider audience online. In other words, Reading (2011) also supports the idea of globital memories, which are the result of globalization and digitization of our everyday memories. The scholar concludes that as compared to the battle of Waterloo, the image of Neda's killing was witnessed in minutes around the world because of the global nature of the digital media.

Also, in the digital age, collective memories not only travel faster and reach wider audiences, such memories get a variety of interpretations simultaneously. For example, in the case of the Neda Soltan's viral video, her memory got different interpretations in different parts of the world. Her image was compared to the Statue of Liberty in the United States, while the same video for citizens in other Muslim countries such as Tunisia and Egypt, reminded them of their own grievances against their dictatorial regimes. Reading (2011) adds that it is because of the global nature of digital media that everyone can now create multiple interpretations of the same event. Thus, the collective memory is not static. Rather, it is porous and takes many shapes, which was not the case in the past.

V Masks as Global Memory Icons

The 2011 political uprisings frequently referred to as the Arab Spring are generators of iconic collective memory in our recent past. These historical events created unstoppable ripples in the stagnant political culture of the Arab region (Arif, 2018; Breuer, Landman & Farquhar, 2015; Khosrokhavar, 2016), and are continuing to affect change across the region. The common global perspective is that these political uprisings started in Tunisia in late 2010, when a Tunisian street vendor, Mohamed Bouazizi, doused himself with gasoline and self-immolated in protest against poor economic conditions and police brutality (Fraleigh, 2018, Harb, 2011; Mir, 2011, Zayani, 2015). This incident paved the way for online and offline (real world) political mobilization and protests in 18 Arab countries in North Africa and the Middle East (Ghannam, 2011). The spread of this online and offline activism points toward a new era of social movements and protests in the digital age and continues to unfold today. (For example, look at the Sudanese and Algerian Springs of 2019.) While looking back at what happened nine years ago in the Muslim-majority countries' landscape, throughout this chapter I would like to highlight an important theoretical paradigm of collective memory, which the majority of mass media scholars failed to recognize while trying to make sense of the unprecedented collective actions in the Arab region.

As I have discussed elsewhere, the term Arab Spring is unnecessarily limiting in scope because of its tendency to interpret the political insurrections that have taken place in many Muslim-majority countries only in the context of the Arabic-speaking Middle East. In fact, the political struggles of 2007 (Pakistan) and 2010–11 (Tunisia & Egypt) in Muslim-majority countries were part of a much bigger phenomenon than the Arab Spring. Social media archives such as YouTube offer us a wonderful opportunity to revisit and reevaluate memories of political activism in Pakistan, the Middle East and North African regions. If we carefully analyze the still and moving images of political protests coming out of these countries, it would be hard to ignore the stark similarities between some of the iconic images of the political uprisings erupting across the Muslim world.

In other words, through an in-depth analysis of the events that unfolded during and after the Arab Spring, it can be argued that political uprisings in the Muslim world were not country-, culture-, or region-specific; rather, they were part of a larger global phenomenon of social movements that continue to spring up around the world with slight variations. During this same period, political unrest has been occurring in both Muslim and non-Muslim countries but has been mostly overlooked as a global phenomenon because of the overuse of the term Arab Spring in academic, political and vernacular discourses. Examples of similar protests are the Occupy Wall Street movement of 2011 in the United States, the 2013 protests against bus-fare increases in Brazil, and the Gezi Park protests, a resistance movement against the construction of a park in Turkey in 2013 (Gerbaudo & Emiliano Treré, 2015; Montague, 2013; Wigmore-Shepherd, 2013; Ogan & Kaptan, 2018; Zakaria, 2013). The techniques and themes used on social media platforms during these movements in the recent past are reminiscent of those observed during the political uprisings in Tunisia (2010–11) and Egypt (2011).

For example, let's focus on one particularly common theme that kept reemerging in both Western and non-Western collective actions. During the political unrests of 2010–11 in several Muslim-majority countries, some of the widely circulated and viewed videos and images on social media, in general, and on YouTube, in particular, showed the protesters holding and/or wearing *V* masks to associate their social movements with the famous movie *V for Vendetta.*

Vendetta is a 2005 film directed by James McTeigue and written by the Wachowski Brothers. It is based on the 1982 graphic novel by Alan Moore and David Lloyd. The movie represents one person's struggle to avenge his government's wrongdoings and abuses of power (Swaminathan, n.d.).

These *V* masked protesters were not exclusive to the Arab Spring—similar *V* masked protesters were also spotted among other political unrests in Western societies, including some parts of Europe and the United States (such as during the Occupy Wall Street movement of 2011). Therefore, the *V* mask became a symbol of resistance not only in the Middle East, but also for Western societies. Let's recall some of the political unrests in societies other than the Arab Spring: *V* masks were seen in Brazil in June 2013 when over 200,000 Brazilians, mostly youth and university students, took to the streets over issues such as the rising cost of 2014 World Cup preparations in that country. The protesters stated that they were "angry about high taxes, corruption, and lavish spending on the upcoming

World Cup soccer tournament, among other complaints" (Castillo & Darlington, 2013, para. 5). It is interesting that the Brazilian protesters used many of the same images and strategies deployed in the two Muslim-majority countries, Tunisia and Egypt. Brazilian protesters wore *V* masks during the demonstrations, relied heavily on social media to promote their narrative of protests and used slogans to attract potential sympathizers to join their struggle, in addition to attempting to gain the attention of a larger global audience by utilizing global cultural and ideological themes.

Likewise, protesters used *V* masks during the Occupy Wall Street movement in 2011 in the United States and the 2013 Gezi Park protests in Turkey. These *V* masks also appeared in Europe in reaction to the recent reports of worldwide U.S. spying on virtually all telephone and Internet communications, and particularly when an American whistleblower, Edward Snowden, leaked highly classified information from the U.S. National Security Agency (NSA) in 2013 (Jordans, 2013; Wigmore-Shepherd, 2013). It is pertinent to mention here that the popularity and iconic power of this symbol of protest led the United Arab Emirates (UAE), Bahrain and Saudi Arabia to ban *V* masks in their countries (Zakaria, 2013). Consequently, the *V* mask has been transformed from a movie prop in England, to a symbol of resistance during the Arab Spring, to a nearly universal symbol of resistance against government and corporate abuse, corruption, and violence—proof that collective memory themes have now become part of a bigger phenomenon. Therefore, in light of this discussion, a strong case can be made that the political uprisings in the Muslim world neither started nor ended with the so-called Arab Spring. YouTube, Facebook, Twitter and other social media were, in fact, helping political activism take place on a global scale, which continues to unfold regardless of the regional limitations.

Moving forward, if we treat this globally recognized *V* mask as a collective memory theme, then the original idea of collective memory as applying only within individual groups or cultures is challenged; collective memory, thanks to the online platforms made available by digital media, now truly extends to virtually everyone on earth. This concept resonates with the ideas of globital and connective memories, then. As has been discussed previously, Reading (2011) coined the term globital memories, instead of collective memories, to include the factors of globalization and digitization seen while studying collective memory in the 21st century. Reading (2001) adds that it is because of the global nature of digital media that multiple interpretations of the same event are created. One implication of this phenomenon is that collective memory is no longer static, but rather something that is porous and able to take many shapes, something that was not possible in the past. Hoskin (2011) holds similar views. He argues that collective memory in this time of digital media is different from that of the past and so should be called "connective memory," instead. Thus, the Internet and social media connectivity should be seen as the determining factors regarding how far a collective memory can travel and can get accessed. At the same time, this factor also leads us to realize that nearly half of the world's population is still without the Internet and social media. So, it can be stated that the connective memory in this digital age has yet to connect the entire population on the globe. Once the entire population on this planet gets complete access to the Internet and digital platforms, we might witness a different era of collective memories that will need to be studied by utilizing theories and approaches that are more global in essence, rather than just relying on Western perspectives, which are currently being applied to the non-Western situations to understand and make sense of the world around us. Also, media and communication scholars studying cultural aspects of communication need to expand their focus on global culture, which is quickly forming and taking a tangible shape on global horizons, thanks to the Internet and social media (Arif, 2017).

In summary, this section of the chapter argues that while studying social media's role and its contributions in social movements, we need to understand these aspects of this phenomenon: social media's role in creating a collective memory that connects the people of one specific country or culture during a political uprising (i.e., the formation of a collective "We"), and social media's role in changing the nature of collective memory in the digital age (i.e., formation of connective memory). Through this chapter, I invite my fellow academics to revisit the events of the so-called Arab Spring and retest our approaches to social movements and collective actions in a global perspective to understand and explore new dynamics and avenues in this digital age. This may help to not only test our existing theoretical paradigms, but also to evolve and improve these theoretical perspectives in the rapidly changing media and communication landscape of the 21st century.

Collective Memory on Digital Platforms

The discussion provided in this section of the chapter is based on the findings and observations of my doctoral work when I analyzed several protest-related YouTube videos of political uprisings in the three countries under investigation (Arif, 2014). Many interesting themes related to collective memory were found that need some in-depth discussion to make sense of the rapidly morphing expectations of what used to be known as the collective memory of a group, tribe, community and/or a nation state. During the political uprisings of Pakistan, Egypt and Tunisia, two kinds of collective memory themes were found in the protest-related videos that were uploaded on YouTube: collective memory themes that were specific to each country's culture and traditions; and memory themes that are known and understood globally. To connect these themes to the theoretical paradigm, we will revisit the definitions of collective memory.

Collective memory refers to the common past that members of a community can associate with (Hoskin, 2011). Also, in journalistic terms, collective memory serves as a tool that media professionals use to interpret new occurrences in a predictable way (Berkowitz, 2010). Hence, in a nutshell, collective memory is generally attributed to a common past or common knowledge of a specific group, its culture and traditions in a society. Let us address the journalistic definition of collective memory first. By revisiting the most frequently shared, or "viral," videos of political protests during the political uprisings, it was observed that most of these videos belonged to independent persons/individuals, not to media professionals. Therefore, in the case of the three uprisings investigated, the chapter argues that a journalistic role was played by the individuals. Unlike media professionals who use collective memory as a tool to tell journalistic stories, these protest-related videos and images, which belonged to non-traditional media sources, were mostly interpreting the political uprisings in a relatively broader context. That is why the whole idea of collective memory played out very differently in the protest-related videos than what I had anticipated at the beginning of my research. Furthermore, during the data analysis, I observed that most of the protest-related videos were using collective memory themes at two levels: first, the videos shared the collective memory themes that could connect the protesters to their fellow citizens (e.g., religious and nationalistic appeals, national language, national flags); second, simultaneously, the protest-related videos were using several global themes to connect to the rest of the world (e.g., Hollywood movie themes and songs, frequent use of English language, images of protesters facing military tanks in a manner that evoked China's Tiananmen Square). Here we need to understand this phenomenon in two ways: social media's role in deploying local, regional and national collective memories to connect people to their fellow citizens during the recent political uprisings (the formation of collective "We"); and second, social media's role in changing the nature of collective memory in the digital age. The following paragraphs will provide detailed discussion on both stages.

The Formation of Collective "We"

Looking at social media's role in utilizing collective memory themes in the three cases, I would argue that social media platforms helped average citizens in these Muslim-majority countries to connect with each other by sharing their grievances online. Thus, social media texts, in this case in the form of YouTube videos of protests and Facebook pages, contributed to create collective "We" that was mostly missing in the region. In Muslim-majority countries with authoritarian regimes, people's frustration against their regimes existed long before the Arab Spring, but because public issues were discussed primarily within private spheres, people could never identify their grievances to each other (Abdelmoula, 2015; El-Nawawy & Iskandar, 2003; Hafez, 2007; 2008; Harb, 2011). When the images of a Tunisian burning man, Bouazizi, and the Egyptian man, Khalid Said (who was tortured and killed by the police for exposing police corruption online) travelled across the Muslim world, it resonated with the grievances and miseries of the entire region. These online stories led to mass political uprisings offline (in the streets). It is interesting to note that while revisiting the protest-related videos and images, I came across a YouTube video of a Pakistani man, Raja Khan, who, like Bouazizi, doused himself with gasoline and self-immolated in front of his government's building in 2012 to protest against unemployment and poor economic conditions. The video report by *CNN* referenced his act of suicide as a copycat to the Tunisian man, Bouazizi. Ironically, the video of Raja Khan's self-immolation did not receive the attention and support the way we had witnessed in the case of Bouazizi. One of the reasons for this video not becoming the most iconic or spreadable on social media platforms could be because the social networking site YouTube was banned in the country for more than three years after the Pakistan's political uprisings of 2007–8, depriving people of an important platform to share their grievances. Even though this discussion is beyond the scope of this chapter, I still found it relevant to discuss in the context of collective memory, which connects this Pakistani man's self-immolation to that of the Tunisian example.

The Formation of "Connective" Memory

Looking exclusively at the concept of collective memory in the digital media age, we start getting somewhat different explanation for this theory. During the Arab Spring, street protesters and online activists on social media platforms used Western popular music and Western movie themes in the protest-related videos on

YouTube, and frequently used English as one of the languages of protests, since the language is globally spoken and understood. For example, I observed that several videos of political protests used the *Gladiator* movie theme song "We are Free Now." Other videos on YouTube showed protesters holding facemasks as a copycat to the famous British award-winning movie, *V for Vendetta*. Some of the protesters, particularly in the case of Tunisian and Egyptian demonstrations, were shown holding placards saying, "Yes, We Can." This slogan was used by the President Obama's election campaign for his first term in the United States. Also, another theme that I found consistent in all the three countries was of unarmed protesters facing tanks and guns the same way we had witnessed in the case of Tiananmen Square's political protests of 1989 in China (Perlmutter, 1998). The image of a Chinese protester facing military tanks became an iconic image of resistance all over the world. Protesters during the political uprisings in the three countries copycatted the Chinese protester's example as if the incident was a part of their collective memory.

If we treat all of these globally understood and recognized themes as collective memory themes, then the whole idea of collective memory itself gets challenged, because then it is no more about the memory and culture of a certain group, community or a nation; rather, this kind of collective memory that is using global memory themes on online platforms such as YouTube, Twitter, Facebook, Instagram, etc., should be interpreted as global memory themes. This discussion also resonates with the works of Reading (2011) and Hoskin (2011) as both scholars promoted the ideas of globital and connective memories, respectively. Building upon the ideas of globital memory and connective memory, this debate leads us to the next important point of discussion for this chapter, which is discussed below.

Recent Political Uprisings as the Part of a Global Movement

The political uprisings in the Muslim world in this age of the social media and the Internet were the part of a bigger global phenomenon that continues to resurrect in many regions of the globe. One of the most recent examples of such a political uprising that was taking place outside of the Muslim world in 2019 is of Hong Kong's pro-democracy demonstrations: "On June 9, more than a million people marched against the [controversial extradition] bill, which they [protesters] fear will allow China to encroach on rights in the semi-autonomous territory"

(Al Jazeera, 2019, Para 2). The political mobilization in this case was so quick that in less than a week (by June 16, 2019) the number of protesters doubled, as about two million people took to the streets, demanding the resignation of the Hong Kong's leader, Chief Executive Carrie Lam and unconditional release of all the arrested participants of these pro-democracy protests (Al Jazeera, 2019). Many of Hong Kong's pro-democracy protesters also wore masks and goggles during these protests. Just like several other examples discussed in this chapter, the Hong Kong protesters also utilized global memory themes in order to mobilize their social movement. For example, several protesters adopted a Christian hymn, "Sing Hallelujah to the Lord," as their protest anthem (Leung, 2019). It is worth mentioning here that "[t]he Christian hymn was written by the Indiana-born Linda Stassen in 1974" (Leung, 2019, Para 5) and carries a deep-rooted collective memory among the Christian communities in the United States.

Shifting our focus back to the social movements of the recent past, this chapter reiterates that the techniques and themes used during the Arab Spring uprisings and later movements of 2011 to 2013 provide stark similarities when it comes to how the protesters deployed the cultural and ideological frames to sustain their collective actions. For example, *V* masks were used as a cultural and ideological frame during not only the social movements of the Muslim world, but also in the cases of political uprisings in the non-Muslim or Western World. As I have already discussed in a separate section of this chapter, the *V* mask has become the symbol of resistance wherever such political protests are emerging in recent times. Therefore, the *V* symbol, which was earlier interpreted as exclusive to the Arab Spring can be seen as a proof that these collective memory themes are actually part of a bigger phenomenon, Hence, calling political uprisings in the Muslim world as being specific and isolated to the Arab Spring would be a miscalculation of the political activism taking place at the global scale.

Conclusion

During the political uprisings of 2007 (Pakistan) and 2010–11 (Tunisia & Egypt), two kinds of collective memories were at play: First, there were collective memories of grievances among the citizens of the three countries under investigation, wherein people could empathize and connect with each other's pain because they had a history of shared social, political and economic injustices under their respective regimes. Second, the global collective memory that was a unique and new phenomenon in the age of the Internet and social media. Protesters were able to share collective themes and memories that were not necessarily a representation or a portrayal of their society or national identity, but, in fact, were more global in nature and outreach. Such memories were deployed as techniques by the protesters to connect with the citizens of the globe at large, rather than just connecting with the fellow citizens of their home countries. Thus, the phrase "fellow human beings" seems more appropriate while studying social movements phenomenon on social media platforms, rather than "fellow citizens." Therefore, this chapter argues that the recent political uprisings are the examples of much bigger and wider phenomena, in terms of their scope and scale, than just being country- or region- specific. Our "glocal" (global plus local) and "globital" memories (global plus digital) are helping us to connect with each other for a common purpose and, whenever needed, take part in collective actions, regardless of the limitations of geographical boundaries. Fast growing means of communication and technologies coupled with the fact of more than half of the planet's population already present on social media and the Internet, are opening new doors of opportunities to collaborate and participate in global social movements commonly seen as online political, social and economic activisms. The success and/or failure of each social movement that takes place on social media platforms, by default, generates a new memory for the online world, which then can be deployed by others during their future activism.

References

Abdelmoula, E. (2015). *Al Jazeera and democratization: the rise of the Arab public sphere.* Routledge.

Al Jazeera. (2019, June 17). Hong Kong protests: All the latest updates. Retrieved August 03, 2019, from https://www.aljazeera.com/news/2019/06/hong-kong-protests-latest-updates-190612074625753.html

Anderson, B. (1991). *Imagined communities: Reflections of the origin and spread of nationalism.* New York, NY: Verso.

Arif, R. (2014). *Social movements, YouTube and political activism in authoritarian countries: A comparative analysis of political change in Pakistan, Tunisia & Egypt* (Unpublished doctoral dissertation). University of Iowa, Iowa City, IA.

Arif, R. (2017). Internet as a hope or a hoax for emerging democracies: Revisiting the concept of citizenship in the digital age. *The Journal of Social and Behavioral Sciences-Procedia,* (236) 4–8. doi: 10.1016/j.sbspro.2016.12.002

Arif, R. (2018). Social networks, social movements and politico-cultural situation of Pakistani media. In Julie Dee (Ed.), *From Tahrir Square to Gezi Park: Social networks as facilitators of social movements*. New York, NY: Peter Lang Publishing.

Bennett, W. L. & Segerberg, A. (2011, August). *The logic of connective action: Digital media and the personalization of contentious politics*. Paper presented at the 6th General Conference of the European Consortium for Political Research, Reykjavik, Iceland.

Berkowitz, D. A. (Ed.) (2010). *Cultural meanings of news: A text-reader*. Los Angeles, CA: Sage Publications.

Birkner, T., & Donk, A. (2018). Collective memory and social media: Fostering a new historical consciousness in the digital age? *Memory Studies*, 1–17. doi: 10.1177/1750698017750012

Castillo, M. & Darlington, S. (2013). Brazilian protesters 'being heard,' president says. *CNN*. Retrieved Jun 08, 2019, from http://www.cnn.com/2013/06/18/world/americas/brazil-protests/index.html

Coman, A., Brown, D. A., Koppel, J. & Hirst, W. (2009). Collective memory from a psychological perspective. *International Journal of Politics, Culture, and Society*, *22*(2), 125–141. doi: 10.1007/s10767-009-9057-9.

El-Nawawy, M. & Iskandar, A. (2003). *Al-Jazeera: The story of the network that is rattling governments and redefining modern journalism*. Boulder, CO: Westview.

Fraleigh, D. (2018). The Tunisian revolution: A social movement of courage assisted by social media. In Julie Dee (Ed.), *From Tahrir Square to Gezi Park: Social networks as facilitators of social movements* (pp. 3–18). New York, NY: Peter Lang Publishing.

Gerbaudo, P. & Treré, E. (2015) In search of the 'we' of social media activism: introduction to the special issue on social media and protest identities. *Information, Communication & Society*, *18*(8),865–871. doi: 10.1080/1369118X.2015.1043319

Ghannam, J. (2011). Social media in the Arab world: Leading up to the uprisings of 2011. *Center for International Media Assistance*, *3*(1), 1–44. Retrieved May 05, 2019, from http://www.cima.ned.org/wp-content/uploads/2011/02/Ghannam-Jeffrey-Arab_Social_Media-Report-10-25-11.pdf

Hafez, K. (2007). *The myth of media globalization*. Cambridge, UK: Polity Press.

Hafez, K., Ed. (2008). *Arab Media: Power and Weakness* (pp. 01–08). New York: Continuum Inc.

Halbwachs, M. (1992). *On collective memory*. Chicago, IL: University of Chicago Press.

Harb, Z. (2011). Arab revolutions and the social media effect. *M/C Journal*, *14*(2). Retrieved October 23, 2019, from http://journal.media-culture.org.au/index.php/mcjournal/article/view/364Two

Hoskin, A. (2011). Anachronisms of media, anachronisms of memory: From collective memory to a new memory ecology. In M. Neiger, O. Meyers, & E. Zandberg (Eds.) *On media memory*. (pp. 278–288). London, England: Palgrave Macmillan.

Jordans, F. (2013, June 30). European officials slam US over bugging report. *AP*. Retrieved May 17, 2019, from https://news.yahoo.com/european-officials-slam-us-over-bugging-report-135703554.html

Leung, H. (2019, June 19). A 1974 Hymn Called 'Sing Hallelujah to the Lord' Has Become the Anthem of the Hong Kong Protests. Time. Retrieved July 20, 2019, from https://time.com/5608882/sing-hallelujah-to-the-lord-protestors-hong-kong-extradition-anthem/

Liu, J. (2018). Who speaks for the past? Social media, social memory, and the production of historical knowledge in contemporary China. *International Journal of Communication, 12*(21), 1675–1695. doi: https://ijoc.org/index.php/ijoc/article/view/7873/2323

Mir, J. (2011). Political and media transitions in Tunisia: A snapshot of media policy and regulatory environment. *Internews Report.* Retrieved June 02, 2019, from https://internews.org/sites/default/files/resources/Internews_Tunisia_MediaLawReview_Aug11.pdf

Montague, J. (2013). World Cup only benefits outsiders, say Brazil protesters. *CNN.* Retrieved January 06, 2019, from https://www.cnn.com/2013/06/18/world/americas/brazil-protests-montague/index.html

Neiger, M., Meyers, O., & Zandber, E. (Eds.) (2011). *On media memory.* London, England: Palgrave Macmillan.

Nora, P. (1989). Between memory and history: Les lieux de mémoire. *Representations, 26*, 7–24. doi: 10.2307/2928520

Nora, P., & Kritzman, L. D. (1996). *Realms of memory: The construction of the French past. Vol. 2, Traditions.* New York, NY: Columbia University Press.

Ogan, C. & Kaptan, Y. (2018). Laughing with tear gas in our eyes: Use of satirical humor in the Gezi Park social movement in Turkey. In J. Dee (Ed.), *From Tahrir Square to Gezi Park: Social networks as facilitators of social movements* (pp. 103–130). New York, NY: Peter Lang Publishing.

Olick, J., & Robbins, J. (1998). Social memory studies: From "collective memory" to the historical sociology of mnemonic practices. *Annual Review of Sociology, 24*, 105–140. doi: https://doi.org/10.1146/annurev.soc.24.1.105

Perlmutter, D. D. (1998). *Photojournalism and foreign policy: Icons of outrage in international crises.* Westport, Conn.: Praeger.

Reading, A. (2011). Memory and digital media: Six dynamics of the globital memory field. In M. Neiger, O. Meyers, & E. Zandberg (Eds.) *On media memory.* (pp. 241–252). London, England: Palgrave Macmillan.

Robinson, S. (2011). Journalism as process: The organizational implications of participatory online news. *Journalism & Communication Monographs, 13*(3), 137–210. doi: https://doi.org/10.1177/152263791101300302

Russell, N. (2006). Collective memory before and after Halbwachs. *The French Review, 79*(4), 792–804. Retrieved June 15, 2019, from http://www.jstor.org/stable/25480359.

Savage, K. (2007). *History, memory, and monuments: An overview of the scholarly literature on commemoration.* Pittsburgh, PA: University of Pittsburgh. Retrieved July 27, 2019, from http://npshistory.com/publications/savage.pdf

Smith, A. (1991). *National identity.* Reno, NV: University of Nevada Press.

Swaminathan, B. K. (n.d.). V for Vendetta (2006): Movie vs Graphic Novel: Explained. *This is Barry.* Retrieved February 17, 2018, from https://www.thisisbarry.com/film/v-for-vendetta-2006-movie-vs-graphic-novel-explained/

Tarrow, S. G. (1998). *Power in movement: Social movements and contentious politics.* Cambridge, England: Cambridge University Press.

Wigmore-Shepherd, D. (2013). Occupy Lancaster: the legacy of a northern protest movement. *The Guardian UK.* Retrieved June 20, 2019, from https://www.theguardian.com/uk/the-northerner/2013/jun/24/occupy-lancaster-legacy-of-protest

Zakaria, F. (2013). Why Turkey protests are a good thing. *CNN World News*. Retrieved May 19, 2019, from http://globalpublicsquare.blogs.cnn.com/2013/06/14/why-turkey-protests-are-a-good-thing/

Zayani, M. (2015). *Networked publics and digital connection: The politics of everyday life in Tunisia*. Oxford, England: Oxford University Press.

14

Aftermath of Online Activism in Pakistan, Egypt & Tunisia

This chapter summarizes the debate on what happened during the popular political uprisings in Pakistan, Egypt and Tunisia and opens the discussion about what lies ahead. This chapter, which is divided in two parts, makes a case that the political uprisings of the three countries should not be seen as the pinnacle of a new era of social change, but actually the precursors of what is to come. In order to make sense of the morphing political, social, economic and media climate in Muslim-majority countries, particularly the Middle East and Pakistan, part one of this chapter summarizes some of the common themes that were observed in the comparative analysis of the three cases.

The second part focuses on the changing trends in these countries and beyond. For example, rulers in these countries have become more aware of the power of social media and are trying to tap into this resource for promoting their own narratives online. It is a shift in approach for these dictatorial regimes, who earlier rejected the power of social networks. Now, they are embracing these digital spheres to reassert their control. The chapter then provides some examples of political uprisings that erupted most recently (in 2019), such as the political uprisings of Algeria, Sudan and Morocco. Finally, the chapter provides an outlook of how future social movements will employ broader collective memory themes and collective cultural and ideological frames. I will make the case that these larger and/or global social movements, rather than small community, country and region-specific ones, will become the norm in the era of social media.

In order to discuss the common themes that were found in the three countries, I will draw some of the highlights from my doctoral research that was based on extensive qualitative and quantitative analyses of large data sets collected during the time when some of the Arab Spring uprisings were actually unfolding nine years ago (Arif, 2014). In this regard, my discussion will revolve around protest-related YouTube videos and images of the three political uprisings. These still and moving images refer to all the amateur content that online activists themselves recorded via their smartphones and uploaded on social media platforms such as YouTube and Facebook to spread their narrative of revolt against their respective regimes. Therefore, any reference in the first part of this chapter to social media and protest-related videos and images should be interpreted in that context. The following paragraphs will discuss these themes and their connection to social media and social movements in further detail.

Part One: Comparative Analysis of Social Movement Themes in the Three Countries

Since this chapter is concluding my argument on social media and social movements in the context of the three political uprisings in Pakistan, Egypt and Tunisia that were the primary focus of this book, it is important that we discuss the highlights of this investigation while tying them back to the theoretical foundations that were presented in the first chapter. Therefore, important findings and observations will be discussed in the context of prominent icons, collective memory, cascades of information, cultural and ideological frames of social movements, contention in social movements, and the economic and traditional logics of collective actions, to name a few (Boudreau & Meyer, 2009; Hirschman, 1970; Hoskin, 2011; Jenkins, 1983; Lohmann, 1994; Perlmutter, 1998; Reading, 2011; Skocpol, 1979; Tarrow, 1998; Tilly, 1992).

Similarities of Themes among Three Countries

An analysis of still and moving images of political protests in the three countries revealed stark similarities: A majority of protest-related videos available on YouTube show violence against protesters. Military, police and security officials are shown beating and torturing unarmed protesters in these videos. Notably, the security officials in the three countries used very similar tactics for attacking, dispersing and torturing the protesters. These videos show protests taking place in the capital cities of the three countries. Furthermore, the majority of the most popular and widely viewed videos do not come from traditional media sources, but rather use raw footage of videos recorded by individuals during the protests. This finding illustrates that traditional media sources were ineffective in their coverage during the political uprisings. The protesters in the three countries relied on alternative media such as YouTube—which served as the best substitute for television media—to tell their stories. Unlike traditional media reports and documentaries, the average length of most of these videos is less than five minutes. This observation also speaks to the overall changing pattern of communication on social media profiles. Online users utilize fewer words and space in favor of faster communication. Twitter is an example of such a communication network. This new pattern of short and to the point communication remains the same when it comes to visual communication on YouTube.

The following paragraphs will discuss six significant themes found across the three countries. Besides providing an in-depth analysis of the overall content of the videos, this discussion will provide further evidence and interpretation of the use of alternative media in promoting and sustaining of social movements against the powerful elites.

If It Bleeds, It Leads. The famous adage in everyday journalism, "if it bleeds, it leads," was very much true in the case of the most viewed YouTube videos of political uprisings in Pakistan, Egypt and Tunisia. This adage basically means that people are fascinated with violence. It is generally believed that mass media including TV, radio, film and even video games with violent content have much higher ratings because people love to watch violence. The same principle seems to apply in the case of social media, particularly the YouTube videos analyzed for this study. The analysis of the most viewed videos in the three countries reveals that images of violence, destruction, torture and chaos dominated the visual content. All these violence-related images showed police and security forces arresting, beating and shooting protesters without mercy. In some cases, videos documented the scenes when protesters were dying from bullets being fired at them at point blank range. Egypt dominated such images, with many videos showing people dying from injuries and bullet wounds from the country's security forces. In other words, security officials who are supposed to protect their citizens were actually killing them in the streets.

Some of the videos show close-up angles of scenes in which police and/or military officials are torturing, beating or arresting their own countrymen. Among other images of violence are the torture-disfigured face of the Egyptian man Khalid Said, the flame-engulfed image of the Tunisian street vendor, Mohamed Bouazizi, and the humiliation of Pakistan's deposed Chief Justice, Iftikhar Chaudhry, were depicted significantly in the videos. Such images of violence not only serve an informative role for viewers of these videos on social media, they also generate sympathy for the protesters and incite anger against the rulers/dictators. Generally, people empathize with others when they realize that what is happening to someone else in their own country may happen to them.

Epicenters of Protests. In the modern world, capital cities of countries symbolize power, collective identity and the rule of law. Because of the importance of capital cities, mass media seem to be more vibrant whenever something unusual happens near and around these power hubs. People in Pakistan, Egypt and Tunisia are well aware of this fact. The three countries have a history of flash protests erupting in the three capitals (Islamabad, Cairo and Tunis) whenever people need the attention of the media and/or of their governments on an important issue. Therefore, the whole idea and motivation of holding protests in national capitals is to get attention to amplify the grievances or demands of protesters. An analysis and comparison of the three political uprisings reveals that capital cities provided the center stage for protests in the three countries. The visual analysis of videos from the three countries revealed in the location and scenes where these protests were taking places. Although the three cases under investigation represent three countries where political uprisings took place at different times, the pattern of the locations and scenes of these protests are strikingly similar. It was observed that the mass uprisings against the three dictatorial regimes took place in highly populated, educated and relatively advanced urban places. I categorized this theme as "the epicenter of protests" to further observe and analyze why people had chosen urban areas for their protests and also explore how this finding is consistent with the theory of informational cascade (Lohmann, 1994).

For Pakistan, all except two of the protests in 2007 occurred in the federal capital, Islamabad. For most of these protests, people gathered in front of the Parliament building and the President's House to stage their protests against President Musharraf. The motivation was not only to get attention, but also to challenge and change the regime. In Pakistan, the three most important buildings symbolizing power and authority in the country (Parliament House, the President's House and the Supreme Court) are located in a row on one street. The official name to this street is *Shahrah-e-Dastoor*, which in English means Constitution Avenue. This name was adopted after Pakistani parliament passed a unanimous constitution in

1973. According to the Constitution, Pakistan is a democratic state and will be governed by the people of Pakistan who emerge through a democratic process.

Thus, the name of this street links to a collective cultural memory for the citizens of the country that remind them of their Constitutional freedoms. In other words, the name of this street, Constitution Avenue, itself challenges the dictatorship of the country. The President's House of Pakistan, where General Musharraf was residing while he was still holding the office as a military chief, also symbolizes the ideology of democracy in the country. Only a democratically elected president has the legal right to live in the President's House. When the mass political uprisings against President Musharraf started to erupt, people chose Constitution Avenue as center stage to express their anger and raise their voices against the regime. Another reason for choosing this location was the fact that the Supreme Court is located on the same Avenue. Since the struggle strove to restore the deposed Chief Justice, Iftikhar Chaudhry, and to free the highest symbol of democracy, the President's House, from the military dictator, it was natural that people joined anti-regime protests in the Federal Capital at the Constitution Avenue. In other words, Constitution Avenue in Islamabad can be seen as Pakistan's Tahrir Square during its political uprisings of 2007.

For Tunisia, only three protests in the videos are shown occurring in Sidi Bouzid, the city of Tunisian street vendor Mohamed Bouazizi. Bouazizi was born in this city, and he immolated himself in the same city to protest police brutality and injustice. Even though the Tunisian revolution was born in this city, the place did not become the epicenter of protests. Instead, the most viewed videos of Tunisian uprisings on YouTube show protests occurring mostly in front of the Presidential Palace, which is in Tunis, the capital city of Tunisia. The videos of these protests show that people are carrying anti-Ben Ali slogans and are trying to reach the gates of the Presidential Palace. One possible motivation for choosing this location to stage most of their protests could be the fact that people came out in the streets to challenge the regime. They blamed their president for Bouazizi's death. Since the Presidential Palace of Tunisia symbolized the power and authority of Ben Ali's regime, protesting in front of this house of power provides a powerful voice of dissent against the regime. Also, since the Tunisian mass media were concentrated in the capital and were under the absolute control of Ben Ali to serve the regime, these media outlets could not ignore anything that happened right in front of the Presidential Palace. In other words, protesters had higher chances of getting their voices heard from the nation's capital. In addition to that, Tunis is the largest city of the country with the highest population. Most of this population comes from the educated elite. Therefore, it is easier to mobilize people who have political awareness and resources in the nation's capital than those who are in other, less populated and relatively less educated parts of the country. Also, because of its historical importance, Tunis is one of the most popular tourism places for foreigners (Brown, 2008), which makes this city a prime location to hold such protests so as to amplify the voices of the voiceless.

For Egypt, all the protest videos, except one in which police are beating a woman, were taken at Tahrir Square in Cairo. Tahrir Square has maintained a historical significance for Cairo since the 13th Century. Tahrir, "which means *liberation* in Arabic is one of the oldest squares in modern Cairo" (AlSayyed, 2011, para. 2). According to a 2011 story by Al Jazeera, the Square has been the traditional site for major protests and demonstrations over the years, including the 1977 Bread Riots.

Originally it was called Maidan Ismailia, after the 19th-century ruler Khedive Ismail who commissioned the new downtown district's design. It was renamed Maidan al-Tahrir or Liberation Square in 1954 after the 1952 Egyptian revolution that changed Egypt from a constitutional monarchy into a republic ("Tahrir Square's," paras. 6–7).

Thus, the so-called Arab Spring protests that erupted at Tahrir Square were not a new phenomenon. The Square is significant in the collective memory of the Egyptian people, who have a cultural and historical association with it. For them, Tahrir Square symbolizes liberation. During the Arab Spring revolution, protesters used Tahrir Square as the epicenter of the protests. As in Pakistan and Tunisia, protesters in Egypt also wanted to amplify their grievances so that their voices of dissent could be heard right in the middle of the country's power hub, Cairo. Just like any other dictator, President Mubarak immediately banned mass media from covering the protests against his regime. However, this time President Mubarak could not stop the protesters from sharing their negative information about the regime with their fellow citizens because they were using social media as an alternate platform of communication. In other words, having the opportunity to record and upload these protests on social media so as to amplify the voices of protesters can be seen as a political opportunity that might have contributed to the informational cascades of these protests for the people of Egypt.

In summary, such political protests were not uncommon in the three countries. Political activists and protesters have a long, uninterrupted history of protests in the federal capitals of Pakistan, Egypt and Tunisia. One possible reason for choosing capital cities—and particularly sites in front of presidential palaces—is that the protesters wanted to get noticed. Also, in all three countries, the mass media cluster in their federal capitals because the traditional media are supposed to serve and report on the activities of rulers, not the plight of people. Therefore, if people manage to wage a protest in front of a parliament building or a presidential palace, they are sure to get national and/or international media attention. This means their dissenting voices have a better chance of being heard at a larger scale.

In the three countries, the dictatorial regimes were well aware of this fact. That's why, when these dictators could not control the political protests, they blocked the traditional media coverage of these protests to suppress the voices of the protesters. However, as discussed earlier, for the very first time in the history of these countries, people had an alternative to traditional media in the form of social media, including YouTube, Facebook, Twitter and blogs. Protesters used their cellphones to record the ongoing protests against their dictators and uploaded and disseminated those videos on social media platforms. Hence, the informational cascade regarding people's unhappiness and disapproval of the regime kept flowing on social media platforms even when the mass media were absent from the scene.

Youth Prevails. The social media videos analyzed for the three countries showed protesters of all ages including men, women and children. However, an in-depth analysis of these videos reveals that an overwhelming majority of participants consisted of youth, both men and women. This finding regarding the dominance of youth among protesters of the three countries can be interpreted in the context of digital media. Put this way, the rise of digital modes of communication corresponds to the average age of younger generations. To understand this finding, we look at some important facts about the rising population of youth in the three countries, as most of these youth are growing up with information and communication technologies in their hands.

The popularity of digital media in the Muslim world is not only because citizens in many of these countries have historically lacked access to traditional media sources, but also because rising youth majorities in countries with a Muslim majority contribute to the phenomenon of *netizens* or the *net generation* (Arif, 2016; Dubai Press Club, 2013; Papacharissi 2010a; Papacharissi 2010b). At the time of the Arab Spring uprisings of 2010–11, the available data on Arab demographics shows that:

> more than 50 percent of the populations of Yemen, Oman, Saudi Arabia, Jordan, Morocco, and Egypt [were] … estimated to be under 25 years of age, while in the rest of the Arab region, the under-25, 'net generation' [made] up between 35 to 47 percent of the total populations. (Ghannam, 2011, p. 6)

More recent statistics indicate similar demographics:

> Young people 15 to 24 constitute approximately 20% of the populations in Egypt, Iraq, Lebanon, Libya, Morocco, Oman, Sudan, Syria, Tunisia, Yemen, Jordan, Algeria, and Saudi Arabia. In the Arab countries' populations, young people are the fastest growing segment, some 60% of the population is under 25 years old, making this one of the most youthful regions in the world, with a median age of 22 years compared to a global average of 28. (Youth Policy, 2019, para. 1)

As for Pakistan, "64% of the nation is younger than 30 and 29% of Pakistanis are between 15 and 29 …. Pakistan now has more young people than it has ever had, and this is forecasted to continue to increase until at least 2050" (Ahmad, 2018, para. 1). This means that future political uprisings in these countries may witness more participation of youth, particularly if the rulers continue to fail to provide economic and employment opportunities to the growing population of educated youth. As discussed earlier, a majority of youth in the Muslim world have access to the Internet and smartphones. In other words, even though mainstream media serves the interests of the ruling elite, youth in Pakistan, Egypt and Tunisia have another avenue for accessing digital media in the form of smartphones, social media and blogs, through which they can express their views and unhappiness toward their respective regimes.

Another aspect of having vibrant youth in the Muslim world is the younger generation's ability to engage politically to change or reform the existing political system in their countries. It is pertinent to mention here that the three countries under investigation (Pakistan, Egypt, Tunisia) are not oil rich as most of the Middle East is. These three countries have a higher number of educated unemployed youth, and the Internet and mobile phone communication in these countries is predominant. A political science scholar, Ross (2001) argues that oil and mineral wealth in countries such as Saudi Arabia, the United Arab Emirates (UAE) and Bahrain actually hinders democracy, since these countries can use wealth to compensate the grievances of citizens. In contrast, since Pakistan, Egypt and Tunisia, are not oil rich, we can argue that their respective regimes could not appease the anger of their youth through economic bribery, which contributed to the political unrest in these countries. Huntington (1993) provides the concept of the snowballing impact of democratization. By snowballing, he means that sometimes a democratic wave in one country may encourage similar movements in neighboring states. To support his argument, Huntington says, "In 1990, for instance, it was reported that the 'upheaval in Eastern Europe' had 'fueled demands for change in the Arab world' and prompted leaders in Egypt, Jordan, Tunisia, and

Algeria to open up more political space for the expression of discontent" (p. 287). Although Huntington proposed the idea of a snowballing impact nearly three decades ago, his work seems to be relevant in the case of recent political uprisings Pakistan, Egypt and Tunisia, particularly since these three countries have political, cultural, religious and economical commonalities besides having access to social media and their ability to communicate in English (Hafez, 2007; Hafez, 2008; Eko, 2012). Hence, the commonality of themes and patterns of protests also correspond to the fact that these three countries share a comparable population of youth protesters who used similar tactics to raise their voices of dissent during the political upheavals under study.

In addition, while analyzing data for this investigation, it was observed that women were equal participants in political protests on the streets in all three countries. The importance of this finding also comes from the fact that in Muslim-majority countries women are usually hesitant to play active roles in their country's politics. For women, coming out in the streets along with their fellow men to protest against their regimes indicates that the majority of protesters in the three countries belonged to elite and/or educated families. Muslim women who belong to the educated, liberal and elite classes in these three countries enjoy relatively more freedom to take part in political activities. Keeping in mind the cultural and social taboo of women's participation in protests in Muslim societies, it can be inferred that a majority of women who participated in these protests belonged to the privileged class, and so they had the opportunity to come out and take part in protests to express their disapproval of a particular regime. However, their participation in these iconic political uprisings set the stage for future uprisings where women could play even a bigger role when it comes to challenge the regime. This will be discussed further in the second part of this chapter under Sudanese political uprisings of 2019.

Symbols. Chants, slogans, symbols, religious and/or cultural references or visualizations serve as important elements of protests. Tarrow (1998) believes that culturally compatible symbols and slogans actually help protesters sustain their movements by encouraging sympathizers to join them. These symbols and slogans directly express grievances and demand something collectively (Gerbaudo, 2015). The three countries revealed an interesting pattern of symbols not only within the videos of each country, but also across the videos of the three countries. Among the slogans and symbols that showed stark commonalities were Islamic religious calligraphic themes, the use of flags to express the love for their countries, anti-regime slogans, and the "V-sign." This last sign appeared not only as a sign for victory, as it is commonly perceived, but also to denote a specific social movement on the Internet (Gerbaudo, 2015). This online social movement is known as "Anonymous." The movement's slogan is "V," which stands for *V for Vendetta*, a famous British movie based on a graphic novel. A detailed discussion has already been provided in the previous chapter about the collective memory of this book.

Symbols of solidarity and brotherhood among Muslim community were also found evident in these videos. For example, the images of protesters offering Friday prayers at Tahrir Square symbolized Muslim unity, regardless of their country's origin. Similarly, the use of religious slogans might have served two objectives for the protesters: to connect to their fellow citizens and to gain support and sympathy of Muslim community across the world. Since most of the protesters in the three countries belonged to the privileged classes, they did not serve as true representatives of their respective countries' larger populations where an overwhelming majority lives under poverty line. By using the term "privileged classes" for these protesters, I mean not only economically privileged, but also privileged in terms of their level of education, their level of access to the digital means of communication and technologies such as smartphones and the Internet, besides being a part of the urban communities, as compared to the rural ones. However, using Islamic chants and religious slogans might have helped these privileged protesters to connect themselves to the rest of their Muslim brothers and sisters on the basis of a shared religion and culture. In other words, using a religious theme actually helped the protesters gain the support and sympathy of their fellow citizens.

Furthermore, this religious narrative not only represents Muslim brotherhood inside a country, but also becomes a powerful theme that unites movements across the Muslim world. The religion of Islam becomes a protest tool in the form of a collective memory of the Muslim community. Regardless of the fact that Muslims across the globe represent multiple cultures and speak several languages, they can all read and understand classic Arabic (the language of the Quran) and connect with religious symbols such as prayers, images of sacred places and Islamic calligraphy. It is interesting to note that during the analysis of the protest-related videos on YouTube and associated social media, not even a single video showed security officials or policemen offering prayers or performing religious acts, even though the policemen and other security officials also belonged to the same religion. In other words, the narrative in these videos depicts protesters as followers of Islam who are fighting the Holy war, known as *Jihad*, against nonbelievers. That is why whenever anyone would get killed by police or other security forces, he/she was commemorated as a martyr.

Similarly, national flags and nationalistic songs used in the videos were also aimed at achieving the same goal of getting more empathizers online. Since national flags represent the unity of a nation, protesters gained more attention and appreciation from their fellow citizens by displaying these flags. This symbolism legitimized their struggle against the powerful opponent, depicting these protesters as fighting for the freedom of their country against a very powerful and cruel enemy.

Good Guys versus Bad Guys. Hollywood's obsession with the dichotomy of good versus evil works not only for the blockbuster movies, but also for the online activists who were engaged in creating and uploading protest-related videos on social media. It was observed that most of the protest-related videos from the three countries carried the same narrative: Good guys (protesters) are fighting the bad guys (dictators in the three countries).

All the videos studied for this investigation portrayed protesters as "heroes" and the law enforcement agencies such as police, military and paramilitary forces as enemies, or "bad guys." The narratives highlighted protesters as brave men and women who were risking their lives by coming out on the streets against the powerful rulers. These protesters are portrayed as being victimized and tortured by security agencies yet refusing to bow in front of the evil. We see brave men courageously facing fast moving police vehicles, military style tanks and guns. As is evident from the videos and news reports, some such protesters lost their lives during these acts of bravery. They were subsequently celebrated as martyrs, which according to Islamic faith is the highest honor that one can get by sacrificing her/her life for a just cause.

Put this way, the central theme or plotline of each video depicted two elements. First, state agencies including police are bad guys who, on behalf of the rulers, are involved in killing their own people to stop them from protesting against the dictatorship. Second, protesters are brave and heroic, facing a cruel enemy in the streets for the sake of their people and to secure freedom for their countries. The videos show that the protesters do not care for their own safety; rather they care more about their country, and their fight is to set the country free from evil (dictators). Many videos repeat the images of protesters who are intentionally facing guns and military-style tanks. The whole narrative portrays these protesters as fearless. They are brave, and they will not give up. Likewise, Tunisian street vendor, Mohamed Bouazizi, Egyptian man, Khaled Said, and Pakistani Chief Justice, Iftikhar Chaudhry, become the three icons of heroism. They are the representation of resistance—those who faced the enemy with courage and stood up against the dictatorship for what they believed was right. Thus, all the protesters who were in the streets were representatives of the same struggle, and if anyone lost their lives during the protests, they were commemorated as Khaled Said and Bouazizi, the martyrs (Buckner & Khatib, 2014).

On the other hand, such protest-related videos treated dictators in the three countries (President Musharraf for Pakistan, President Ben Ali for Tunisia, and President Mubarak for Egypt) as criminals. Several chants and slogans in the protest-related videos blamed Ben Ali for the Tunisian burning man's death. Also, President Mubarak was depicted as the murderer of Khaled Said. Likewise, President Musharraf was portrayed as a Nazi leader in some of the videos, and sometimes he was depicted as a vampire who loves to suck the blood of his own people. In the videos, the images of the Pakistani Chief Justice's humiliation and arrest, and Musharraf's images of pride in his military uniform were shown side by side. The plotline showed Musharraf as the criminal who attacked Pakistan's independent judiciary by sacking the Chief Justice, whereas, Iftikhar Chaudhry became a hero who decided not to bow in front of the dictator even when facing arrest and humiliation at the hands of country's law enforcement agencies.

Message of Resistance. In a nutshell, the overall communicative intention or persuasive goal of online activists during these political uprisings was to gain sympathy for those protesting against their dictatorial regimes. The social media in their hands provided them an excellent opportunity to craft and promote their own narrative and disseminate it. The social media activists used techniques such as emotional music and songs that were put together with extremely disturbing images such as the torture-disfigured face of Khaled Said, burning images of Bouazizi, a woman who was beaten to death by policemen, images of protesters leading funerals of fellow protesters, and several other images showing injured and bleeding protesters. When put together, the combined narrative communicates the message of resistance. The videos amplified the voice of dissent by showing thousands of protesters pouring into the streets of the three capital cities, Islamabad, Tunis and Cairo. Also, the videos targeted the support and sympathy of people in the online world so as to sustain these protests and encourage more people to join the struggle. Simultaneously, since protest-related narratives were being spread by activists on the Internet, visual and textual descriptions, by default, became the omnipresent examples of *collective* and *connective* memories for future generations.

The final communicative intention of these videos connects us back to the whole idea of informational cascades. We shall revisit the facts. In the three countries, dictators had banned mass media in order to hide the negative information about their regimes. The three dictators (President Musharraf, President Mubarak and President Ben Ali) did not want others to see that people are unhappy with their policies and that the people were protesting against them.

However, even with the absolute ban on traditional media sources, including Al Jazeera TV, dictators could not stop the message of resistance because people now had an alternative in the form of social media. When people could not get the attention of mass media, they used their own smartphones to record the ongoing protests and upload and disseminate these raw videos on YouTube and other social media platforms. Others (online viewers and potential challengers) got the information of resistance and protests against their regimes via these new and non-traditional sources of information. Therefore, the informational cascade kept flowing even in the absence of mainstream media. These findings highlight the cultural and ideological frames used in the most viewed videos of each revolution, the contribution of YouTube videos as informational cascades, and Al Jazeera's use of YouTube as alternative platform to disseminate its content. The findings also documented how social media, including YouTube videos, gave voice to the protests and left us with the most iconic images of each revolution. In short, the comparative analyses of the repeatedly emerging themes in the three cases of the political uprisings suggest that in the absence of traditional media sources, social media became an alternative platform of information, communication and dissent. Social movements in the three countries (The Lawyers' Movement of 2007 in Pakistan, the so-called Jasmine Revolution of Tunisia in 2010, and the Arab Spring of Egypt in 2011) exploited social media tools as alternate channels of communication to disseminate information on political protests against the dictatorial regimes for purposes of promoting resistance.

English Language, Violence and Emotions as Political Opportunities

As I have discussed earlier, Tarrow (1998) suggests that social movements form when common people who are unhappy with their rulers perceive the existence of an opportunity for political change, and social movements build when people succeed in communicating cultural and ideological frames, grievances and successful instances of resistance in a way that engages and mobilizes masses of potential protesters. An in-depth analysis of social media content related to the three social movements in Pakistan, Egypt and Tunisia revealed multiple factors present in the political opportunity structures that helped protesters in the three countries to form sustained social movements. These factors included the use of English as the common language of communication, violent repression by authoritarian regimes, and emotional appeal to gain sympathy of the online community.

English as the Common International Language. Historians have no choice but to acknowledge the fact that the rise of the 21st Century is founded upon a revolution in the field of information and communication technologies. The Internet has interconnected the world, and English, by default, has become the international language of information and communication technology, science and business. Since the Internet and associated social media are predominantly the inventions of the 21st century global West, English continues to dominate as the language of communication on digital platforms around the globe. Since Pakistan and Egypt were former British colonies, the politically powerful elites of these countries, as well as the elites of Tunisia, had mastered English to communicate with their rulers long ago. This trend continued even when their colonial masters left these countries as a result of nationalist freedom movements. It is therefore not surprising that while analyzing the protest-related still and moving images (such as YouTube) and social media pages (such as Facebook), I observed that English was the language most commonly heard in the soundtracks and seen on the protest signs displayed in the hands of the protesters in the three countries, along with their national languages (Urdu for Pakistan, and Arabic for Egypt and Tunisia). Sometimes both languages appeared simultaneously. It appears that the use of the English language during the protests was not a random decision. Rather, online and street protesters in the three countries were sending messages to two publics: the international community (via English) and their fellow citizens (via national languages, Arabic and Urdu). The high prevalence of English in the readable signage illustrates that protesters in all three countries understood that English would more effectively grab international attention during the political crises. Having social media in their hands as an alternative to traditional media, protesters were well aware of the fact that the Internet was a political opportunity for them to get international attention so as to put an external pressure on their rulers.

As we have already discussed in detail, the political uprisings of the three countries were not a new phenomenon. In fact, Pakistan, Egypt and Tunisia have a history of political protests and social movements against their regimes well before the uprisings of 2007, 2010–11. Most of those protests died down without even getting international attention for two reasons. First, traditional media were under state control and did not provide coverage to any anti-government protests or rallies. The second reason was that people in the three countries lacked a common communication platform to interact directly to the international community.

However, during the political uprisings under study, the whole scenario was different. Protesters did not only have alternative media for communication (the Internet and social media), they were also comfortable communicating in the English language, as a majority of these protesters were educated youth. These young educated protesters were not only aware of how to use social media and the Internet, they were also well-versed in speaking and writing standard English. The younger generations of the three countries grew up with information and communication technologies. They are adept at using YouTube, smartphones, Facebook, Instagram, Snapchat, Twitter, Pinterest and other technologies. Most of these technologies were developed in the United States and have English as their native underlying language. The social media archives of the three countries' political protests are full of examples that carried slogans in English language such as: "Pakistan belongs to the Pakistanis"; "Go Musharraf Go"; "Ben Ali: The Game is Over"; and "Mubarak will Fall," to name a few. In addition to gaining the attention of the international community, the use of English can also be seen as a language that might have attracted educated elites of each country to come out and join their fellow protesters, who also spoke and understood this language of elites.

Violence: A Tool in the Hands of Elites, or an Opportunity for Protesters? While analyzing the protest-related videos, images and social media pages for this study, I intended to understand whether the political uprisings in the three countries were examples of violent protests, or if they were representations of peaceful protests. My assumptions, however, took a completely new direction when I observed that the online activists utilized the theme of violence not to scare off the potential sympathizers (which the ruling elite had intended), but as an opportunity to gain support of people and encourage them to join the protests. This would not have been possible if the protesters did not have access to their own media (social media), which was there to help them craft their own storylines of the protests.

The dominance of the theme of violence in the social media archives supports Tarrow's (1998) assumption that people (unorganized protesters) commonly use violence as a resource to sustain their social movements. The online archives of protest-related images and videos, particularly available on YouTube, contain images of government-perpetrated violence to incite people to anger. It is important to note that in these YouTube videos, Tarrow's (1998) idea of the use of violent tactics by the common people takes an entirely different form from what he had predicted. For Tarrow (1998), since poor people lack money and other resources, they use violence or violent tactics as a resource to sustain their social movements. However, in the case of these protest-related YouTube videos of the three countries, protesters instrumentalized the images of violence by security forces to document their repressive tactics, attempting to get the attention of viewers in the online world. Therefore, in the case of these protest-related YouTube videos, Facebook pages and Tweets, the depiction of violence was aimed at generating sympathy among viewers and followers of social media toward the protesters with the hope that international condemnation would end their government's acts of violence and repression.

It was observed that an overwhelming majority of the protest-related YouTube videos were filled with images (both still and moving) of violence, torture and police brutality. For example, one such video, was based on a screenshot of a cell phone-recorded video of Egyptian protests against the Mubarak regime. This video shows a military crackdown on a group of protesters at Tahrir Square. The most disturbing part of the video shows military officials beating two unarmed protesters to death. It showed military officials beating one of the female protesters as well. In the video, they rip her clothes apart and do not stop beating her until she passes out. The video stands out because of the fact that security forces in Egypt are shown targeting an unarmed and nonviolent female protester. This visual depiction of cruelty went viral and became an iconic example of violence against protesters that spread around the globe with the speed of light, shocking the international community over how women were being treated in Egypt during the political uprisings. Apart from the aspect of brutality, we need to interpret the iconic nature of this figure both in terms of religion and politics. In Islamic traditions, women occupy a special place of modesty. Men who are not part of their families cannot touch them. This image, however, is a complete shock to this ideology and so was received as outrageous across the Muslim world. Politically, the image tells a story of how women are treated in Egypt and testifies that the struggle for women's rights in Egypt has a long way to go (Eltahawy, 2011). According to different media reports, during the political uprisings in Egypt, military officers were accused of arresting women protesters, "beat[ing] them, [giving] them electric shocks and subject[ing] them to strip searches. [The women] were then forced to undergo 'virginity tests' and threatened with prostitution charges" ("Egypt: A year after," 2012, para. 1).

Clearly, the violent and repressive tactics of the security forces in Pakistan, Egypt and Tunisia were used as opportunities to further the aims of the protesters. YouTube and Facebook images of police violence were used to rally international public opinion against and build condemnation of the three regimes. They were also used to rally the elite and young people against these authoritarian governments.

Emotional Appeal as a Political Opportunity. Political opportunity structure, in Tarrow's theorization of social movements, refers to the opportunities that social movement organizations and protesters may find advantageous to gain the support of fellow citizens. Tarrow argues that political opportunity structures are not static and may change with the changing circumstances. Keeping Tarrow's definition of political opportunity structures in context, this investigation finds that social movements in the three countries utilized emotional images of protests as a new form of political opportunity to gain the support of potential sympathizers. For emotional appeals, the social media archives analyzed for this study were full of still and moving images of blood, violence and security forces' torturing and killing of unarmed protesters. Not only this, the online narratives of protests were also feeding into the images of hunger and poverty themes so as to expose the deteriorating living conditions of average people under these authoritarian regimes. An example of this is found in an image of a child from a protest-related video uploaded to YouTube during the political uprisings of Pakistan (Arif, 2014). The image shows a child with a small piece of bread in his mouth. It does not show any element of violent interaction between security forces and protesters. The image, however, is aimed at depicting growing hunger in Pakistan. According to World Bank statistics, more than 60% of the population of Pakistan is living under the poverty line. Poverty and hunger were among the factors that contributed to the political uprisings of 2007 in the country. The references to bread and poverty were also common in the cases of Egypt and Tunisia. In the videos, people were shown waving bread in their hands to show that they don't even have bread to eat under their regimes, while the rulers are living in luxurious palaces. In short, protesters in the three countries utilized the images of brutality and violent suppression by authoritarian regimes, nationalistic theme songs and slogans, and the visual representation of poverty to garner emotions of viewers so as to sustain their movements against their particular regimes.

Cultural and Ideological Frames of the Three Social Movements

In the previous chapters of this book, we discussed in detail the idea of collective memory and cultural and ideological frames, which many scholars term as integral to social movements (Anderson, 2006; Hoskin, 2011; Neiger, Meyers & Zandber, 2011; Tarrow, 1998). According to Tarrow (1998), the idea of cultural and ideological frames refers to new but familiar symbols, slogans and themes used by protesters/political activists that resonate with an individual's belief system in order to mobilize them for participating and sustaining a social movement. The scholar argues that "social movements attempt to replace a dominant belief system that legitimizes the status quo with an alternative mobilizing belief system that supports collective action for change, movement leaders proffer the symbols of revolt to gain support and mark themselves off from opponents" (p.106). While analyzing data for this investigation, three content categories (i.e., frames) were found to be of primary significance. These content categories are: 1) the presence of religious slogans during the protests, 2) the presence of strong nationalistic symbols such as the country's flag, and 3) the presence of secular and/or nationalistic songs in the protest-related videos. Each content category is discussed separately below.

Presence of Religious Slogans

While discussing political uprisings in countries with a Muslim majority, it is important to understand that Islam, plays an important role in political resistance. Traditionally, in these Muslim-majority countries, the term "Muslim brotherhood" is used to connect fellow citizens in order to gain sympathy and support on certain issues. People use different religious symbols and slogans including Quranic calligraphy and the images of Holy places (such as the *Kaaba* in Mecca, Saudi Arabia), which connect them to the rest of the Muslim community on the basis of Islamic ideology and Islamic culture. While analyzing protest-related videos on YouTube, I observed that such videos included many references to Islam. Such references ranged from calling "*Allah-o-Akbar*," to offering prayers during protests, to holding signs with Quranic verses inscribed on them, to portrayals of Islamic symbols and places of worship such as the *Kaaba* in Mecca, Saudi Arabia. During the analysis, it was observed that even though religious symbols and references were frequently used, a majority of protesting youth wore Western-style clothing and demonstrated an ability to speak and understand English, which, in the three countries, is generally considered as the language of Western and modern values. Yet, Pakistan, Egypt and Tunisia are part of the Muslim world. It is only natural that religion would be an ingredient in the anti-government protests. Holding Arabic and English placards and posters with religious slogans such as "*Allah-o-Akbar*" or other verses from the Holy Quran, mostly represented religious appeals. In certain videos, the English translation of the Arabic text was present. In some cases, protesters were shown holding their hands with their faces raised toward the sky, which in Muslim culture symbolizes calling on God for help. The analysis found that a majority of the religious-appeal videos used common religious symbols to connect to their fellow citizens. Religion was used as a weapon of inspiration and resistance. Another way to interpret this finding could be that protesters in the three countries used religion and religious values as a political opportunity not only to recruit potential sympathizers, but also to sustain their movements against their regimes.

Presence of Strong Nationalistic Symbols

Nationalistic symbols, such as countries' flags, national anthems, monuments, etc., are another important tool that governments and people deploy to unite their fellow citizens. In other words, national symbols and themes serve as a collective memory of a group, nation state or a community. For nationalistic appeals, protest-related videos on YouTube showed images of people kissing their national flags or holding signs and placards to show respect and love for their country.

Secular/Nationalist versus Religious-Themed Songs. Music and chants were very important elements during the political uprisings. Protesters utilized these songs as another tool of cultural and ideological persuasion. An extensive analysis of data for this investigation suggests that the addition of secular or nationalistic songs to a protest-related YouTube video indicates an intent to appeal broadly to all members of the society, while religiously themed songs added to a video indicates an intention to appeal to members of a specific religious faith or tradition. We may also understand that the religious theme songs were used to connect to the fellow citizens on the basis of common religion, Islam. The analysis of frequency of musical genre in the videos revealed that secular songs were used much more frequently. Applying Tarrow's (1998) lens of cultural and ideological frames to this finding, it can be argued that online activists (video creators and/or uploaders) in the three countries preferred using wider and nationalistic themes and secular songs to make their protest message more universal. In addition to the nationalistic songs, it was observed that some of the protest-related videos in the three countries used Western music as an overlay with the still and moving images of protesters. Also, this logic of cultural and ideological frames can be seen in the global context as well. Analyzing these videos of protests, we can see an effort to make a connection to global culture rather than just narrowly focusing on the videos' specific country. Looking at the examples of Pakistan, Egypt and Tunisia, we find the social movements in these countries used slogans such as "People want to bring down the regime" and "Leave, leave, leave." They also used images of the Tunisian burning man (Bouazizi) and the Egyptian man (Khaled Said) who died of police torture in Egypt (Mendel, 2011). Although Pakistan's political crisis occurred earlier than the Tunisian and Egyptian revolution, people in that country used very similar images of police brutality and anti-regime slogans to mobilize the potential challengers.

Data analyses of the protest-related videos selected for this investigation revealed that Tarrow's (1998) logic of cultural and ideological frames takes on a somewhat new definition and direction when it comes to the videos of political protests on YouTube, the online world. For example, during the analysis of data, it was observed that there was not only country- and culture-specific music but also Western/Hollywood songs in some of the viral videos. For example, "We are Free Now" from the movie *Gladiator* was found in many videos from both Egypt and Tunisia. Another famous song, "Imagine," by John Lennon was also present as a background to some of the Tunisian protest-related videos. Even though Pakistan's political uprisings took place three years before the Arab Spring, Western songs were present in some of the Pakistan-specific protest videos as well.

This finding suggests that the video clips with Western secular songs as background were actually intended to appeal not only to their own citizens, but also to gain the attention of people in other countries, particularly the Western world. Also, in terms of cultural and ideological frames, the use of international music on the digital platform should be interpreted as *connected* cultural and ideological frames because the message of these videos is understood globally (Hoskin, 2011). Clearly, the idea of cultural frames is becoming more complex when applied to social media platforms. Further discussion to this aspect appears in Chapter 13 of this book.

Part Two: Uprisings of 2019

Sudanese Political Uprisings & Women as the Leading Face of Protests

The political uprisings of 2007, 2010–11 did not only change the political and media landscape of the three countries forever, but also social and cultural landscapes of the Muslim world. The three uprisings, which were clearly dominated by youth in Pakistan, Egypt and Tunisia, also saw participation by a considerable number of women during street protests against their respective regimes. This was, in fact, a powerful statement about women's political role and participation in countries where cultural and religious taboos have left little to no room for them to come out and demand their basic human rights. Therefore, when the narratives of protests carried female protesters' images on social media such as Facebook, Twitter and YouTube, people in other Muslim-majority countries received them as cascades of information. These signals of informational cascades were not only about joining such uprisings to revolt against authoritarian regimes, but also, they were sending signals to the female populations of some of these countries to participate in political activism, despite all the social, cultural and religious barriers put in place to minimize their role in the society. Who knew these informational cascades would not only contribute toward women's participation in the Muslim world, but would lead us to witness an era of political uprisings that are being mobilized, formed, sustained and led by women. Sudan, a country located in the northeast of Africa, is an iconic example in this regard. The recent political uprisings of Sudan surprised the world when the images of women protesting and leading protests started to emerge on traditional and social media platforms, particularly on Twitter. Some of these images—which were recorded on smartphones and were disseminated by social media platforms—have already become icons of Sudanese political uprisings.

To put things in perspective, the month of December seems to remain a primary choice of protesters when it comes to discuss political uprisings in the Middle East and Muslim-majority countries. Sudanese protests that started on December 19, 2018 against President Omar al-Bashir were suppressed by the authoritarian ruler via the use of force, arrests, killings of protesters and traditional media and Internet censorships (Elmileik, 2018; Mahmoud, 2018). Omar al-Bashir, who had ruled the country for around 30 years (since 1989), came to power as a result of a military coup against elected Prime Minister Sadiq al-Mahdi (Warburg, 2003). Just like Pakistan, Egypt and Tunisia, Sudanese protests were also against the rising living costs, corruption of political elites, authoritarian regime, and denial of basic human rights such as freedom of expression and speech, among others (Elmileik, 2018; Mahmoud, 2018; Mezzofiore, 2019).

These political demonstrations against al-Bashir took a new turn when a majority of women, despite threats to their lives, came out on the streets in March of 2019 and demanded the president to step down. Alaa Salah, a 22-year-old engineering and architecture student, became an iconic symbol of protest against the regime when she led a protest rally in the streets of the Sudanese capital, Khartoum:

> On Monday [April 08, 2019] evening, as thousands of people took to the streets in the capital of Khartoum demanding that President Omar al-Bashir step down,

> local photographer Lana Haroun captured 22-year-old Alaa Salah standing on top of a car above a sea of people with her arm raised in the air, finger pointed toward the sky. Dozens of people surrounding her can be seen recording her with their phones. (Griffin, 2019, para. 3)

Alaa Salah's image of protest against the regime gained its iconic status not only because a young woman was challenging the most powerful man on the throne, but also because her white outfit carried multiple interpretations to the collective memories of Sudanese women's history. Salah's white robe had a connection to working class women in Sudan and was also "linked w/ cotton (a major export of Sudan), so it represents women working as professionals in cities or in the agricultural sector in rural areas" (Mezzofiore, 2019, para. 12). Along with white cotton outfit, Salah also wore gold earnings that connected with Sudanese women's memories of their mothers and grandmothers, who protested against the military dictatorships of 1960s, 1970s, and 1980s (Mezzofiore, 2019). Lena Haroun, who captured the iconic image of Salah and then Tweeted this image on social media, said:

> Sudanese everywhere are referring to female protesters as 'Kandaka,' which is the title given to the Nubian queens of ancient Sudan whose gift to their descendants is a legacy of empowered women who fight hard for their country and their rights. (Mezzofiore, 2019, para. 14)

Within days of these women-led protests, al-Bashir was ousted from his presidency on April 11, 2019 (Walsh & Goldstein, 2019). The ousting of al-Bashir, however, does not mean a change of the system, as the country is still being ruled by the former president's team. Even though Sudan has a long road ahead to walk in order to become a genuine democracy, the country has already set an example of women's leadership role in successful political protests against the most powerful men in the history of dictatorial regimes. No other protests were led by women in the recent history of political uprisings in the Muslim world. Therefore, these cascades of women's political activism will not only continue to inspire political activism in the region, but will also serve as a collective and connective memory of women's role, courage, valor and leadership in Muslim-majority countries. Perhaps we can refer to this evolving phenomenon as the "Arab Spring 2.0," where deprived factions of the closed societies—such as women—are not only finding their ways to express themselves via online and offline (real world) collective actions, but also, they are actually leading such political social movements, as it was witnessed in the case of the Sudanese uprisings of 2019.

Another important observation in the case of the Sudanese political protests is about the use of symbols and slogans that the protesters reinvented to sustain their collective action against the powerful elite. One such slogan was "We are All Darfur" (Rosenberg, 2019). I would like the readers to recall the discussion about "We are All Khaled Said" in Chapter 7 in order to find a connection to this newly created cultural memory, which already exists on social media platforms, particularly in the form of a Facebook page with the same slogan. The Egyptian Arab Spring took place over nine years ago, and the Khaled Said incident occurred 10 years ago, but when the people of Sudan decided to come out on the streets to protest their regime, they had a collective memory of protest-related slogans that already exist on social media platforms.

Aurat *[Women's] March of Pakistan*

Pakistan, likewise, witnessed a women's movement during the same year of 2019. In fact, the Pakistani women's movement started exactly one month before the Sudanese women's protests flared up. On March 8, 2019, thousands of Pakistani women from all walks of life came out in the streets of major cities across the country as part of the "*aurat* march," which in English means "women's march" (Chughtai, 2019). This women's initiative, which demanded safety and better working conditions for women, has already produced a big impact on Pakistani society as "a growing number of working-class women [are] joining the initiative to help facilitate political action on women's rights and gender justice" (Chughtai, 2019, para. 5). One difference that needs to be noted here, however, is the fact that the Pakistani women's march was not aimed at regime change, rather it was aimed more broadly at getting women incorporated into society. On the other hand, the Sudanese women's march and protest rallies were not demanding women's incorporation into the existing political and social infrastructure, rather their demand was regime change. That is why, contrary to the Sudanese case, the Pakistani women's march did not witness any arrests or the use of force by Pakistani security forces.

The Algerian Spring

Coincidently, while I was compiling this book, the Algerian Spring started to erupt during late February of 2019. The events that unfolded with the mass political uprisings of Algerians and the outcome of these protests were extraordinarily similar and pertinent to what has already been discussed in this book, particularly in the context of Pakistan, Egypt and Tunisia. Let us quickly revisit the Algerian Spring and its connection to the political uprisings of 2007, 2010–11.

Just like all other cases discussed in this book, the primary reasons for the Algerian protests were related to a dictatorial regime and poor economic conditions. The country's top leader, President Abdelaziz Bouteflika, had ruled the country since 1999 and was seeking a fifth presidential term when the protests against him erupted in the streets of the Algerian capital, Algiers (Mezahi, 2019). Also, corruption, denial of basic human rights to the citizens and poor economic conditions of the people of Algeria remained the same as we witnessed during the cases of Pakistan, Egypt and Tunisia. Unable to withstand the political pressure and demands of Algerian protesters, the 82-year-old ruler, Abdelaziz Bouteflika, resigned from his office on April 03, 2019 ("Abdelaziz Bouteflika," 2019).

Protest Songs (Netflix). The discussion about global connective memories and global themes that were being applied during the Arab Spring of 2010–11 becomes more relevant and refreshed when looking at the most recent political uprisings in Algeria, commonly referred to as the Algerian Spring. For example, one of the most influential protest songs that gave voice to protesters during the Algerian protests was "La Casa del Mouradia," "named after Netflix's La Casa de Papel (Money Heist) TV series [, the song] lambasts Bouteflika's four terms of governance" (Mezahi, 2019, para. 11). This can be interpreted in two ways. First, because of the Internet, people all around the world, including Algeria, have access to the same shows on *Netflix*, *HBO*, etc., that we can access in the United States. Such TV media productions are not specific to one culture or country but share global audiences. Second, the protesters might have intentionally made their song after *Netflix*'s "La Casa de Papel" ("Money Heist") TV series, to attract the Western world and gain support for their narrative against the regime. In any case, the Algerian struggle was able to achieve its goal of getting rid of their dictatorial leader, Abdelaziz Bouteflika. However, the country may witness more episodes of political uprisings before the will of its people is exercised in its full essence.

Morocco, an Active Volcano for Political Uprisings

The political uprisings in Muslim-majority countries are far away from being over. For example, Morocco has witnessed multiple waves of social uprisings during the past three years. The most recent one was in late April of 2019. The Moroccan Rif Movement, also known as *Hirak Rif*:

> organised protests in 2016 and 2017 after the death of a fishmonger in Al-Hoceima, a town in Rif. Fishmonger Mohcine Fikri was crushed to death by

> a rubbish lorry whilst trying to recover his fish which had been confiscated by local police. ("Morocco protests," 2019, para. 9)

This sad incident reminds us of the Tunisian man, Mohamed Bouazizi, who was also mistreated and embarrassed by the local police authorities. Bouazizi's attempted suicide ignited the Tunisian Jasmine Revolution, and Mohcine Fikri's incident triggered protest movements in Morocco. In the case of Morocco, however, the ruling elite were quick to suppress the movement by arresting and punishing the protest leaders, and "[i]n June 2018, a [Moroccan] court sentenced Nasser Zefzaki, the leader of Hirak Rif, to 20 years in prison" ("Morocco protests," 2019, para. 7). This sentence had been challenged in the country's legal system. Another wave of protests erupted when a court upheld the sentence of 42 arrested activists of the Rif Movement on April 22, 2019 ("Morocco protests," 2019). Just like other countries, the Rif Movement also blamed the country's ruling elite for corruption and poor economic conditions and associated the fishmonger's death with police brutality and corruption. What will happen in Morocco's political arena has yet to be seen. The king of Morocco, Mohammed VI, has been in power since 1999. Only time will determine whether the people of Morocco will be able to see a democratic future for themselves. At this point, however, one thing is for sure: the recent political uprisings of Morocco are the presages of what is to come in terms of mass political uprisings and collective actions both online and in the streets (offline).

Moving Forward: Flash Social Movements

Historically, political uprisings and social movements were seen and studied as something that occur not randomly, but as a result of deep-rooted processes that take years, sometimes decades, to erupt. These social movements were looked at as part of extended processes and required several components for the movements to be either successful or to fail, depending upon the circumstances. Some of these components include whether or not a movement is aimed at a regime change (for example, Arab Spring movements) or if its demand is for incorporation into the existing system (mostly Western examples such as the Women's Suffragist Movement in the United States and recent gay rights movements in the West). Because of these assumptions of what it takes to create a successful movement, the existing scholarship is mostly focused on understanding the motivations of people who choose or decline to participate in a collective action. Both traditional and modern scholars studying social movements have either applied an a-rational approach or economic logic (rational choice models) to study collective actions and social movements. (For examples, look at the works of Boudreau & Meyer, 2009; Hirschman, 1970; Jenkins, 1983; Olson, 1965; Skocpol, 1979; Tarrow, 1998; Tilly, 1992). None of these scholars had to deal with scenarios wherein a social movement and/or a political collective action emerged as an overnight phenomenon and disappeared from the scene with the same pace. That's why most of the scholarship in existing political science and mass media archives on social movements treats communication as peripheral rather than central when investigating any collective action. Throughout this chapter, I propose new approaches and lenses to study these novel phenomena of social movements wherein communication, particularly the Internet and social media, is central to understanding the motives of a collective action.

Elaborating further, in today's world, we are witnessing novel examples of social movements erupting like flash floods on digital media platforms of human communication. Using the term "flash floods" as a metaphoric explanation here, we are aware that such floods involve the element of suddenness whenever the term is used to describe heavy rain and its catastrophic implications on a particular region. Current online social movements mimic this same phenomenon. For example, some of these social movements recently erupted on Twitter within minutes of an incident to mark a protest against that incident. These movements caught enough attention of people around the world in remarkably less time and then disappeared just as quickly. One such example of a flash movement arose in response to a 14-year-old 'clock boy', Ahmed Mohamed, which took place on Twitter on September 14, 2015 in response to events at MacArthur High School in Irving, Texas (Chow, 2015; Schuppe, 2016). Ahmed, the son of a Sudanese Muslim immigrant family, had brought a homemade clock to his school, which got him arrested and suspended from the school on the charges of carrying a hoax bomb. Once the news broke out, social media, especially Twitter users, commonly referred to as Twitterati, reacted to it strongly and termed the incident as racially and religiously motivated action on the part of the school and the Dallas police department. The hashtag #IStandWithAhmed went viral on Twitter and was followed and supported by thousands of Twitter users. In less than 24 hours, "close to a million people … jumped on his bandwagon and sent out tweets with the supportive hashtag #IstandwithAhmed" (Muskal, 2015, para. 3).

Making the time factor, which had always been extremely important for the building (mobilization) and sustainability of a social movement, almost irrelevant in this case, this reactionary social movement to support Ahmed immediately became one of the most discussed and debated issues on social media platforms.

As a result of the amplification of this incident on social media, Ahmed was later invited by the White House and the Google World Headquarters (Schuppe, 2016). This social movement, which was at one point supported by over a million people on Twitter subsided as quickly as it had started, particularly when social media activists determined that they have achieved their goal. Likewise, other online social movements such as #MeToo, #BlackLivesMatter, #BringBackOurGirls, #IceBucketChallenge, #Ferguson, #TakeAKnee and #Covfefe, etc., keep on emerging on Twitter platform as flash floods and then disappear quickly when something else distracts the online activists to shift their attention to another issue of importance to them. In other words, today's online activists and social movements are unique in that an individual or a participant can be a legitimate and an influential part of multiple social movements simultaneously. This was never possible in the past. Street protesters could never afford to be a part of multiple movements all at once. Street protests and physical social movements require more focus, time, resources, loyalty and effort to sustain a collective action, while online activism does not have to be contained in all of these chains. People on social media platforms can perform their activist roles efficiently without committing themselves to one particular movement for an extended period of time. In other words, Hirschman's (1970) theorization of "loyalty" as an integral component of a collective action, also begins to get challenged when applied on the flash movements of today's digital age. Thus, online social activism is mostly based on a principle of being available *whenever needed*. Therefore, such flash movements have some of the following common elements, which are described below:

Virtual Spaces. Flash movements are virtual in nature. Even though such movements, sometimes, may be triggered in response to an incident that takes place in a physical space, these flash movements usually do not get translated into offline or street protests because they have already achieved their goals online, and activists feel no need for them to have an offline version of the political activism. Take for example, #MeToo Movement, which has received the most attention on digital social media platforms around the world, was never transformed into an organized real-world social movement in any part of the globe.

Ease. Ease to participate, produce, disseminate and communicate via online platforms of information and communication technologies, is another characteristic of flash movements. Everyone and anyone who has access to the Internet and social media platforms of communication can join such collective actions without having to get out of their comfort zones. Hence, even while sitting on your comfy and cozy couches, you can be a part of the most devastating political actions.

Suddenness. Such movements represent a quick yet strong response in a relatively short span of time. Therefore, everything, in terms of people's reaction to an issue of importance to them, takes place so suddenly that it leaves little to no room for the powerful elites to react or respond accordingly.

Short-lived, yet Long Lasting. In spite of the fact that such movements appear so much amplified on social media platforms and get an incredible number of followers and empathizers around the globe, they tend to be short-lived. These movements disappear as quickly as they originate, particularly when their goals are achieved. Despite their short-lived nature, these movements, however, become a permanent archive of online activists' collective memories, which then serve as the cultural and ideological frames for future online activists, whenever needed.

Instant Gratification. The element of instant gratification may be considered as an important component while studying flash movements. Because of the social media factor and the sophisticated pace of human communication via electronic and digital platforms, people participate, comment and react on an issue of importance to them far more quickly than in real life situations. This aspect of being able to express their views online may be a contributing factor in achieving their instant gratification. On the contrary to online social movements, street protests and collective actions don't yield quick outcomes and, thus, may not offer any instant gratification to the participants.

Individual, yet Collective Actions. Flash movements represent an oxymoron phenomenon when it comes to talk about collective actions. One of the most important elements of flash movements is the fact that people participate in such collective actions while maintaining their individual physical spaces. Not only this, but they don't even share their tools and technologies—such as smartphones, tablets and laptops/desktops—with others while participating in online activism. Hence, future scholars need to acknowledge the fact that the repertoire of collective actions have also been changed by technologies such as smartphones, which are designed for individuals, not for a group. The introduction of facial recognition technologies on people's smartphones is a step forward in the direction of individuality of communication technologies. Second, participants in flash collective actions maintain their physical spaces as individuals while they create collectiveness in virtual spaces. Thus, such flash movements are to be looked at isolated from the physical and geographical realities of people participating in them.

Flash Movements Are Communication Technologies Dependent. Finally, these *flash* movements were only possible because of the advancements in communication technologies. Had it not been for social media and digital modes of communication, there would be no such a thing as flash movements. That is why these movements will only be seen in societies where the basic infrastructure for the Internet and social media networks of communication exist and function. Areas which have yet to join the digital age of human communication may not witness such a political, social and cultural activism known as flash movements.

Conclusion

This chapter has discussed the new era of global common themes emerging as a result of political activism on social media platforms, which keep generating and morphing new collective memories to be used for future protesters in similar collective actions. Such phenomena are not only helping protesters and political activists, but also ruling elites and dictatorial forces are quickly learning and adapting to the new means of communication and are trying to re-exert their control via new modes of technology of surveillance (Dencik, Hintz & Carey, 2018; Treré, 2016). For example, in a recent turn of events, it was revealed that military and intelligence agencies in countries like Pakistan and India are using the same tactics and social media tools to promote their agenda and narratives to the online world. Ironically, the same ruling forces reject and resist the use of these very same tools of expression for their citizens. For example, during April 2019, Facebook "removed 103 pages, groups and accounts that were part of a network it said was linked to employees of the Pakistani military's public relations arm" (Sayeed, 2019, para. 1). The social media site also "announced the removal of 687 pages and accounts linked to India's main opposition Congress party which had engaged in 'coordinated inauthentic behavior' on its social media platform" (Sayeed, 2019, para. 8).

Such revelations of the ruling elites' anonymous uses of social media highlight another important aspect to which we need to pay attention. Not only the civilian protesters, but the authoritarian regimes and ruling elites also send signals through a cascade of information among the rulers of other countries. If a social movement succeeds in one particular country, it sends signals to other authoritarian rulers to be vigilant and adopt new strategies before it's too late for them. That is why, a strategy that works in one country is adopted and implemented in another neighboring state by the ruling elite. For example, when Saudi Arabia banned anonymous masks, the United Arab Emirates (UAE) soon followed the move.

This chapter also puts forward the idea of flash movements in the digital age, which future researchers should test against trends in digital social movements to determine its applicability in multiple scenarios. Furthermore, the chapter highlights an important feature of Tarrow's (1998) theorization of political opportunity structures, which future scholars need to revisit in the context of cultural and ideological frames. For example, the political opportunity structures deployed by online and street protesters and activists in Pakistan (involving the Chief Justice), Egypt (involving Khaled Said) and Tunisia (involving Mohamed Bouazizi) can also be seen as cultural and ideological frames, particularly once the three movements were over. Therefore, future researchers should look at this new dynamic in which political opportunity structures transition into cultural and ideological frames on digital media platforms, which then, serve to inspire potential sympathizers for future uprisings in the form of collective and connective memory themes.

Furthermore, all the social movements discussed in this chapter highlighted the common plights of people, regardless of the geographical locations, as motivations for forming and/or joining a social movement. These commonalities include poverty, unemployment, educated but unemployed youth, lack of freedom of expression, a state-controlled mass media, a history of human rights violations, dictatorial regimes and the advent of the Internet as an alternative to traditional media sources. Finally, the chapter makes the case that Pakistan served as the epicenter of social media inspired protests, not Tunisia or Egypt. Hence, social media and social movement scholars should look at the example of Pakistan's political activism while studying mass uprisings in the age of the Internet. It may be noted that Iftikhar Chaudhry (Pakistan), Khaled Said (Egypt) and Mohamed Bouazizi (Tunisia) were not participants in the movements, but were the reason for uprisings in the three countries. Therefore, these three icons of outrage were not only catalysts to bring people to action, but were in fact serving as political opportunity structures for social movements to form and be sustained in the three countries. Metaphorically speaking, these three mass uprisings of Pakistan (2007), Egypt (2010–11) and Tunisia (2010) were the examples of a fission chain reaction of social movements, not fusion. This chain reaction is destined to continue in other societies in the days to come. Further, because the Internet has yet to connect half of the population of the planet, we may witness much bigger and wider social movements in the near future. Once it's achieved, the whole idea of online political activism will transform the entire meaning of activism itself.

Contribution to the Scholarship

As a final word, I put forward two significant contributions of this book to the existing scholarship on social media and social movements in the Muslim world.

My first contribution relates to reversing the order of Muslim world's political activism. It is commonly perceived that the recent political uprisings in Muslim-majority countries started from Tunisia in 2010, and the success of Tunisian revolution originated political protests in Egypt in 2011, which then triggered political uprisings in several other Muslim-majority countries. I challenge this perception and invite scholars to amend this order by putting Pakistani political uprisings in their proper context. My scholarly contribution argues that the political uprisings of 2007 in Pakistan were among the first organized efforts to utilize the Internet and social media to form and sustain their social movements. Such online political activism was then witnessed in June of 2010 in Egypt, which was followed by street protests. Tunisia came last in this order as its Jasmine Revolution started in December of 2010.

My second most significant contribution is to bring communication to the center stage of political activism and social movements. In order to do that, I propose a new model of political collective action, which is entirely based on communicative phenomena in the digital age. A pictorial display of this new model is provided below.

According to this new model of collective action, I put forward six basic roles of this new form of digital communication in our information age: (1) introduction of the Internet and social media, (2) low cost communication, (3) expansion of public domain, (4) formation of collective "We," (5) amplification of voice, and (6) political activism and social movements. The placement of communicative processes at the center of this new model positions it as significantly different from other models of collective action which identify political motives and actions as the key components of social change (e.g., Tilly, 1978).

Based on this new model, the success of political uprisings in the three countries (Pakistan, Egypt and Tunisia) hinged upon the single most important factor: digital communication. The model asserts that the introduction of the Internet and social media in countries like Pakistan, Egypt and Tunisia resulted in lowering the cost of communication in the society, both in terms of control and access. Before the age of the Internet, mass media sources were directly or indirectly controlled and operated by the authoritarian regimes in these countries. They were subservient to the state, with little to no representation of the problems and plights of common people. The Internet changed that. With smartphones in their hands and able to create and disseminate their own content, people of these oppressive regimes found an extremely inexpensive and a relatively more sophisticated way of telling their own stories to the world, whenever and however they wanted. This low cost of communication resulted in an immediate expansion of

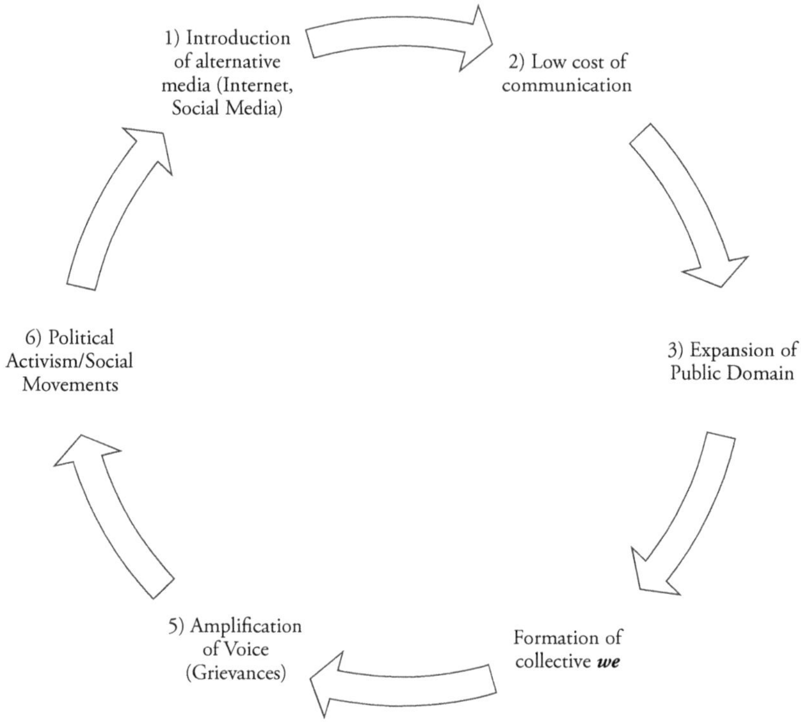

Figure 14.1: New Model of Collective Action for the Digital Age. Source: Author, Copyright 2019 by Rauf Arif, PhD.

their public domain in these relatively closed or less free societies. When stories of people's plights, miseries and suppression by their own regimes travelled online, other users also shared their experiences, not only with their fellow citizens, but also to the globe. This phenomenon segued to the formation of a collective "We" (Gerbaudo & Treré, 2015). When people on social media platforms learned that it was not only them, but many other citizens who had similar experiences—such as humiliation, torture, corruption of their rulers, and denial of basic human rights by their regimes—there were no more individual stories; their voices were becoming a collective "We." When people found out that it was *Us*, not *Me,* who was going through similar challenges, they started to come out to form a collective action against their oppressive regimes. The Facebook social media campaign of 2010 in Egypt, "We are all Khaled Said," was the most powerful example of this formation of a collective "We" phenomenon. People in these societies, for the very first time in history, could realize the fact that if it could happen to Khaled

Said, it can happen to them. The formation of collective "We" was amplified on social media platforms of communication so quickly that the oppressors could no longer suppress these amplified voices by merely banning or controlling the traditional media outlets (Milan, 2015). All these factors led to political activism and social movements in these countries that are still ongoing. I invite future researchers and scholars to apply and test this model in other scenarios where freedom of information, speech and expression is prohibited to see whether changes in political opportunity in the form of digital communication (such as the Internet and social media) would contribute to the formation and sustainability of social movements as it was witnessed in the cases of Pakistan, Egypt and Tunisia.

References

Abdelaziz Bouteflika: Algerian leader resigns amid protests. (2019, April 3). *BBC News*. Retrieved April 05, 2019, from https://www.bbc.com/news/world-africa-47795108

Ahmad, S. (2018, July 24). Unleashing the potential of a young Pakistan. United Nations Development Programme: Human Development Reports. Retrieved May 15, 2019, from http://hdr.undp.org/en/content/unleashing-potential-young-pakistan

AlSayyed, N. (2011, April 1). A History of Tahrir Square [Blog post]. *Harvard University Press Blog*. Retrieved June 05, 2019, from https://harvardpress.typepad.com/hup_publicity/2011/04/a-history-of-tahrir-square.html

Anderson, B. (2006). *Imagined communities: Reflections on the origin and spread of nationalism* (revised ed.). Brooklyn, NY: Verso Books.

Arif, R. (2014). *Social movements, YouTube and political activism in authoritarian countries: A comparative analysis of political change in Pakistan, Tunisia & Egypt* (Unpublished doctoral dissertation). University of Iowa, Iowa City, IA.

Arif, R. (2016). Internet as a hope or a hoax for emerging democracies: Revisiting the concept of citizenship in the digital age. *Procedia-Social and Behavioral Sciences, 236*, 4–8. doi: https://doi.org/10.1016/j.sbspro.2016.12.002

Boudreau, V. & Meyer, D. S. (2009). Social Movements. In T. Landman and N. Robinson (Eds.) *The Sage Handbook of Comparative Politics*. Thousand Oaks, CA: Sage Publications Inc.

Brown, K. (2008). Tunis. In M. R.T. Dumper & B. E. Stanley (Eds.) *Cities of the Middle East and North Africa: A historical encyclopedia* (pp. 369–373). Santa Barbara, CA: ABC-CLIO.

Buckner, E., & Khatib, L. (2014). The martyrs' revolutions: The role of martyrs in the Arab Spring. *British Journal of Middle Eastern Studies, 41*(4), 368–384. doi: https://doi.org/10.1080/13530194.2014.918802

Chow, K. (2015, September 16). Texas high school student arrested after homemade clock mistaken for bomb. *NPR*. Retrieved July 03, 2019, from https://www.npr.org/2015/09/16/440914070/texas-high-school-student-arrested-after-homemade-clock-mistaken-for-bomb

Chughtai, A. (2019, March 8). Pakistani women hold '*aurat* march' for equality, gender justice. *Al Jazeera*. Retrieved April 04, 2019, from https://www.aljazeera.com/news/2019/03/pakistani-women-hold-aurat-march-equality-gender-justice-190308115740534.html

Dencik, L., Hintz, A., & Carey, Z. (2018). Prediction, pre-emption and limits to dissent: Social media and big data uses for policing protests in the United Kingdom. new media & society, 20(4), 1433–1450.

Dubai Press Club. (2013). *Arab Media Outlook 2009–2013: Inspiring Local Content*. (3rd. Ed). Retrieved February 16, 2016, from https://fas.org/irp/eprint/arabmedia.pdf

Egypt: A year after 'virginity tests'. (2012, March 9). *Amnesty International*. Retrieved April 05, 2019, from https://www.amnesty.org/en/latest/news/2012/03/egypt-year-after-virginity-tests-women-victims-army-violence-still-seek-justice/

Eko, L. (2012). *New media, old regimes: Case studies in comparative communication law and policy*. Lanham, MD: Lexington Books.

Elmileik, A. (2018, December 26). What prompted the protests in Sudan? *Al Jazeera*. Retrieved May 07, 2019, from https://www.aljazeera.com/news/2018/12/prompted-protests-sudan-181224114651302.html

Eltahawy, M. (2011, June 2). These 'virginity tests' will spark Egypt's next revolution. *The Guardian*. Retrieved April 05, 2019, from https://www.theguardian.com/commentisfree/2011/jun/02/egypt-next-revolution-virginity-tests

Gerbaudo, P. (2015). Protest avatars as memetic signifiers: Political profile pictures and the construction of collective identity on social media in the 2011 protest wave. *Information, Communication & Society*, *18*(8), 916–929. doi: 10.1080/1369118X.2015.1043316

Gerbaudo, P. & Treré, E. (2015). In search of the 'we' of social media activism: Introduction to the special issue on social media and protest identities. *Information, Communication & Society*, *18*(8), 865–871. doi: 10.1080/1369118X.2015.1043319

Ghannam, J. (2011). Social media in the Arab world: Leading up to the uprisings of 2011. *Center for International Media Assistance*, *3*(1), 1–44. Retrieved October 24, 2019, from http://www.cima.ned.org/wp-content/uploads/2011/02/Ghannam-Jeffrey-Arab_Social_Media-Report-10-25-11.pdf

Griffin, T. (2019, April 9). People can't stop talking about this iconic photo from the protests in Sudan. *BuzzFeed News*. Retrieved May 05, 2019, from https://www.buzzfeednews.com/article/tamerragriffin/sudan-protests-woman-car-iconic-photo-alaa-salah

Hafez, K. (2007). *The myth of media globalization*. Cambridge, UK: Polity Press.

Hafez, K. (Ed.) (2008). *Arab media: Power and weakness*. New York, NY: Continuum, Inc.

Hirschman, A. O. (1970). *Exit, voice, and loyalty: Responses to decline in firms, organizations, and states*. Cambridge, Mass: Harvard University Press.

Hoskin, A. (2011). Anachronisms of media, anachronisms of memory: From collective memory to a new memory ecology. In M. Neiger, O. Meyers, & E. Zandberg (Eds.) *On media memory* (pp. 278–288). London, England: Palgrave Macmillan.

Huntington, S. P. (1993). *The third wave: Democratization in the late twentieth century* (Vol. 4). Norman, OK: University of Oklahoma Press.

Jenkins, J. C. (1983). Resource mobilization theory and the study of social movements. *Annual Review of Sociology*, *9*(1), 527–553.

Lohmann, S. (1994). The dynamics of informational cascades: The Monday demonstrations in Leipzig, East Germany, 1989–91. *World Politics*, *47*(1), 42–101.

Mahmoud, O. (2018, December 25). 'It's more than bread': Why are protests in Sudan happening? *Middle East Eye*. Retrieved May 05, 2019, from https://www.middleeasteye.net/news/its-more-bread-why-are-protests-sudan-happening

Mendel, T. (2011). *Political and media transitions in Egypt. A snapshot of media policy and regulatory environment*. Retrieved June 22, 2019, from http://hrlibrary.umn.edu/research/Egypt/Internews_Egypt_MediaLawReview_Aug11.pdf

Mezahi, M. (2019, March 16). Algeria protests, politics loom over derby of Algiers. *Al Jazeera*. Retrieved April 06, 2019, from https://www.aljazeera.com/news/2019/03/mass-protests-politics-loom-derby-algiers-190315181654770.html

Mezzofiore, G. (2019, April 10). This woman has come to symbolize Sudan's protests. *CNN World*. Retrieved April 12, 2019, from https://www.cnn.com/2019/04/09/africa/photo-woman-chanting-sudan-uprising-scli-intl/index.html

Milan, S. (2015). From social movements to cloud protesting: the evolution of collective identity. *Information, Communication & Society*, *18*(8), 887–900.

Morocco protests: Thousands demand release of activists. (2019, April 22). *BBC News*. Retrieved May 16, 2019, from https://www.bbc.com/news/world-africa-48008463

Muskal, M. (2015, September 17). How student Ahmed Mohamed went from suspected bomb maker to overnight celebrity. *Los Angeles Times*. Retrieved July 10, 2019, from https://www.latimes.com/nation/la-na-ahmed-mohamed-clock-arrest-20150917-story.html

Neiger M., Meyers O., Zandberg E. (2011). On Media Memory: Editors' Introduction. In: Neiger M., Meyers O., Zandberg E. (Eds.) On Media Memory. Palgrave Macmillan Memory Studies. Palgrave Macmillan, London.

Olson, M. (1965). *Logic of collective action*. Cambridge, MA: Harvard University Press.

Papacharissi, Z. (Ed.) (2010a). A networked self: Identity, community, and culture on social network sites. New York, NY: Routledge.

Papacharissi, Z. (2010b). *A private sphere: Democracy in a digital age*. Cambridge, UK: Polity Press.

Perlmutter, D. D. (1998). *Photojournalism and foreign policy: Icons of outrage in international crises*. Westport, Conn.: Praeger.

Reading, A. (2011). Memory and digital media: Six dynamics of the globital memory field. In M. Neiger, O. Meyers, & E. Zandberg (Eds.) *On media memory* (pp. 241–252). London, England: Palgrave Macmillan.

Rosenberg, P. (2019, January 27). Uprising in Sudan: Does this African nation offer a window of hope onto the future? *Salon*. Retrieved April 09, 2019, from https://www.salon.com/2019/01/27/uprising-in-sudan-does-this-african-nation-offer-a-window-of-hope-onto-the-future/

Ross, M. L. (2001). Does oil hinder democracy? *World Politics*, *53*(3), 325–361. doi: https://doi.org/10.1353/wp.2001.0011

Sayeed, S. (2019, April 1). Facebook removes accounts linked to Pakistani military employees. *Reuters*. Retrieved June 26, 2019, from https://www.reuters.com/article/us-facebook-accounts-pakistan/facebook-removes-accounts-linked-to-pakistani-military-employees-idUSKCN1RD1R6

Schuppe, J. (2016, August 8). 'Clock boy' Ahmed Mohamed sues Texas City for accusing him of making bomb. *CBS News*. Retrieved May 17, 2019, from https://www.nbcnews.com/news/us-news/clock-boy-ahmed-mohamed-sues-texas-city-accusing-him-making-n625401

Skocpol, T. (1979). *States and social revolutions: A comparative analysis of France, Russia, and China*. Cambridge, England: Cambridge University Press.

Tahrir Square's Historic Past. (2011, February 1). *Al Jazeera*. Retrieved July 01, 2019, from http://www.aljazeera.com/news/middleeast/2011/02/2011211035225O8343.html

Tarrow, S. G. (1998). *Power in movement: Social movements and contentious politics*. Cambridge, England: Cambridge University Press.

Tilly, C. (1978). *From mobilization to revolution*. Reading, Mass.: Addison-Wesley Pub.

Tilly, C. (1992). *Coercion, capital, and European states, AD 990–1992*. Hoboken, NJ: Blackwell.

Treré, E. (2016). The dark side of digital politics: Understanding the algorithmic manufacturing of consent and the hindering of online dissidence. *IDS Bulletin*, *1*(47). Retrieved April 20, 2019, from https://opendocs.ids.ac.uk/opendocs/handle/123456789/7697

Youth Policy (2019). Middle East and North Africa: Youth Facts. Retrieved August 04, 2019, from http://www.youthpolicy.org/mappings/regionalyouthscenes/mena/facts/

Walsh, D. & Goldstein, J. (2019, April 11). Sudan's President Omar Hassan al-Bashir is ousted, but not his regime. *The New York Times*. Retrieved April 13, 2019, from https://www.nytimes.com/2019/04/11/world/africa/sudan-omar-hassan-al-bashir.html

Warburg, G. R. (2003). *Islam, sectarianism and politics in Sudan since the Mahdiyya*. Madison, WI: University of Wisconsin Press.

Index

A

B

E

F

G

H

I

M

N

T

www.ingramcontent.com/pod-product-compliance
Ingram Content Group UK Ltd.
Pitfield, Milton Keynes, MK11 3LW, UK
UKHW020217290926
15470UKWH00001B/233

9 781433 16669